WHAT THE HELL ARE CRYPTOCURRENCIES?

What The Hell are Cryptocurrencies?

MARCO BEFFA

This book is dedicate to the loved persons who made it possible. To my dearest wife, Laura, the love of my life, whose unwavering support and boundless love have made every step of this journey possible.
And to my four incredible children, Beatrice, Camilla, Aurora and Matteo, who fill my days with laughter, wonder, and purpose. You are my light, my joy, and my reason for everything I do. Each of you carries a piece of my soul, and I am endlessly proud to be your husband and father.

Marco Beffa

CONTENTS

~ 1 ~

LEGAL DISCLAIMER

Author Disclaimer

Dear readers and friends! Before we dive into this exciting adventure together, I just want to quickly remind you to carefully read the legal disclaimer that follows. It's important to enjoy the ride responsibly, without any hiccups. Let's make this journey awesome, keep things cool and safe! Enjoy every moment!

Legal Disclaimer

No Financial Advice: The information contained in this book is for general informational and educational purposes only. It reflects the personal opinions and perspectives of the author and is not intended to constitute, and should not be construed as, financial, investment, or trading advice. The author is not a licensed financial advisor, and the content of this book should not be interpreted as a recommendation or endorsement of any particular investment strategy, financial product, or asset.

Investment Risks: The field of cryptocurrencies and digital assets is highly speculative and subject to significant volatility. Investing in digital assets involves substantial risks, including the risk of losing your entire investment. The author makes no representations or warranties regarding the accuracy, completeness, or reliability of the information presented in this book. Readers should conduct their own research and consult with a qualified financial advisor before making any investment decisions.

No Guarantees: The author does not guarantee the accuracy, completeness, or timeliness of the information provided. The views expressed in this book are based on the author's opinions and are subject to change without notice. The author shall not be held liable for any losses, damages, or expenses incurred as a result of the use or reliance on the information provided in this book.

No Endorsements: Any mention of specific cryptocurrencies, digital assets, companies, Exchanges or investment strategies is not an endorsement or recommendation of those entities or practices. The author does not receive any compensation or incentive for mentioning or discussing any particular assets or services.

Legal and Regulatory Compliance: The legal and regulatory environment surrounding cryptocurrencies and digital assets is constantly evolving. Readers are responsible for ensuring that they comply with all applicable laws and regulations in their jurisdiction. The author assumes no responsibility for any legal or regulatory issues that may arise from the use of information contained in this book.

Professional Advice: The information in this book is not intended to replace the professional advice from qualified financial, legal, or tax advisors. Readers should seek professional advice tailored to their individual circumstances before making any financial or investment decisions.

No Liability: In no event shall the author, publishers, or any affiliated parties be liable for any direct, indirect, incidental, special, or consequential damages arising from the use or inability to use the information contained in this book, even if advised of the possibility of such damages.

Forward-Looking Statements: The book may contain forward-looking statements or projections regarding future performance of cryptocurrencies or digital assets. Such statements are inherently uncertain and should not be relied upon as guarantees of future results.

By reading this book, you acknowledge that you understand and agree to this Legal Disclaimer.

Thanks!

$$\sim 2 \sim$$

YOUR COOL, FRESH PATH TO
DIVE IN

Dear Readers and Friends, Welcome to the ultimate reading experience! This reading guide is here to make sure you get the most out of each chapter, every insight, and all the knowledge packed in this book. My goal is to make the content as accessible as possible, while still being professional and comprehensive. However, tackling advanced and complex topics like the ones we are going to explore here is no small feat. That's why I've designed this guide to give you the best tools to approach these challenging subjects step by step, just like easing into a cold ocean, inch by inch, sometimes walking back one step to step forward again with more confidence.

Throughout the book, I revisit key concepts multiple times from different angles. This gentle repetition isn't meant to bore the more experienced readers, but to ensure that everyone, regardless of their level of expertise, can grasp even the trickiest ideas. Navigating the world of crypto space can make you feel like exploring a mysterious, uncharted planet, filled with unknowns and potential risks, where the boundaries are uncertain. And it is during these moments of feeling lost or overwhelmed that encountering a familiar concept on your way brings back comfort, reigniting your courage and restoring the strength to press forward with renewed enthusiasm.

And here comes another help for you: in addition to the main content, you'll find several in-depth analyses on particularly complex topics, marked by the title "What the Hell are..." *and presented in italics.* Feel free to dive into those sections whenever you need a deeper understanding or want to revisit a difficult concept. And remember: there's no pressure here, no need to rush. You feel it from the very first page. The words invite you to take your time, to move at your own pace. Some days, you may only turn a single page, while other days, you fly through the chapters, each one pulling you deeper. But no matter how fast or slow, the message is clear: enjoy the ride.

~ 3 ~

PROLOGUE

As we stand at the threshold of a digital revolution, one thing becomes clear: the future of finance is being reshaped by cryptocurrencies and digital assets. These are not just buzzwords or fleeting trends, they represent a profound shift in how we think about money, property, and ownership. My love for this new financial world goes beyond mere interest, it's a belief in a better future. A future where people have more control over their finances, assets, and destinies. A future where central intermediaries no longer dictate the rules, but where individuals are empowered to directly manage, protect, and grow their wealth. At its core, the world of cryptocurrencies and digital assets offers more than just an alternative currency.

It offers the promise of democratization of finance, of ownership, and of opportunity. And as someone who has spent years exploring this space, I am driven by a mission to share its potential with as many people as possible. To help others see what I see: that this is not just about investing in Bitcoin or Ethereum but about taking part in a financial renaissance that will reshape how the world operates. This book is my way of giving back to the community and providing an easy-to-understand and complete guide to the world of cryptocurrencies and digital assets. Whether you're a complete novice or someone with a bit of background knowledge, my goal is to simplify the complexities and make this emerging field accessible to everyone. You don't need to be a tech expert or financial guru to grasp the enormous potential that lies ahead—you simply need curiosity and an open mind.

Throughout this book, I will take you on a journey that covers the history, technology, use cases, and future of cryptocurrencies and digital assets. From the earliest concepts of decentralized money to the rise of blockchain technology, you'll gain insight into the forces that have shaped this space. We will explore the fundamental technologies that underpin cryptocurrencies, explaining in simple terms how the blockchain works and why it's such a game-changer for finance and beyond. But we won't stop there. This book is about understanding how cryptocurrencies are already being used today. From transferring value across borders in a matter of seconds to enabling decentralized applications that remove the need for trusted intermediaries, digital assets are already transforming industries.

We will look at real-world use cases that demonstrate the power and potential of these technologies, highlighting how they are impacting everything from finance and real estate to supply chains and governance. And, of course, we will gaze into the future. The road ahead for cryptocurrencies and digital assets is filled with both promise and challenges. Will governments embrace or resist them? How will regulatory frameworks evolve to accommodate this new paradigm? And perhaps most importantly, what role will these technologies play in empowering individuals and communities around the globe? As we answer these questions, you will gain a clear picture of where the industry is headed and how you can be a part of this exciting transformation.

At the heart of this book is a commitment to making cryptocurrencies and digital assets understandable for everyone. Too often, the language used to explain these concepts is overly technical, filled with jargon, or designed to intimidate rather than inform. That's not my approach. My mission is to break down barriers to understanding so that anyone, regardless of background can grasp the power of digital assets. I want to foster widespread adoption by showing that the world of crypto is not reserved for experts, but is open to everyone. Whether you're looking to understand how to buy your first Bitcoin, explore the possibilities of decentralized finance (DeFi), or simply want to grasp the broader implications of blockchain technology, this book will provide you with the tools and knowledge to do so. As you read through the pages that follow, you will find clear explanations, real-world examples, and step-by-step guides that will help you navigate the world of digital assets.

By the end of this book, you will not only understand the fundamentals but also feel confident in your ability to engage with this new financial landscape. You will be ready to make informed decisions about your own digital assets and participate in this evolving world with confidence. The future of finance is here, and it's more inclusive, more efficient, and more empowering than anything we've seen before. This book is your gateway to understanding that future. Whether you are a skeptic, a beginner, or someone looking to deepen your knowledge, my goal is to provide you with the clarity and insight needed to thrive in the world of cryptocurrencies and digital assets. Welcome to the journey. Together, let's explore, understand, and embrace the next frontier of finance

~ 4 ~

LOVE

I stepped into the world of cryptocurrency by chance, in the midst of the great surge of 2017. It all began during a casual conversation with an old high school friend, now teaching at the Normale University of Pisa in the Department of Mathematics and Computer Science. He started talking about the crypto space, blockchain technology, digital assets, and cryptocurrencies. What initially seemed like a technical and somewhat complex discussion about emerging technologies quickly took a turn as he began explaining how this new frontier was revolutionizing personal and corporate finance. The concept of full ownership over one's own assets, the ability to conduct transactions between peers without the need for a central authority, and the notion of true financial freedom immediately sparked my interest. Little did I know, this conversation would ignite a passion within me that has only grown stronger with time.

But the moment I truly began to fall in love with crypto was when my friend dove deeper into the idea of decentralization, interconnection, and the power of a worldwide network. He spoke of nodes sparkling across the globe, each participating in a system where no single entity held control, and of smart contracts—self-executing agreements coded into the blockchain, removing the need for intermediaries. This vision of a decentralized world, where individuals and businesses could operate freely and securely, struck a chord with me. As someone who had always been captivated by the boundless possibilities of science fiction, from Star Trek to Star Wars, my imagination took flight. I felt as though I had been transported into a space suspended between stars, planets, and intergalactic journeys, a place where freedom and innovation reigned supreme. I began to see crypto as more than just a financial tool, it felt like the manifestation of the futuristic worlds I had dreamed of as a child. In Star Trek, the crew of the USS Enterprise traversed the galaxy, exploring new frontiers with the aid of advanced technology. In Star Wars, the Rebel Alliance fought against a centralized empire, striving for freedom and justice. These stories had always resonated with me, but I never imagined that I would one day see a parallel in the real world. The crypto space, with its promise of decentralization, self-governance, and peer-to-peer transactions, felt like the embodiment of these ideals. It was as if the world of crypto was offering me a ticket to a future where individuals could break free from the constraints of traditional financial systems and take control of their own destinies.

My fascination quickly turned into obsession. I immersed myself in the world of blockchain and cryptocurrency, devouring white papers, essays, and opinion pieces from experts in the field. I attended conferences and meetups, eager to learn more about this new frontier that seemed to hold endless potential. I became an active participant in online forums, where discussions about the latest developments in the crypto world flowed as freely as the digital assets themselves. I wanted to understand every aspect of this rapidly evolving space, from the technical intricacies of blockchain architecture to the philosophical implications of decentralization. It wasn't long before I decided to invest in Bitcoin. At the time, Bitcoin was on its first major surge, and though I was cautious, I couldn't resist the pull of this exciting new asset class. I knew that investing in Bitcoin was a risk, but it felt like the right kind of risk, the kind that could pay off in more ways than just financial gain. Bitcoin represented a revolution in the way we think about money, ownership, and power, and I wanted to be a part of that revolution.

As I watched the value of Bitcoin rise, I felt a rush of excitement that was unlike anything I had experienced before. It wasn't just about the potential for profit, it was about being part of something bigger, something that had the power to change the world. The more I learned about the underlying technology and the vision of those who were building the crypto ecosystem, the more I realized that this was more than just a passing trend, it was a movement. A movement toward a future where financial systems are open, transparent, and accessible to everyone, regardless of their background or location. But what truly cemented my love for crypto was the realization that it wasn't just about the technology, it was about the people. The crypto community is a diverse, passionate, and innovative group of individuals who are united by a shared belief in the power of decentralization. Whether they are developers building the next generation of blockchain protocols, investors looking to support the most promising projects, or enthusiasts simply eager to learn more, they are all part of a global movement that is working to create a better, fairer financial system. This love for crypto continues to blow wind into my sails even now. Over the years, I've witnessed incredible advancements in the space, new blockchain platforms, decentralized finance (DeFi) projects, non-fungible tokens (NFTs), and countless other innovations that have expanded the boundaries of what's possible. I've also seen the challenges and setbacks, from market crashes to regulatory hurdles, but these have only strengthened my belief in the long-term potential of the technology. In many ways, my journey with crypto feels like an epic adventure, a journey through uncharted territory where the possibilities are endless and the stakes are high. But it's also a deeply personal journey, one that has reshaped the way I think about money, technology, and the future. Falling in love with crypto wasn't just about embracing a new investment opportunity, it was about embracing a vision of the future where individuals have the power to shape their own financial destiny.

Toward the end of 2017 I decided to partially liquidate my crypto holdings and to invest into my first crypto venture. Armed with ambition and a vision, I assembled a small but dedicated team, a skilled software engineer and a sharp marketing specialist, and together, we embarked on our journey. Since then, I've never looked back. Starting with a solid tenure, I've continually expanded, exploring new horizons and launching multiple ventures in the dynamic world of crypto, and I'm still going on today. As I continue to explore this exciting and ever-evolving world, I am reminded of the words of Captain Jean-Luc Picard from Star Trek: "The sky's the limit." In the world of crypto, that sentiment rings truer than ever. We are on the cusp of a new frontier, one that promises to reshape not only the way we think about finance, but the way we think about freedom, ownership, and possibility. And just like those intergalactic explorers I've admired for so long, I am ready to boldly go where no one has gone before.

~ 5 ~

EXPLORATION

Cryptocurrencies are digital assets enabling decentralized transactions among peers. In other way, a different form of exchanging money (digital) from one person to another. First of all we should clear the air from some major misconceptions and common mistakes that are usually storming anyone who is attempting to get closer to the crypto space. First thing first: it's crucial to differentiate between blockchain technology, the underlying framework, and the various products built upon it, such as cryptocurrencies, tokens, and NFTs.

What the hell are all these?

Blockchain: A decentralized, digital ledger of transactions maintained by a network of computers (nodes), which records information in blocks that are securely linked together.

Transactions: A blockchain records transactions, which can represent many types of information, such as:

- *Transfer of assets (e.g., cryptocurrencies)*
- *Ownership of digital goods (e.g., NFTs)*
- *Smart contracts execution*

Example: Alice sends 1 Bitcoin to Bob. This transaction is broadcast to the entire network.

Transaction Block Creation: *Transactions occurring over a period are bundled together into a "block." Each block contains:*

- *A list of validated transactions*
- *A timestamp, a digital record that indicates the exact date and time an event occurred*
- *A cryptographic hash of the previous block (linking them together)*
- *A cryptographic proof (like Proof of Work in Bitcoin) or some form of consensus verification.*

Validation and Consensus: *Before a transaction can be added to the blockchain, it must be validated by nodes on the network. Different blockchains use different consensus mechanisms for this process. Once consensus is reached (i.e., most nodes agree that the transactions in the block are valid), the block is added to the blockchain.*

Chaining of Blocks: *Each new block is linked to the previous block by including its cryptographic hash. This chain of blocks forms the "blockchain." The cryptographic hash ensures that if anyone tries to alter a block, it will break the link between that block and the next, alerting the entire network to the tampering attempt. Example: Block 5 has a reference (hash) to Block 4, ensuring they are linked. If anyone tries to change Block 4, the hash in Block 5 won't match, making the alteration evident.*

Schematic Diagram: Blockchain as a System of Blocks and Walls

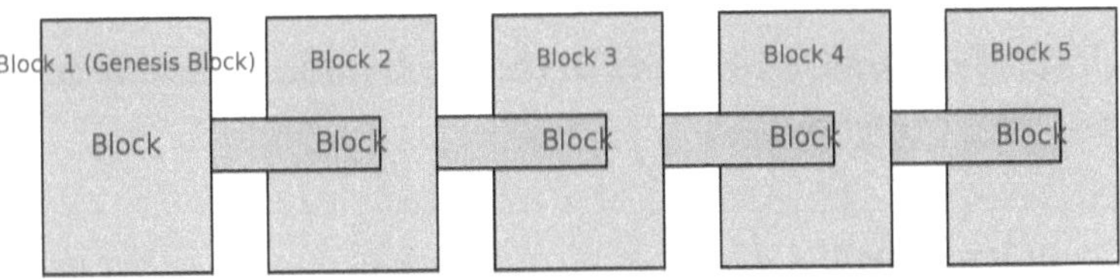

Blockchain Formation Process

Distribution and Synchronization: *After a new block is validated and added to the blockchain, it is distributed across all nodes in the network. Each node updates its copy of the ledger, ensuring that all participants have the same version of the blockchain. This decentralized synchronization eliminates the need for a central authority to control the ledger, making it resilient to attacks or failures.*

Security and Cryptography: *Blockchain uses strong cryptography to secure transactions and ensure the integrity of the data. There are two major cryptographic concepts used:*

Hashing: *Each block is represented by a cryptographic hash (a fixed-length string of numbers and letters). Any slight change to the data in the block produces an entirely different hash, making tampering detectable.*

Public and Private Keys: *Participants on the blockchain use cryptographic keys to sign transactions.*

Private Key: *A cryptographic key that allows users to access and manage their cryptocurrency holdings. It must be kept secure, as anyone with access to it can control the associated assets.*

Public Key: *A cryptographic code associated with the private key, which can be shared with others to receive cryptocurrency. It acts as an address for transactions*

Cryptocurrency: *A digital or virtual form of currency that uses cryptography for security and operates independently of a central authority. Examples include Bitcoin, Ethereum, and Litecoin.*

Altcoins: *Any cryptocurrency other than Bitcoin.*

Stablecoins: *A type of cryptocurrency designed to maintain a stable value by being pegged to a reserve asset, such as fiat currencies like USD or commodities like gold. Examples include Tether (USDT) and USD Coin (USDC).*

Stablecoin Collateralization: *The method by which a stablecoin maintains its peg to a fiat currency or other asset. This can be done through fiat reserves, cryptocurrency collateral, or algorithms.*

DeFi (Decentralized Finance): *A financial system built on blockchain technology that removes intermediaries like banks, enabling peer-to-peer transactions using smart contracts. Examples include lending platforms like Aave and decentralized exchanges (DEXs) like Uniswap.*

CeFi (Centralized Finance): *A financial system where a central entity (such as an exchange) manages cryptocurrency transactions and services. Popular CeFi platforms include Binance and Coinbase.*

App (Application): *Software designed to run decentralized services or enable cryptocurrency transactions, often via a smartphone or web platform. DeFi apps are commonly referred to as* **dApps** *(decentralized applications).*

Decentralized Application (dApp): *An application that runs on a decentralized blockchain, typically using smart contracts. Examples include DeFi platforms and NFT marketplaces.*

DAO (Decentralized Autonomous Organization): *A blockchain-based organization governed by smart contracts, with decisions made through a collective vote by token holders.*

Wallet: *A digital tool or app used to store and manage cryptocurrencies. Wallets can be hot (online) for easy access, or cold (offline) for secure, long-term storage.*

Tokens: *Digital assets built on top of a blockchain, representing various things, from currency to voting rights to ownership of digital or physical assets.*
Cryptocurrencies: *Yes, they can be considered a type of token.*

Utility Tokens: *Tokens used to access a product or service on a platform (e.g., Basic Attention Token, BAT).*

Security Tokens: *Tokens that represent ownership in an asset, such as a stock or real estate, and are subject to securities regulations.*

Governance Tokens: *Tokens that give holders voting rights in the development of a project or protocol (e.g., Uniswap's UNI token).*

Non-Fungible Tokens (NFTs): *Unique digital assets representing ownership of items such as digital art, collectibles, or virtual real estate.*

Staking: *The process of locking up a certain amount of cryptocurrency to support the operations of a blockchain network (such as validating transactions), often in return for rewards.*

Validation Nodes: *Computers or entities participating in the network to validate transactions and add new blocks to the blockchain. In exchange, they may receive rewards in the form of cryptocurrency.*

Consensus Mechanism: *a protocol used to achieve agreement among distributed nodes on the validity of transactions and the state of the ledger. It ensures network security, data integrity, and trust without relying on a central authority. Here the most used (in order of importance):*

Proof of Work (PoW): *Participants (miners) solve complex mathematical puzzles to validate transactions and add new blocks to the blockchain. PoW is energy-intensive. Examples: Bitcoin, Ethereum (before Ethereum 2.0 upgrade).*

Proof of Stake (PoS): *Validators are chosen to create new blocks based on the number of tokens they hold and are willing to "stake" as collateral. PoS is more energy-efficient compared to PoW. Examples: Ethereum (after Ethereum 2.0), Cardano, Solana.*

Delegated Proof of Stake (DPoS): *Token holders vote to elect a small number of delegates to produce blocks on their behalf. It's faster than PoS and PoW but can be more centralized. Examples: EOS, TRON.*

Practical Byzantine Fault Tolerance (PBFT): *Consensus is reached via a majority agreement among nodes, even if some nodes act maliciously or fail. This is a low-latency, high-throughput mechanism used in permissioned blockchains. Examples: Hyperledger Fabric, Zilliqa.*

Proof of Authority (PoA): *Validators are pre-approved and must maintain a reputation to act in the network's best interest. This is mostly used in private or consortium blockchains. Examples: VeChain, Microsoft's Azure Blockchain, POA Network.*

Proof of Elapsed Time (PoET): *Participants wait for a randomly chosen period before producing a block. The first participant to finish waiting wins the right to create the block. Examples: Hyperledger Sawtooth.*

Proof of Burn (PoB): *Participants "burn" tokens (send them to an unrecoverable address) to earn the right to mine or validate transactions. The more tokens burned, the higher the chances. Examples: Slimcoin, Counterparty.*

Proof of Capacity (PoC): *Description: Also known as Proof of Space, participants allocate hard drive space to mine blocks. The more storage you allocate, the better your chances of creating the next block. Examples: Burstcoin, Chia.*

Proof of Weight: *Similar to PoS but uses additional factors (besides the number of tokens) like ownership of resources or importance within the network. Examples Algorand, Filecoin.*

Proof of Activity: *Combines PoW and PoS, where miners perform PoW, but instead of mining a full block, they create an empty block header. Validators then add transactions based on PoS. Examples: Decred.*

Proof of Reputation: *Validators are chosen based on their reputation, which is built over time through honest participation. Examples: Some private blockchain networks, but not widely implemented in public blockchains.*

Proof of Importance (PoI): *Validators are selected based on various factors, including the number of coins held, transactions made, and overall network activity. Examples: NEM.*

Tendermint: *Tendermint uses a PBFT-like consensus algorithm optimized for high-performance blockchain platforms. It achieves consensus within a limited number of validator nodes. Examples: Cosmos.*

Federated Byzantine Agreement (FBA): *Instead of a single validator set, FBA allows participants to choose whom they trust, creating overlapping "quorum slices" that lead to consensus across the network. Examples: Stellar, Ripple.*

Proof of History (PoH): *This is a new consensus mechanism introduced by Solana that uses a verifiable delay function to create a historical record proving that an event occurred at a specific moment in time. Examples: Solana.*

Proof of Space-Time (PoST): *Participants must prove that they have stored data for a certain amount of time, combining the concepts of Proof of Capacity and time to secure the blockchain. Examples: Filecoin.*

Protocol: *refers to a set of rules and standards that define how data is exchanged and how operations are carried out on a blockchain or decentralized network. These protocols establish the foundational structure for various blockchain networks and decentralized applications (dApps).*

Smart Contract: *Self-executing contracts with the terms of the agreement directly written into code. These contracts automatically enforce themselves once predetermined conditions are met.*

Liquidity: *The availability of assets in a market to be bought or sold without significantly affecting the asset's price. In DeFi, liquidity providers earn rewards by supplying assets to a liquidity pool.*

Liquidity Pool: *A pool of tokens locked in a smart contract that provides liquidity for decentralized trading, lending, and other activities on DeFi platforms.*

Mining: *The process of using computational power to validate transactions and add them to the blockchain in PoW systems. Miners are rewarded with cryptocurrency for their efforts.*

Halving: *A predetermined event where the reward for mining a block in a PoW blockchain (like Bitcoin) is cut in half. This happens roughly every four years and reduces the rate of new Bitcoin entering circulation.*

Gas: *A fee paid to execute transactions on a blockchain network, most commonly on Ethereum. Gas fees compensate miners for validating and securing the network.*

Encryption: *is the process of converting plain, readable data into an encoded format (ciphertext) to prevent unauthorized access. It uses algorithms and keys to scramble the data, ensuring that only those with the correct decryption key can interpret it. This protects sensitive information during transmission or storage. Encryption is fundamental to securing digital communications, online transactions, and personal data. It is widely used in applications like emails, messaging, and financial systems.*

Fork: *A split in the blockchain where a new version of the blockchain is created, often resulting in two separate cryptocurrencies. Forks can be soft (compatible with the old chain) or hard (not compatible, creating a new chain).*

Airdrop: *The distribution of free tokens to holders of a particular cryptocurrency, often as a marketing tool to promote a new project or reward early adopters.*

Whale: *A term used to describe individuals or entities holding large amounts of cryptocurrency, whose actions (buying/selling) can significantly impact the market.*

HODL: *A term originating from a misspelling of "hold," which has become slang for holding onto cryptocurrency through market volatility instead of selling.*

Initial Coin Offering (ICO): *An ICO is a fundraising method where a company or project issues its own cryptocurrency tokens directly to investors in exchange for capital, often using blockchain. Here the accountability remains on the issuer, who handles the entire process independently.*

Initial Exchange Offering (IEO): *An IEO is a fundraising method conducted through a cryptocurrency exchange, which acts as an intermediary. Investors purchase tokens directly on the exchange platform. Here the accountability is shifted to the Exchange, who offers an extra layer of who performs due diligence, adding an extra layer of credibility and security, and facilitates the entire process, including listing the token post-offering.*

Non-Fungible Tokens (NFTs): *are unique digital assets stored on a blockchain, representing ownership or proof of authenticity of a specific item, such as art, music, or virtual goods, that cannot be replicated or exchanged on a one-to-one basis like cryptocurrencies.*

Fungible tokens: *are digital assets that are interchangeable and identical in value. Each unit of a fungible token is indistinguishable from another, meaning one token can be exchanged for another without any loss* *or change in value. Cryptocurrencies like Bitcoin and Ethereum are examples of fungible tokens, where each coin has the same value as another coin of the same type.*

Difference Between Fungible and Non-Fungible Tokens:

Fungible Tokens

- *Interchangeable: each token is identical to another of the same type*
- *Divisible: Can be broken down into smaller units (e.g., 0.5 Bitcoin)*
- *Use Case: Primarily used as currency or store of value (e.g., Bitcoin, Ethereum).*

Non-Fungible Tokens (NFTs):

- *Unique: Each token represents a distinct item with its own value and characteristics.*
- *Indivisible: Cannot be split into smaller units (you can't divide a digital art piece)*
- *Use Case: Used to represent ownership of unique digital assets like art, music, or virtual items.*

Metaverse: *is a collective virtual space, combining augmented reality (AR), virtual reality (VR), and all the tools offered by Web3, where users can interact with each other and digital environments in real-time. It serves as a shared, immersive digital universe where people can socialize, work, play, and create, often using avatars and digital assets such as NFTs. The metaverse blends the physical and digital worlds, enabling experiences like virtual meetings, gaming, commerce, and cultural events.*

Web3: *is the next generation of the internet, built on decentralized technologies like blockchain. It enables peer-to-peer interactions without relying on centralized intermediaries, giving users more control over their* *data, identity, and digital assets. Web3 aims to create a more open, transparent, and user-driven web by integrating concepts such as cryptocurrencies, decentralized applications (dApps), and smart contracts. It marks a shift from the centralized web (Web2) to a decentralized, user-empowered ecosystem.*

Web 1.0 (The Static Web):

- *Time Period: 1990s to early 2000s*
- *Read-only, static web pages*
- *Limited interactivity for users*
- *Information was primarily consumed rather than created*
- *Centralized servers hosted content*
- *User Role: Consumers of content with little ability to interact (e.g., early websites, static HTML pages).*

Web 2.0 (The Social Web):

- *Time Period: Mid-2000s to present*
- *Interactive and social web, where users can create and share content (e.g., social media, blogs, forums)*
- *Centralized platforms controlled by tech companies (e.g., Facebook, Google)*
- *Dynamic content, responsive web applications, and real-time interactions*
- *Heavy reliance on user-generated content*
- *User Role: Active participants and creators of content, but data and platforms are controlled by centralized entities.*

Web 3.0 (The Decentralized Web):

- *Time Period: Emerging in the 2020s*

- *Decentralized systems powered by blockchain and distributed technologies*
- *Users control their own data, identity, and digital assets (e.g., through decentralized apps, crypto wallets)*
- *Peer-to-peer interactions without intermediaries*
- *Incorporates concepts like tokenization, decentralized finance (DeFi), and digital ownership (NFTs)*
- *User Role: Owners of data and digital assets, with more autonomy over their online interactions and transactions.*

Whitepaper: *a detailed document that outlines the technical specifications, goals, and structure of a cryptocurrency or blockchain project. It typically provides in-depth information about the project's technology, problem it aims to solve, use cases, tokenomics (the economic model of the token), and the roadmap for development. White papers are used to educate potential investors, developers, and users about the purpose and functionality of the project, offering transparency and credibility in the decentralized ecosystem.*

Yield farming: *in the context of cryptocurrency is a process where users lend or stake their crypto assets to generate returns or rewards, typically in the form of additional cryptocurrency. It is primarily associated with decentralized finance (DeFi) platforms.*

Centralized Exchange (CEX): *is a platform where users can buy, sell, and trade cryptocurrencies through an intermediary or central authority. These exchanges, like Binance, Coinbase, or Kraken, manage users' funds and private keys, facilitating transactions and ensuring liquidity. CEXs often provide additional services like margin trading, staking, and lending, and require users to trust the platform for security and custody. While they offer ease of use and high liquidity, centralized exchanges are susceptible to hacks and regulatory oversight.*

Decentralized exchange (DEX): is a type of cryptocurrency exchange that operates without a central authority or intermediary, allowing users to trade directly with one another via blockchain-based smart contracts. Unlike centralized exchanges, DEXs do not hold users' funds, and trades are conducted peer-to-peer, enhancing privacy and security. Popular DEXs include Uniswap and PancakeSwap. They often offer lower fees and reduced regulatory oversight but may have lower liquidity and slower transaction times compared to centralized platforms.

Blockchain explorer: is a web-based tool that allows users to view and search the public ledger of a blockchain in real-time. It provides detailed information on transactions, blocks, wallet addresses, and smart contracts, offering transparency and insight into blockchain activity. Users can track the status of their transactions, check wallet balances, and view historical data. Popular blockchain explorers include Etherscan for Ethereum and Blockchain.com for Bitcoin. These tools are essential for monitoring and verifying blockchain activity.

Cryptocurrency data aggregator: is a platform that collects, organizes, and displays real-time data on various cryptocurrencies, including prices, market capitalization, trading volume, and rankings. These tools provide comprehensive insights into market trends, historical data, and exchange listings, helping users and traders make informed decisions. The three most popular cryptocurrency data aggregators are CoinMarketCap, CoinGecko, and Nomics. These platforms serve as essential resources for tracking and analyzing the global crypto market.

The Epic of Crypto Space

From a futuristic vision, the dream of a decentralized currency, cryptocurrencies leverage blockchain technology to offer transparent, secure, and borderless transactions. Over the years, the crypto ecosystem has expanded to include thousands of coins, tokens, and applications, reshaping industries from finance to gaming. The history of cryptocurrency is a journey of technological innovation, economic disruption, and regulatory challenges. Understanding this evolution provides key insights into the future of digital finance and decentralized systems.

The story of blockchain technology didn't begin in some high-tech lab in the 21st century. No, its roots stretch back, deep into the fertile ground of cryptography and distributed systems, disciplines that quietly evolved over decades. Like the slow, patient growth of a tree, these two fields gradually developed the tools that would one day form the foundation for something far bigger, a decentralized digital ledger that would change the world. From the 1970s through the 1990s, cryptographic innovations and the concept of decentralization began to take shape, each step forward paving the way for the blockchain technology we know today. At the heart of this early development was cryptography, the quiet giant that laid the cornerstone of security. The 1970s and 1980s saw a revolution in how we think about secure communications, with public-key cryptography emerging as a key player. It was a game-changer, encryption wasn't anymore just a secret between two parties, but a dynamic, secure exchange, safeguarded by advanced algorithms and mathematical elegance. Public-key cryptography was the first spark, the whisper of a revolution that would eventually lead to the blockchain's robust, impenetrable system of trust. And so, in the hushed corridors of research labs and the minds of cryptographers, the foundations of blockchain were quietly being laid, brick by brick, algorithm by algorithm.

What the Hell is Cryptography?

Cryptography is the science of securing communication and data from unauthorized access, ensuring confidentiality, integrity, authenticity, and non-repudiation. It has been used for centuries, evolving from simple substitution ciphers in ancient times to highly advanced algorithms in modern computing. In the digital age, cryptography is fundamental to securing information, especially in sectors like finance, communication, and military operations. One of the most transformative applications of cryptography has been its use in blockchain technology, which underpins cryptocurrencies like Bitcoin and decentralized systems. Cryptography primarily deals with two key operations: encryption (the process of converting plaintext into ciphertext) and decryption (the process of converting ciphertext back into plaintext). There are various forms of cryptographic techniques that ensure the secure transmission and storage of data:

__Symmetric Key Cryptography:__ In symmetric key cryptography, both the sender and the receiver share the same key for encryption and decryption. The key must remain confidential for the system to be secure. While symmetric cryptography is efficient and fast, the challenge lies in securely distributing the key. Example: __The Advanced Encryption Standard (AES)__ is a widely used symmetric encryption algorithm.

__Asymmetric Key Cryptography:__ Also known as public-key cryptography, uses two keys: a public key (which can be shared with everyone) and a private key (which remains confidential to the owner). The public key encrypts the data, while the private key decrypts it, or vice versa. This system solves the key distribution problem of symmetric cryptography.

__Cryptographic Hash Functions:__ A cryptographic hash function is a mathematical algorithm that takes an input (or message) and returns a fixed-size string of bytes. The output, often called a hash or digest, is unique to the input data. They are:

__Deterministic:__ The same input always produces the same output.

Irreversible: It's computationally infeasible to derive the original input from the hash.

Collision-resistant: It's difficult to find two different inputs that produce the same output.

Cryptography in Blockchain Technology: plays a critical role in the operation of blockchain technology, ensuring that transactions are secure, immutable, and decentralized. Blockchain relies on cryptographic principles to create trust in a distributed network without a central authority.

Here's how cryptography is integrated into blockchain:

Public and Private Keys in Blockchain: In a blockchain network, every participant has a public key and a private key. The public key is used to generate a blockchain address and is publicly visible. The private key is used to sign transactions, proving ownership and authorization to transfer assets like cryptocurrencies. This public-private key system ensures that only the owner of the private key can authorize a transaction from their account. Example: In Bitcoin, users generate a wallet (which is essentially a pair of cryptographic keys) that allows them to send and receive Bitcoin securely.

Digital Signatures: Are used to verify the authenticity and integrity of a message, transaction, or data. In blockchain, digital signatures ensure that only the rightful owner of a cryptocurrency can authorize the transfer of funds. Each transaction is signed with the sender's private key, and anyone in the network can verify the signature using the corresponding public key. Example: *ECDSA (Elliptic Curve Digital Signature Algorithm)* is commonly used for digital signatures in blockchain systems, including Bitcoin and Ethereum.

Proof of Work (PoW): *In blockchain systems like Bitcoin, Proof of Work consensus algorithms rely on hash functions to create new blocks. Miners compete to solve a cryptographic puzzle by finding a nonce that, when hashed with the block data, produces a hash that meets specific difficulty criteria (usually starting with a certain number of leading zeros). This process secures the network and ensures immutability.*

Merkle Trees: *A Merkle tree is a cryptographic structure that organizes data into a tree of hashes, where each leaf node represents a data block's hash, and non-leaf nodes represent hashes of their child nodes. This ensures efficient and secure data verification by allowing any modification to be detected with minimal recalculations. Cryptographic hash functions are used in Merkle trees to structure transaction data efficiently. In a Merkle tree, each transaction is hashed, and these hashes are recursively combined to create a root hash, which summarizes all the transactions in a block. This helps ensure that the transactions are valid without storing the entire transaction history.*

Cryptographic Hash Functions: *A hash function takes an arbitrary input and produces a fixed-length output (the hash or digest). These functions are deterministic and ensure that even a minor change in input produces a radically different output. In blockchain technology, hash functions are used for various purposes:*

Hashing of Transactions: *Every transaction in a blockchain is hashed and included in a block.*

Linking of Blocks: *Each block in a blockchain contains the hash of the previous block, creating a secure and immutable chain.*

Proof of Work: *The process of mining requires solving cryptographic hash puzzles, where miners find a nonce that, when combined with the* *block data, generates a hash with certain properties (e.g., a specific number of leading zeros).*

Cryptographic Algorithm SHA-256 *is one of the most widely used cryptographic hash functions and is the backbone of Bitcoin's Proof of Work system. It takes an input of any length and produces a fixed 256-bit (32-byte) output. SHA-256 is highly secure and collision-resistant, making it ideal for cryptographic applications in blockchain.*

Elliptic Curve Cryptography (ECC): *Is a public-key cryptography system based on the algebraic structure of elliptic curves. ECC provides the same level of security as RSA but with much smaller key sizes, making it more efficient for use in blockchain systems. Most modern blockchains, including Bitcoin and Ethereum, use ECDSA (Elliptic Curve Digital Signature Algorithm) for securing transactions.*

Zero-Knowledge Proofs (ZKPs): *Is a cryptographic method that allows one party (the prover) to prove to another party (the verifier) that they know a certain piece of information without revealing what that information is. ZKPs are gaining popularity in blockchain for their privacy-preserving features. They are used in privacy-focused blockchains like Zcash, which allows users to hide transaction amounts and addresses while still verifying that the transaction is valid.*

Homomorphic Encryption: *Is a type of encryption that allows computations to be performed on encrypted data without needing to decrypt it first. This concept has enormous potential for blockchain and decentralized finance (DeFi), as it would allow sensitive financial data to be processed while remaining encrypted.*

Threshold cryptography: *Allows a group of participants to jointly perform cryptographic operations such as signing a transaction or de-*

crypting a message. It has applications in blockchain governance, where multiple parties must come to a consensus to approve changes.

__Quantum-Resistant Cryptography:__ As quantum computing evolves, it poses a threat to classical cryptographic algorithms. Blockchain developers are exploring quantum-resistant algorithms to future-proof blockchain networks.

__Multi-Party Computation (MPC):__ MPC allows multiple parties to jointly compute a function over their inputs while keeping those inputs private. MPC has the potential to enhance privacy and security in decentralized networks.

Public-key cryptography was first introduced by Whitfield Diffie and Martin Hellman in their landmark 1976 paper. Their method allowed secure data transmission across unsecured networks by using a pair of cryptographic keys, one public and one private. The breakthrough in public-key cryptography solved the problem of secure communication over open networks like the internet, which became increasingly relevant in the late 20th century. Traditional methods of encryption relied on a single, shared secret key, which had to be distributed securely before encrypted communication could take place. Diffie and Hellman's approach eliminated the need for such secure key distribution by creating a system where one key (the public key) could be openly shared, while the private key remained confidential. Anyone could use the public key to encrypt a message, but only the holder of the private key could decrypt it.

This system became fundamental to the blockchain's architecture, particularly for ensuring the security of transactions and data exchanges in decentralized networks. Public-key cryptography enables the use of digital signatures, a key feature in blockchain technology. Digital signatures ensure the authenticity and integrity of data, allowing participants in a decentralized system to verify the identity of senders and the accuracy of the information without relying on a centralized authority. By the 1980s, digital signatures were gaining wider attention as a tool for securing electronic communications, setting the stage for their future use in distributed systems. The ability to create verifiable and secure digital identities was a major step toward building decentralized systems where trust could be established without intermediaries.

While cryptography addressed the problem of secure communication and data integrity, the development of distributed systems provided the structural foundation for decentralization. The concept of distributed systems emerged in the 1980s as computer scientists sought to design systems that could operate efficiently and securely without relying on a single, centralized server. In a distributed system, data is stored and processed across multiple computers (or nodes) that work together as a network. This approach improves the resilience and fault tolerance of the system. If one node in a distributed network fails, the other nodes can continue to operate, making the system more resistant to outages, attacks, or other failures that could cripple a centralized system. Distributed systems also improved security. In centralized systems, a single point of failure, such as a data breach or a compromised server, can lead to catastrophic consequences. However, in distributed systems, no single point of failure exists, since the data is replicated across multiple nodes. This redundancy and decentralization make distributed systems more robust and difficult to compromise.

The concept of **Byzantine Fault Tolerance (BFT)** was also a major development in distributed systems theory during this period. BFT refers to a system's ability to continue functioning correctly even in the presence of some faulty or malicious nodes. The **Byzantine Generals Problem**, introduced in 1982, explored how a group of nodes could reach a consensus on a decision even if some nodes were unreliable. This problem was crucial for the development of decentralized consensus algorithms, which would later become a key feature of blockchain technology. At the same time, peer-to-peer (P2P) networks were becoming more common as a way to distribute data across multiple computers. P2P networks allow users to directly share files and information without relying on a centralized server. These networks embody the decentralized principles that blockchain would later adopt: participants contribute resources to the network, and data is distributed across all participating nodes, making the system more resilient and resistant to censorship or failure.

While cryptography and distributed systems were advancing in parallel, the issue of digital privacy became increasingly important. One of the leading figures in this space was David Chaum, a cryptographer who pioneered the idea of digital anonymity. In his 1983 paper, "Blind Signatures for Untraceable Payments," Chaum introduced a technique that would allow for anonymous transactions in a digital environment. His work laid the groundwork for future developments in both privacy-focused technologies and decentralized digital ledgers. Chaum's blind signatures enabled users to send and receive payments without revealing their identities, protecting privacy while ensuring the transaction's validity. This idea was revolutionary at a time when electronic communications were becoming more widespread, and concerns about personal privacy were growing. The concept of anonymous, decentralized transactions would later become a key feature in blockchain technology, where privacy and security are paramount concerns. In addition to his work on digital cash, Chaum founded **DigiCash**, a company that aimed to create a practical application of his privacy-preserving cryptographic techniques. While DigiCash ultimately failed to achieve widespread adoption, Chaum's innovations played a significant role in advancing the conversation around decentralized, secure systems.

By the 1990s, the stage was set for the development of blockchain technology. Cryptographic techniques such as public-key cryptography and digital signatures were widely understood and applied in various fields, while distributed systems and peer-to-peer networks demonstrated the power of decentralization. However, the specific architecture of a blockchain, a decentralized, immutable ledger that could record transactions across a distributed network, had not yet been fully realized. During this period, researchers and developers continued to experiment with new ways to create decentralized networks that could operate without relying on a trusted third party. These experiments laid the foundation for blockchain by addressing two key challenges: trust and consensus. In decentralized systems, trust is distributed across the network, meaning that participants must have a way to verify information and ensure that it has not been tampered with. At the same time, consensus algorithms were developed to enable distributed nodes to agree on the state of the system without relying on a centralized authority. In the late 1990s, these ideas began to coalesce, and the technological building blocks necessary for blockchain were in place. While the term "blockchain" would not be coined until the early 2000s, the cryptographic techniques, distributed systems, and decentralized consensus algorithms developed during this period laid the foundation for the emergence of blockchain technology.

And then comes the visionary Satoshi Nakamoto. Yes, it is perfectly true, much like Homer in ancient Greece, no one knows whether Satoshi Nakamoto truly existed or if he is merely part of an epic, Iliad-like myth. Yet, just as Homer's legacy transformed human culture, Nakamoto's influence has irrevocably changed the world of finance. However it went, legend tells us that in 2008, amidst the global financial crisis, an anonymous individual or group under the pseudonym Satoshi Nakamoto introduced a radical idea that would forever change the landscape of finance and technology. This vision was articulated in a white paper titled "Bitcoin: A Peer-to-Peer Electronic Cash System." Nakamoto's document proposed a decentralized digital currency, based on blockchain technology, that would allow direct transactions between individuals without the need for intermediaries like banks or governments. This revolutionary concept promised financial autonomy, transparency, and security, marking the birth of blockchain technology and its first practical application: Bitcoin. The timing was significant. The collapse of large financial institutions and the loss of trust in centralized systems had created a fertile environment for a new form of currency that could operate outside traditional control. Nakamoto's blockchain technology, which served as the backbone for Bitcoin, introduced a system that could independently verify, secure, and record transactions on a distributed ledger. This ledger, or blockchain, was maintained by a network of computers (nodes) across the globe, ensuring no single entity could manipulate or control it. It was the embodiment of decentralization, a dream that had been the domain of visionaries but had never before been realized. On January 3, 2009, Nakamoto mined the first Bitcoin block, known as the **Genesis Block**, with the inscription "The Times 03/Jan/2009 Chancellor on brink of second bailout for banks." This was a powerful statement, a reflection of Bitcoin's purpose as a reaction against the failures of the traditional financial system. The blockchain, for the first time, was alive. Bitcoin's genesis marked the beginning of a new financial era, but in the early days, few understood its significance. On October 31, 2008, when Nakamoto published the white paper, the idea was initially met with skepticism. However, a small group of cryptographers, known as cypherpunks, quickly recognized the potential of a decentralized digital currency. These early adopters would play a pivotal role in supporting and refining Bitcoin in its infancy. In 2009, Nakamoto released the first Bitcoin software, which allowed users to mine Bitcoin by solving complex mathematical problems, adding new blocks to the blockchain. During these early days, Bitcoin had no established market value. It was traded among enthusiasts as an experiment, a proof of concept for decentralized money. The first recorded exchange of Bitcoin for real-world goods occurred in May 2010, when Laszlo Hanyecz famously paid 10,000 BTC for two pizzas. At the time, the value of Bitcoin was fractions of a cent, but this event marked a turning point—it demonstrated that Bitcoin could function as a medium of exchange. Bitcoin may have been the trailblazer, carving the path into uncharted territory, but it didn't take long for others to follow.

Between 2011 and 2013, a wave of new cryptocurrencies, known as **Altcoins**, began to emerge. Each one built on the foundation Nakamoto had laid, but with its own unique twist, offering a glimpse into the vast possibilities of blockchain technology. **Namecoin** was the first to break free from Bitcoin's shadow in 2011. Its ambition? To decentralize the domain name system (DNS) and create censorship-resistant websites. It was bold, innovative, if not entirely successful. But Namecoin introduced something powerful: the idea that blockchain could be used for more than just currency. Later that year, **Litecoin** entered the scene. Created by Charlie Lee, it was designed to be Bitcoin's quicker, lighter counterpart, offering faster transaction times and using a different hashing algorithm, Scrypt. Litecoin became known as the silver to Bitcoin's gold, and unlike many early altcoins, it endured, solidifying its place in the crypto world. In 2012, **Ripple** took a different approach. It wasn't designed to challenge Bitcoin but to complement traditional finance. Ripple's mission was clear: to enable instant, low-cost international payments between banks, serving as a bridge between the old financial system and the rising world of cryptocurrency. That same year, **Peercoin** emerged with a focus on sustainability. It introduced the concept of proof-of-stake, a significant departure from Bitcoin's energy-hungry proof-of-work system. This innovation sought to reduce the need for massive computational power, planting the seed for future environmentally-conscious blockchains. And then came **Dogecoin** in 2013. What started as a joke, based on the beloved Doge meme, unexpectedly grew into something far more significant. With its fun, friendly community, Dogecoin became a symbol of the rapidly evolving and increasingly diverse world of digital assets. It proved that in this new landscape, even a meme could have staying power. Each of these altcoins, in its own way, added a new chapter to the unfolding story of cryptocurrency, showing that the possibilities for blockchain extended far beyond Bitcoin. These early cryptocurrencies expanded the potential use cases of blockchain technology, moving beyond the concept of digital currency to explore applications in domains like DNS, banking, and energy-efficient consensus mechanisms.

As Bitcoin and altcoins grew in popularity, the need for a way to trade them became apparent. In 2010, **BitcoinMarket.com** was launched, becoming the world's first Bitcoin exchange. Soon after, in 2011, **Mt. Gox**, initially a platform for trading **Magic**: The Gathering cards, pivoted to become the largest Bitcoin exchange. This marked the beginning of an era where cryptocurrencies could be traded for traditional fiat currencies like the U.S. dollar and euro. In the early days, trading Bitcoin was a challenge. Without established exchanges, transactions were often conducted through forums or peer-to-peer platforms, with participants negotiating prices and methods of exchange. However, the launch of exchanges like Mt. Gox made it easier to buy and sell cryptocurrencies, catalyzing the market's growth. At this time, Bitcoin's value remained relatively low. In 2010, it was still worth less than a dollar, but the establishment of exchanges helped its value steadily increase. By 2011, Bitcoin had risen to $1, and by 2013, it had crossed the $1,000mark for the first time, sparking mainstream media attention. In 2015, the blockchain world took a significant leap forward with the launch of **Ethereum**, created by Vitalik Buterin. Unlike Bitcoin, which was primarily designed as a currency, Ethereum introduced a revolutionary new concept: smart contracts. These self-executing contracts could automate transactions and agreements, enabling developers to build decentralized applications (dApps) on top of the Ethereum blockchain. Ethereum's introduction of smart contracts expanded the blockchain's potential, allowing for applications in industries such as finance, supply chain management, and even digital identity verification. Ethereum also pioneered the concept of tokens, enabling the creation of new cryptocurrencies and decentralized assets through initial coin offerings (ICOs). Ethereum's impact on the blockchain space was profound. By 2017, it had become the second-largest cryptocurrency by market capitalization, second only to Bitcoin. The introduction of smart contracts made Ethereum a platform for innovation, spawning countless decentralized projects that would later shape the world of decentralized finance (DeFi) and non-fungible tokens (NFTs).

In 2017, blockchain and cryptocurrencies exploded into the mainstream consciousness. This was the year of the Initial Coin Offering (ICO) boom, where startups and blockchain projects raised billions of dollars by issuing new tokens on platforms like Ethereum. ICOs allowed companies to raise capital quickly and without the need for traditional venture funding, but they were also unregulated, leading to a mix of legitimate projects and fraudulent schemes. As new tokens flooded the market, cryptocurrency prices skyrocketed. Bitcoin hit an all-time high of nearly $20,000 in December 2017, and Ethereum reached $1,400. Altcoins like Ripple (XRP) and Litecoin also saw massive gains. This bull market brought millions of new investors into the space, and media outlets around the world began covering the "crypto revolution" extensively. However, the rapid rise in prices was not without its drawbacks. Many ICOs were speculative ventures or, even worst, scams, and by early 2018, the market experienced a significant correction, with many tokens losing the majority of their value and some others disappearing. Despite this, the technological advancements and innovations of 2017 laid the groundwork for the next phase of blockchain's evolution.

As the world of cryptocurrencies continued to evolve, a new phenomenon took center stage: non-fungible tokens (NFTs).

What the Hell are NFTs?

Non-Fungible Tokens (NFTs) are a type of digital asset that represents ownership or proof of authenticity of a unique item, typically built on blockchain technology. Unlike cryptocurrencies such as Bitcoin or Ethereum, which are fungible (each unit is identical and interchangeable), NFTs are non-fungible, meaning each token has distinct attributes that make it unique and not interchangeable. NFTs can represent a wide range of assets, including digital art, collectibles, music, virtual real estate, and more. NFTs have gained significant attention in recent years, especially in the realms of art, gaming, and entertainment. The ability to tokenize and prove ownership of digital content has opened up new markets and opportunities for creators, collectors, and investors.

History:

Early Concepts of Digital Scarcity: *The concept of digital scarcity, creating a limited supply of digital assets, began before the introduction of NFTs. In the early 2010s, projects like **Colored Coins** on the Bitcoin blockchain explored how blockchain could be used to represent real-world assets and ownership of digital assets.*

CryptoKitties and the Birth of NFTs (2017): *The modern era of NFTs began with CryptoKitties in 2017, a blockchain-based game where users could collect, breed, and trade virtual cats. Built on the Ethereum blockchain using the **ERC-721** token standard, CryptoKitties demonstrated the potential of NFTs for representing unique digital items. The game became so popular that it famously congested the Ethereum network, drawing attention to the scalability challenges of blockchains but also establishing NFTs as a promising new category in the crypto space.*

2018–2020: Early NFT Adoption: *Between 2018 and 2020, a number of NFT platforms emerged, focusing on digital art, collectibles, and virtual real estate. Projects like **Decentraland**, **Axie Infinity**, and **SuperRare** began building communities around the concept of digital ownership. Although these platforms saw moderate success, NFTs remained relatively niche during this period, primarily attracting crypto enthusiasts.*

2021, The NFT Boom: *In 2021, NFTs exploded into mainstream consciousness, driven by major sales, celebrity endorsements, and widespread media coverage. The sale of **Beeple's** digital artwork "Everydays: The First 5000 Days" for $69 million at Christie's auction house in March 2021 became a landmark moment for NFTs. Other high-profile sales included NFT collectibles like **Bored Ape Yacht Club** and **CryptoPunks**, further cementing NFTs' role in the digital economy.*

Tokenomics of NFTs: *Tokenomics refers to the economic and structural characteristics of a token, including how it is created, distributed, and used. In the case of NFTs, tokenomics revolve around scarcity, utility, and ownership.*

Scarcity: *is one of the core principles behind NFT value. NFT creators can control the supply of tokens by minting a limited number of copies or ensuring that each item is a 1-of-1 edition. For example, a digital artist* can create a single NFT representing their artwork, ensuring that only one person can own the original, much like a physical piece of art.

Utility: Some NFTs are not just collectibles but also have utility within ecosystems. For instance, in gaming, NFTs can represent in-game assets, such as characters, weapons, or skins, that players can use within a game. In virtual worlds like Decentraland, NFTs represent land parcels that users can develop or monetize.

Ownership and Royalties: One of the most revolutionary aspects of NFTs is the ability to embed royalty structures directly into the token's smart contract. This means that creators can earn a percentage of each subsequent sale of their NFT, providing a continuous revenue stream. For example, if an NFT is sold in the secondary market, the original creator could automatically receive 10% of the sale price.

Technology Behind NFTs: NFTs are primarily built on blockchain technology, and Ethereum is the most common blockchain for creating and trading NFTs, though other blockchains like **Flow, Binance Smart Chain,** and **Solana** are also gaining popularity.

Ethereum and ERC-721 Standard: The vast majority of NFTs are created using the ERC-721 standard on Ethereum. ERC-721 defines the minimum interface required for a smart contract to manage, trade, and verify ownership of NFTs. It allows each token to have a unique identifier and metadata, ensuring its uniqueness.

ERC-1155 Standard: was introduced to improve on the limitations of ERC-721. ERC-1155 allows for the creation of both fungible and non-fungible tokens within the same smart contract, making it more efficient for projects that require both types of assets, such as games where you may need fungible tokens (e.g., in-game currency) and non-fungible tokens (e.g., unique items or characters).

NFTs are powered by smart contracts, *self-executing agreements with terms directly written into code. These smart contracts automatically verify ownership, handle transfers, and enforce royalty payments. The transparency and immutability of blockchain ensure that once an NFT is minted, the data on its ownership and provenance is permanently recorded and publicly accessible.*

Interoperability: *NFTs can function across different platforms and applications. For example, a sword represented as an NFT in one game could potentially be transferred and used in another game. While full interoperability remains a challenge, some projects and standards are working toward this vision.*

Most Important and Successful NFT Projects:

CryptoPunks: *Launched in 2017 by Larva Labs, CryptoPunks is one of the earliest and most iconic NFT projects. It features 10,000 unique pixel art characters, each with different traits and attributes. CryptoPunks have been highly sought after by collectors and investors, with individual punks selling for millions of dollars.*

Bored Ape Yacht Club (BAYC): *is a collection of 10,000 unique Bored Ape NFTs created by Yuga Labs in 2021. Each Bored Ape grants its owner access to a private "yacht club," including exclusive events, merchandise, and additional NFTs. BAYC has garnered widespread attention from celebrities and collectors, with individual apes selling for six to seven figures.*

Beeple's "Everydays: *The First 5000 Days" Beeple (real name: Mike Winkelmann), a digital artist, made history when his NFT artwork "Everydays: The First 5000 Days" sold for $69 million at auction in March 2021. This event was a major milestone in bringing NFTs into the main-*

stream art world, showing that digital art could command prices similar to traditional artworks.

Decentraland: *Is a decentralized virtual world where users can buy, sell, and develop virtual land parcels, all represented as NFTs. Users can build structures, host events, and create experiences within the virtual world. Each parcel of land is unique, and ownership is tracked via the Ethereum blockchain. Decentraland is a prime example of how NFTs can extend beyond art and collectibles to virtual real estate.*

Axie Infinity: *is a blockchain-based game where players collect, breed, and battle fantasy creatures called Axies. Each Axie is represented as an NFT, and players can earn rewards by participating in the game's ecosystem. Play-to-earn mechanics have made Axie Infinity incredibly popular, especially in developing countries where players can earn income by playing the game.*

In 2021, NFTs became a cultural phenomenon, with digital artworks selling for millions of dollars. Musicians, athletes, and brands also began exploring NFTs as a way to engage with their audiences in new and innovative ways.

~ 6 ~

LANGUAGE

Computer Languages Used in Crypto Cryptocurrencies and blockchain technology rely on various programming languages to create decentralized applications (dApps), smart contracts, and the underlying blockchain infrastructure. Each language has its strengths, suited to different aspects of blockchain development, from building smart contracts to constructing consensus mechanisms. We will cover the major languages used in crypto, in order of priority or prominence, starting with Solidity and moving on to others like Vyper, Rust, Golang, and more.

Solidity emerges as the language that shapes the very fabric of the Ethereum blockchain. It's the tool of choice for developers crafting the intricate web of smart contracts that power decentralized systems. Its reach extends beyond Ethereum, weaving through platforms like **Binance Smart Chain (BSC) and Polygon**, binding these networks with the same elegant precision. Born from the mind of Gavin Wood, a visionary co-founder of Ethereum, Solidity is now under the stewardship of the **Ethereum Foundation.** Its purpose is singular yet powerful: to give life to smart contracts. Solidity is the language that brings them to life, dictating how agreements will unfold in a world where code is law. Solidity stands out with its key features, offering developers a powerful tool that feels familiar yet designed for a revolutionary purpose.

It carries the high-level structure of languages like JavaScript or C++, statically typed to ensure precision, while allowing for the creation of complex logic within smart contracts. Every function, every operation, carefully constructed to follow exact rules, brings those contracts to life in ways both simple and intricate. At its core, Solidity integrates seamlessly with the **Ethereum Virtual Machine (EVM)**, the heartbeat of the Ethereum network, where these contracts are executed. Solidity's power doesn't stop there. It supports inheritance, letting contracts borrow from others, making them more efficient and modular. It also offers libraries and user-defined data types, expanding the possibilities for developers. The use cases are vast. Solidity is the backbone of decentralized applications (dApps), helping developers create systems that operate autonomously on the blockchain. It's the language behind the coding of Initial Coin Offerings (ICOs) and widely adopted token standards like **ERC-20** and **ERC-721**, which fuel the world of tokens and NFTs. Some of the most transformative projects in the crypto space owe their existence to Solidity. **Uniswap**, the decentralized exchange where users trade without intermediaries, and **Compound**, a decentralized finance (DeFi) platform for lending and borrowing, are just two shining examples of what Solidity makes possible.

Vyper emerges from the Ethereum landscape, carved with precision and intent. It stands as an alternative to Solidity, designed not with complexity in mind, but with an unwavering focus on simplicity and security. Where Solidity weaves intricate logic, Vyper strips things down, offering a cleaner, more deliberate path for developers who prioritize safety over feature-rich code. Born from the hands of the Ethereum community, Vyper exists to answer a need, an alternative that reduces the risk of vulnerabilities. It avoids the lure of complexity, recognizing that with too many features, the cracks in security begin to show. Its key feature is its

Python-like syntax, making it a comfortable transition for developers who have worked in the Python world. Vyper's strength is in what it doesn't have. There are no complicated tricks, no function overloading, recursion, or inheritance to navigate. This conscious limitation ensures fewer opportunities for things to go wrong. In this world of smart contracts, where every vulnerability is a door left open, Vyper locks it tight. The use cases for Vyper are clear: it shines in environments where security is paramount, where the cost of complexity is too high. It's used to write smart contracts that must function with utmost precision, particularly in high-security applications. Among the projects that trust Vyper's simplicity is **Curve Finance**, a decentralized finance protocol focused on stablecoin trading. Here, in the quiet precision of its code, Vyper proves its worth, safeguarding transactions in a space where stability is everything.

Rust stands tall in the world of systems programming, a language forged with precision and care. It's known not just for its raw power, but for its ability to ensure safety in the most critical of areas: memory. In a field where speed and security often clash, Rust brings harmony. It's the trusted language for several of the newer blockchains, like **Solana** and **Polkadot**, where performance is everything, and the stakes are high. Birthed by **Mozilla Research**, Rust isn't just another programming language, it's a solution. Built to handle the demands of high-performance systems, it finds its place perfectly in the infrastructure of blockchains, where every nanosecond and every byte counts. Rust's defining features shine through in every line of its code. It offers memory safety without relying on a garbage collector, guarding against bugs that have plagued developers for decades, null pointer dereferencing, buffer overflows, all prevented by Rust's careful design. It doesn't stop there. Rust's built-in concurrency ensures that systems can run in parallel, safely and efficiently, making it a natural fit for the decentralized, distributed worlds of blockchains. Rust finds its purpose in writing the very core infrastructure of these blockchains, the foundational code that keeps everything running. It also steps into the realm of smart contracts, offering developers a tool for building on platforms like Solana, where speed and reliability are critical. In the hands of developers, Rust is more than just a language, it's a way to build systems that are fast, safe, and unbreakable, the perfect companion for the future of blockchain.

Golang, or simply Go, emerges from the halls of **Google** with a quiet confidence. It's a language born for efficiency, designed to handle the complexities of server-side applications and blockchain platforms with the same calm precision. Statically typed and compiled, it moves with the speed and reliability needed in a world where every process matters. Created by Google, Go's purpose is clear from the outset: to build systems that are both scalable and secure. It's a language that doesn't get tangled in complexity. Instead, it thrives on simplicity, letting developers write clean, readable code that won't collapse under its own weight. And behind that clean syntax lies the power that supports the concurrent handling of processes, the lifeblood of blockchain nodes. Multiple processes run efficiently, side by side, without missing a beat. Go compiles fast, it executes even faster, making it an ideal choice for systems that can't afford to slow down. Go's true strength shows in its use cases. It is the foundation upon which blockchain node software is built, the language trusted to write consensus algorithms and manage transaction validation. Projects that demand stability and precision turn to Go. In the world of blockchain, **Hyperledger Fabric** stands as a testament to Go's capabilities, an enterprise-grade platform built on permissioned networks. **Cosmos SDK**, a framework designed to build interconnected blockchains, also leans on Go's strengths, ensuring that every piece of the puzzle fits together seamlessly. Go doesn't shout—it works, efficiently and quietly, its fingerprints all over the systems that drive the future of blockchain technology.

C++ stands as one of the oldest giants in the programming world, a language renowned for its raw power and relentless efficiency. It's been the backbone of countless systems, and in the realm of blockchain, it's the foundation upon which the pillars of decentralized technology are built. Created by the visionary Bjarne Stroustrup, C++ was designed to offer deep control over memory and CPU resources, making it the perfect fit for the demanding, performance-critical world of blockchain nodes. The language's true strength lies in its low-level memory control, allowing developers to extract every ounce of performance from their machines. It's the kind of control that blockchains need, where every byte, every cycle, can mean the difference between success and failure. C++ also brings multi-threading to the table, giving it the ability to handle complex operations and distributed systems, the lifeblood of blockchain infrastructure. Its use cases are as powerful as the language itself. C++ builds the very core of blockchain software, driving some of the most high-performance blockchains in existence. It's also trusted to craft the intricate cryptographic libraries and consensus mechanisms that underpin the security and reliability of decentralized networks. Some of the most iconic projects owe their existence to C++. **Bitcoin**, the original cryptocurrency, has its entire core software, **Bitcoin Core**, written in this language, a testament to C++'s enduring strength. **EOS.IO**, a platform designed for building scalable decentralized applications, also taps into the power of C++, trusting it to handle the vast scale and complexity that its network demands. In the world of blockchain, C++ doesn't just endure, it thrives, shaping the systems that power the future of decentralized technology with the same precision and power it's always had.

Python enters the scene quietly, with a simplicity and elegance that belies its power. It's a language known not for raw speed or efficiency like C++ or Rust, but for its accessibility. Developers of all levels are drawn to Python's clear, readable syntax, finding it easy to learn yet versatile enough to handle the complexities of blockchain development. Created by Guido van Rossum, Python's purpose is clear: to be a tool that anyone can pick up, a language designed for scripting, automation, and data analysis. Though Python may not race ahead in performance, it thrives in areas where speed isn't the sole focus. It plays a pivotal role in scripting, testing, and prototyping, the behind-the-scenes work that brings blockchain projects to life. Its readable syntax makes it an ideal choice for collaboration, where developers can easily share and build upon each other's work. And Python's vast array of extensive libraries, from cryptography to data science, makes it a go-to tool for a wide range of tasks, giving it a versatility that few other languages can match. In blockchain, Python finds its place. It writes testing frameworks for smart contracts, making sure everything runs smoothly before those contracts go live. It scripts automation for blockchain integration with web applications, making the complex seem effortless. Python is also the backbone for lightweight blockchain applications, where ease of development and iteration are key. Some of the most important projects in the blockchain world turn to Python for its unique strengths. **Ethereum's PyEthereum**, the original Python implementation of Ethereum, was used for testing, a critical part of Ethereum's development. **Truffle**, a development framework for Ethereum smart contracts, uses Python for automation and scripting, proving that even in a space where performance is paramount, Python's simplicity and power have their own indispensable role to play. In the hands of its developers, Python becomes more than just a language, it's a bridge between ideas and execution, offering a smooth path through the complexities of blockchain development.

JavaScript, a language born for the web, finds itself woven into the fabric of the blockchain world. Its journey starts with creating interactive websites, but it evolves, expanding its reach into decentralized applications, or dApps, where users interact with the blockchain seamlessly. Brendan Eich first brought JavaScript into existence, and over time, it becomes indispensable not just for building engaging frontends, but also for shaping the architecture behind the scenes. Enter **Node.js**, the runtime that allows JavaScript to step beyond the browser. Developed by Ryan Dahl, it brings JavaScript to the backend, where it powers services that dApps rely on. Its event-driven architecture thrives in an environment where asynchronous operations are the norm. In the world of decentralized apps, where every interaction with the blockchain happens in real-time, this feature is critical. Node.js handles the complex dance of requests and responses with ease, making sure the system runs smoothly without missing a beat. Together, JavaScript and Node.js offer something unique, an ability to build both the frontend and backend of a dApp. A developer can use a single language to create the entire ecosystem, from the user interface to the backend services and APIs that interact with smart contracts on the blockchain. It's an elegant solution for a complex problem, and developers embrace the simplicity of working with a unified toolset. JavaScript's influence is felt in some of the most widely used blockchain projects. **Metamask**, the popular Ethereum wallet and dApp browser extension, is built with JavaScript, making it easy for users to interact with their digital assets. **Web3.js**, the JavaScript library that connects users to the Ethereum blockchain, allows developers to create browser-based blockchain applications, from wallets to exchanges. It's a language that has found its place not only in the world of the web but at the heart of blockchain technology, where it bridges the gap between users and the decentralized world. **JavaScript and Node.js**, once tools for web developers, now power some of the most important innovations in blockchain, shaping the way people connect with decentralized systems. Their story is one of transformation, adapting to new challenges and thriving in the fast-paced world of dApps.

Simplicity enters the blockchain world with a quiet sense of purpose, a language crafted with precision and safety at its core. It's not like the others, born from complexity and speed. Instead, Simplicity emerges with a singular focus, security, ensuring that every line of code written for smart contracts is not just functional but flawless. Created by **Blockstream**, a company known for pushing the boundaries of blockchain technology, Simplicity is designed for those who seek certainty in an uncertain digital landscape. In its essence, Simplicity offers something rare, a formal verification. This isn't just code that runs, it's code that can be mathematically proven to be correct. Developers no longer have to hope their smart contracts will work as intended, they can know. By stripping away potential pitfalls like loops and recursion, Simplicity reduces complexity and the risks that come with it. It's a language that doesn't allow for ambiguity, where every contract is crafted with exacting care. Simplicity finds its use in the realm of smart contracts where security and correctness are paramount. It is especially tailored for platforms built on the **Bitcoin blockchain**, where stability and trust are more important than fast-moving innovations. This language becomes the tool of choice for developers working on systems that need to be bulletproof, where mistakes aren't an option. One of the key projects embracing Simplicity is the **Liquid Network**, the Bitcoin sidechain platform developed by **Blockstream**. Here, Simplicity's strengths are put to the test, providing the foundation for contracts that demand absolute reliability and security. It is the language of those who prioritize safety over speed, precision over flash, building systems that can stand the test of time in the ever-evolving world of blockchain.

Haskell stands apart in the world of programming, a language defined by its mathematical precision and elegance. It isn't just built for speed or simplicity, it's crafted for those who value correctness above all. Born from the minds of academics and nurtured as an open-source project, Haskell is a functional programming language where every computation is treated with the care of a mathematical proof. For those working on blockchain projects that prioritize security and correctness, Haskell becomes the tool of choice. Its purpose is clear: Haskell offers a world of formal verification and safe code execution, making sure that every line of code behaves exactly as expected. There's no room for ambiguity. With strong static typing, Haskell ensures that the code is type-safe, catching errors before they ever reach runtime. Its use of immutable data aligns perfectly with the concept of blockchain's immutable ledger, where every transaction is etched permanently into the record. Haskell's use cases are steeped in security. It's trusted to write secure smart contracts, where a single flaw could mean the difference between success and disaster. Developers turn to Haskell when they need to build blockchain infrastructure that not only works but works flawlessly, with a focus on correctness and reliability. One of the most prominent projects leaning on Haskell's power is **Cardano**. The smart contract platform **Plutus**, built on Cardano, uses Haskell as its foundation. It's no coincidence that a blockchain project so focused on formal methods and security would choose Haskell, a language that embodies those values in every function, every immutable line of code. Haskell isn't just a tool for developers, it's a statement of intent. It says that in a world of ever-growing complexity, some things—like security and correctness, are non-negotiable.

Java steps into the scene as a versatile, object-oriented language that has made its mark across countless industries, and blockchain is no exception. Created by **Sun Microsystems**, Java carries with it a legacy of portability and scalability that makes it a reliable choice for large-scale applications. Its power lies in its ability to transcend platforms, a language that fulfills the promise of "write once, run anywhere." For blockchain developers, this portability means that nodes can operate seamlessly across different systems, a crucial feature in the world of decentralized networks. Java's purpose is clear from the outset: it's built to be platform-independent, a language designed to handle the complexities of large, distributed systems. Scalability is where Java shines, allowing developers to create expansive blockchain networks that can grow and evolve without losing stability or performance. Java's strengths find their use in the core of blockchain development, from building the very nodes that keep the network alive, to designing intricate consensus algorithms that ensure everything runs smoothly. For enterprise-level blockchain applications, where scale and reliability are key, Java provides the foundation. One of the notable projects harnessing Java's power is **IOTA**, a cryptocurrency project with its sights set on the **Internet of Things (IoT)**. In this world, where devices connect and communicate seamlessly, Java's portability and scalability prove to be invaluable, offering the stability needed to manage such an interconnected vision. Java is more than just a programming language, it's a cornerstone for developers building the future of blockchain, a tool that offers both reliability and flexibility in an ever-expanding digital landscape.

Clarity is a smart contract language designed to run on the **Stacks** blockchain, anchored to Bitcoin's immutable foundation. Unlike other languages, Clarity is built on one core principle: decidability. Every outcome is known before the code runs, ensuring certainty. Its syntax, reminiscent of **Lisp**, embraces structure, with parentheses encasing every expression. The journey begins simply: an integer variable called counter, initialized at zero. A function forms to increase its value. In Clarity, functions are called explicitly, returning a single immutable result. Once set, values remain unchanged, ensuring stability as the contract evolves. Data types like integers, booleans, lists, and tuples are precisely defined, shaping the contract's reality. For instance, a balance of one hundred units is declared and maintained throughout the contract's life.

Contracts are more than containers; they house public functions and variables, open to interaction. A public function sets the balance and returns a promise of success. Meanwhile, private functions remain hidden, essential but accessible only from within. Assertions enforce certainty at execution. If a condition fails, the contract halts. Tuples group related values, like "Alice" and her balance of one hundred, into cohesive units. When errors occur, the contract throws an error, refusing to proceed until resolved. Mapping transforms lists, applying private functions to each value, like multiplying each by ten, altering the data's course. Conditional statements guide the flow: if the amount is greater than zero, success, if not, an error halts progress.

Transfers are central to a smart contract's role, enabling asset movement. A single command transfers tokens, as reliably as Bitcoin's blocks. Contracts interact with one another, calling methods from other contracts and forming a web of cooperation. Finally, Clarity mandates an explicit return. Success is declared with an "Ok," or failure with an "Err." In Clarity, there are no loops or risks of endless execution, it always walks a straight line, knowing its end before it begins. This is Clarity: a language of certainty, predictability, and trust.

Cairo, developed by **StarkWare**, stands at the forefront of blockchain innovation, tailored for zero-knowledge proofs with a focus on scalability, privacy, and efficiency. It addresses the limitations of existing blockchains like Ethereum, where slow transactions and high gas fees are persistent challenges. As a language optimized for **STARKs (Scalable Transparent Arguments of Knowledge)**, Cairo enables developers to build decentralized applications (dApps) that operate efficiently off-chain while providing verifiable proofs on-chain.

Cairo, short for **Cairo Arithmetic Intermediate Representation for Zero-Knowledge**, is a low-level programming language resembling assembly code, designed to generate STARK proofs for verifiable computations without executing them directly on the Ethereum mainnet. It serves as a bridge between traditional blockchain constraints and the potential of Layer-2 solutions such as **StarkEx** and **StarkNet**, processing transactions off-chain to lighten Ethereum's load. Built for efficiency and transparency, Cairo bypasses the need for trusted setups by leveraging raw mathematical proofs. It powers highly scalable dApps, reducing the impact of Ethereum's gas fees and transaction delays. General-purpose and Turing-complete, Cairo is equipped to handle everything from simple financial transactions to complex decentralized applications with precision. In Layer-2 solutions like StarkEx, Cairo processes transactions in batches, converting the computational load into efficient STARK proofs that are verified on Ethereum at a fraction of the cost. StarkNet, a permissionless ZK-Rollup, further demonstrates Cairo's potential by enabling scalable smart contracts and dApps to thrive without hitting Ethereum's limitations.

Cairo's low-level control allows developers to fine-tune computations for maximum efficiency, though this comes with a steeper learning curve. Those who master Cairo unlock the ability to optimize their code and transform high-level computations into sleek, verifiable proofs. StarkEx, for example, uses Cairo to batch thousands of transactions into a single on-chain action, dramatically lowering costs. StarkNet, powered by Cairo, creates an ecosystem where DeFi protocols, NFT platforms, and complex dApps can scale effortlessly. Cairo's efficiency also extends to privacy-preserving applications, generating zero-knowledge proofs that validate computations without revealing sensitive data, balancing privacy and decentralization. In short, Cairo is a powerful tool for building scalable, efficient, and privacy-preserving applications, driving innovation in the decentralized world.

~ 7 ~

ESSENCE

Cryptocurrencies are highly diverse, each with its own unique purpose, project vision, underlying technology, and blockchain infrastructure. They differ in their functions, governance models, reward mechanisms, and the specific rules that guide their operation. It means that when you decide to buy or sell a specific coin, you must Do Your Own Research very well and in a in-depth way. These variations create a broad spectrum of digital assets, each designed to address different needs or use cases in the financial and technological ecosystem. One of the most significant distinctions within the cryptocurrency space is between decentralized finance (DeFi) and centralized finance (CeFi) cryptocurrencies. These two categories represent fundamentally different approaches to managing and governing digital assets. DeFi-based cryptocurrencies emphasize decentralization, removing intermediaries, and empowering users with direct control over their assets. In contrast, CeFi cryptocurrencies rely on centralized platforms and institutions to manage transactions and governance, often offering more traditional, familiar financial services. The philosophical and functional differences between DeFi and CeFi often place them in opposing positions, each reflecting a distinct vision of how financial systems should operate in the digital age. But let's dive in.

The CeFi Family

Centralized Finance, commonly referred to as CeFi, represents a financial system where centralized institutions, like Exchanges, play a significant role in controlling and managing assets. In CeFi, users trust intermediaries, **Exchanges**, to facilitate transactions, manage security, and handle custody of their digital assets, offering a more familiar financial experience for those used to traditional banking systems. CeFi platforms, such as **Binance**, **Coinbase**, and **Kraken**, offer cryptocurrency trading, lending, borrowing, and other financial services similar to those in traditional finance (TradFi).

What the Hell are Centralized Exchanges?

*Centralized exchanges (CEXs) are digital platforms that facilitate the buying, selling, and trading of cryptocurrencies. Unlike decentralized exchanges (DEXs), CEXs operate under a centralized authority, meaning a company or organization manages the exchange, sets rules, and controls user assets while providing security and liquidity. The concept of centralized exchanges for cryptocurrencies began after the launch of Bitcoin in 2009. Early exchanges provided a means for users to trade cryptocurrencies in a controlled environment, similar to stock exchanges. The first prominent CEX, **Mt. Gox**, was launched in 2010, initially designed for trading Magic: The Gathering cards before pivoting to crypto. However, the early history of centralized exchanges was marred by scandals and security breaches, most notably the collapse of Mt. Gox in 2014, which lost approximately 850,000 Bitcoin due to hacking and poor internal controls. This event highlighted the need for better security, regulation, and governance in the CEX space.*

Key Technology:

Order Book: *is a real-time, digital ledger that lists buy and sell orders for a particular cryptocurrency. It shows the prices at which traders are willing to buy (bids) or sell (asks), along with the amounts they wish to trade. The order book helps match buyers with sellers, facilitating transparent and efficient trading. It continuously updates as new orders are placed and executed.*

Order Matching Engines: *The core of any CEX is its order-matching engine, which facilitates trades between buyers and sellers. The engine matches orders based on price, time, and volume, ensuring efficient trading.*

Custodial Wallets: *Unlike decentralized exchanges, CEXs offer custodial wallets, where the exchange holds users' private keys and assets. This makes it easier for users to trade, but they must trust the exchange with their funds.*

Liquidity Pools: *CEXs often have liquidity pools or partnerships with market makers to ensure there is sufficient liquidity for trades, helping reduce* **slippage** *(the difference between the expected and actual trade price, caused by market volatility or low liquidity) and ensuring efficient market conditions.*

User Interface (UI) and User Experience (UX): *CEXs typically offer more user-friendly interfaces than DEXs, catering to a broader audience, including new users. They often provide features like charts, market data, and analytics tools to assist with trading.*

Security: *CEXs invest heavily in security measures, such as multi-signature wallets, cold storage for assets, 2-factor authentication (2FA), and* encryption protocols. However, as custodians of large amounts of crypto, they remain a significant target for hackers.

10 Most Popular Centralized Exchanges:

Binance: Founded in 2017, Binance quickly became the largest crypto exchange by trading volume.

Coinbase: Launched in 2012, Coinbase is a publicly traded company and one of the most widely used exchanges in the US.

Kraken: Founded in 2011, Kraken is one of the longest-standing crypto exchanges.

KuCoin: Launched in 2017, KuCoin is known for listing a wide variety of altcoins.

Gemini: Launched in 2015 by the Winklevoss twins, Gemini focuses heavily on compliance.

Bitfinex: Established in 2012, Bitfinex is known for its liquidity and trading volumes, especially in Bitcoin.

Crypto.com: Founded in 2016, Crypto.com is more than an exchange; it offers a wide range of financial services.

Huobi: Founded in China in 2013, Huobi now operates globally.

OKX (formerly OKEx): Launched in 2017, OKX is a major player in crypto derivatives and spot trading.

Bitstamp: One of the oldest exchanges, founded in 2011.

KYC/AML: *Centralized exchanges must implement Know Your Customer (KYC) and Anti-Money Laundering (AML) policies to prevent illegal activities like money laundering and terrorism financing. Failure to comply can lead to fines, sanctions, or legal action.*

Licensing: *Many countries require exchanges to obtain licenses to operate. For example, the US requires registration with agencies like **FinCEN**, and the EU has frameworks like **MiCA (Markets in Crypto-Assets)**.*

Data Privacy: *Exchanges are subject to data privacy laws such as GDPR (General Data Protection Regulation) in the EU, requiring them to protect users' personal information.*

Risk Assessment:

Custodial Risk: *As custodians of user funds, CEXs carry the risk of mismanagement or fraud. Users who keep assets on exchanges are vulnerable to hacks or internal failures, leading to loss of funds.*

Geopolitical Risks: *Regulatory environments differ across jurisdictions, and a CEX operating in multiple countries must constantly navigate changing laws. For instance, China's ban on crypto trading forced exchanges like **Binance** and **Huobi** to exit the country.*

Security Breaches: *As centralized entities holding significant crypto assets, CEXs are prime targets for hackers. High-profile hacks (e.g., **Mt. Gox, Bitfinex**) underscore the importance of security protocols.*

Regulatory Arbitrage: *Some exchanges attempt to operate in regulatory gray areas by setting up offshore entities, which can expose them to significant legal risks and potential shutdowns.*

CeFi has become a prominent model for digital asset management due to its ease of use, regulatory oversight, and range of services that often resemble traditional financial products. Unlike its decentralized counterpart, DeFi, which eliminates the need for intermediaries, CeFi introduces a layer of centralized control, providing services that many users are accustomed to in their daily financial lives. CeFi operates by providing users access to cryptocurrencies through Centralized Exchanges (CEXs) and platforms that handle all aspects of the process, from transaction processing to asset custody. These Exchanges function as intermediaries between buyers and sellers, handling order matching, liquidity provision, and ensuring transactions are processed efficiently. Users create accounts, deposit funds (either fiat currencies or cryptocurrencies), and trade within the platform. Unlike decentralized exchanges (DEXs), where transactions occur directly on a blockchain, CEXs maintain custody of user funds, executing trades off-chain, and later settling them on-chain.

As we said, CEXs usually offer Custodial Services. When users hold their digital assets on a centralized exchange, they are entrusting the exchange to manage the security and control of these assets. Users receive access to the funds through their accounts, but the actual control of the private keys (which grant full ownership of the assets) remains with the exchange. This is similar to how banks operate, where customers can access their funds through online banking but do not directly hold their cash. But CeFi platforms offer several layers of security and compliance: they usually operate under specific regulatory frameworks, depending on the jurisdiction in which they are based. This regulation ensures compliance with Anti-Money Laundering (AML) laws, Know Your Customer (KYC) protocols, and other legal requirements designed to protect consumers and the financial system. CeFi institutions generally require users to verify their identities before they can trade or withdraw large amounts of funds, adding a layer of security and compliance with government authorities. Moreover, CeFi platforms typically employ various security measures to protect user assets. These include two-factor authentication (2FA), encryption, and cold storage (offline wallets) to store the majority of customer funds. By using these security protocols, centralized platforms aim to prevent unauthorized access, hacking, and theft, although the custodial nature of CeFi can be a double-edged sword. Users must trust the platform to maintain security standards, and history has shown that breaches can still occur.

Buying cryptocurrencies through CeFi platforms is a process that feels almost intuitive, as these platforms are designed with simplicity in mind, catering to users of all experience levels. Let's take a walk through the steps involved. First, it all begins with creating an account. Users step into the world of centralized exchanges like Binance or Coinbase by providing their email addresses and crafting a secure password. A quick verification via email or SMS follows, confirming the legitimacy of the account. It's as if the door to a new digital marketplace swings open with just a few keystrokes. But before stepping too far inside, there's a checkpoint: KYC, or Know Your Customer. Most CeFi platforms require users to complete this process, especially if they're planning on diving deep into the world of large transactions. This step feels like an identity check at the gates, personal documents like a passport or driver's license, maybe even a proof of residence, must be submitted. It's a brief pause, a necessary formality before the adventure truly begins. With the formalities behind them, users are ready to deposit funds. Here, the platforms offer flexibility, fiat currencies like USD or EUR can be transferred via bank accounts, credit cards, or other payment methods, seamlessly converting into digital currency.

For those who are already seasoned in this world, the option to deposit existing cryptocurrencies is also available. Now the real action begins: the moment to buy cryptocurrencies. With their accounts funded, users navigate through the platform, browsing real-time market prices. It's a thrilling moment, much like shopping in a bustling market square. The choices are varied, and users can either buy cryptocurrencies instantly or place limit orders, patiently waiting for the price to reach a point that feels just right. Once the trade is made, there's a sense of accomplishment as the transaction confirmation rolls in. The purchased assets appear in their exchange wallet, like treasures safely tucked away in a vault. But buying is only the beginning of the journey—next comes the task of storing cryptocurrencies securely. In the realm of CeFi, users are faced with a decision: to leave their digital wealth in the exchange's wallet or to move it to an external one. It's a choice of comfort versus control, convenience versus security, as each storage method offers its own unique protection.

What the Hell is a Wallet?

*Cryptocurrency wallets are an essential component of the crypto ecosystem, where a wallet address is technically a **hashed version of the public key** and acts as a unique identifier for receiving cryptocurrencies. They allow users to store, manage, and transact with digital assets like Bitcoin, Ethereum, and other cryptocurrencies. In the crypto world, wallets don't actually store coins or tokens but rather manage the private keys that give you access to your digital assets on the blockchain. When a user initiates a transaction (e.g., sending Bitcoin), the wallet signs the transaction with the private key, which proves that the user is the rightful owner of the funds. This signed transaction is broadcast to the blockchain, where miners or validators confirm and add it to the ledger. There are various types of wallets, each designed with specific functionalities, levels of security, and convenience. We will explore the different types of cryptocurrency wallets, how they work, the key components involved, and their pros and cons.*

*A **cryptocurrency wallet** is a tool that allows users to interact with blockchain networks, sending, receiving, and managing digital assets. It comes in two essential forms:*

***Public Keys:** A public key is similar to an account number. It is a cryptographic code that allows users to receive cryptocurrencies. It is derived from a private key and is publicly shareable.*

***Private Keys:** The private key is the critical piece of data that proves ownership of your assets. It is secret and should never be shared. The private key allows the user to sign transactions and access their funds on the blockchain.*

***Types of Crypto Wallets:** Cryptocurrency wallets can be broadly into two categories: hot wallets and cold wallets. Each category has subtypes based on its functionality, security, and usage.*

***Type 1, Hot Wallets (Online Wallets):** Hot wallets are wallets connected to the internet and are accessible from various devices. They offer convenience for quick access and transactions but are also more vulnerable to online threats like hacking. They come in different options:*

Web Wallets:** Web wallets are wallets that are hosted online, typically by a cryptocurrency exchange or a third-party platform. These wallets are accessible through a web browser and do not require any software installation. Examples: **Coinbase, Binance, Kraken

***Pros:** Easy access, user-friendly, integrated services like trading and staking.*

***Cons:** Custodial by nature (the platform holds your private keys), subject to hacking or regulatory intervention.*

***Mobile Wallets:** Mobile wallets are applications installed on smartphones that allow users to send, receive, and store cryptocurrencies. They* are ideal for on-the-go transactions. Examples: **Trust Wallet**, **MetaMask** (also available as a browser extension), **Exodus**

Pros: Convenient, portable, supports QR code scanning for payments, often supports dApps.

Cons: Vulnerable to device loss, malware, and phishing attacks.

Desktop Wallets: Desktop wallets are software applications installed on a computer. They give users full control over their private keys and provide more advanced features compared to mobile wallets. Examples: **Electrum, Atomic Wallet, Exodus**

Pros: More secure than web wallets, good for users who prefer full control over their funds.

Cons: Susceptible to malware, hacks, and phishing if the computer is not secure.

Type 2, Cold Wallets (Offline Wallets): Cold wallets are not connected to the internet, making them highly secure against online threats. They are ideal for long-term storage of large amounts of cryptocurrencies. They come in different options:

Hardware Wallets: Hardware wallets are physical devices, typically resembling a USB drive, that store private keys offline. To make transactions, users connect the device to a computer or mobile device. Examples: **Ledger Nano X, Trezor, KeepKey.**

Pros: High security, even if connected to a malware-infected device, the private keys remain secure.

Cons: More expensive, less convenient for frequent transactions.

Air-Gapped Wallets: Air-gapped wallets are a specialized type of cold storage where the wallet never connects to the internet or any network. The wallet may be a computer or hardware device completely isolated from any external communications. Examples: Some advanced hardware wallets offer air-gapping, such as **Coldcard.**

Pros: *Extremely secure against online threats.*
Cons: *Complex setup, inconvenient for regular use.*

Feature	Custodial Wallet	Non-Custodial Wallet
Control	Private keys held by a third party	User has full control over private keys
Security Responsibility	The platform is responsible for security	User is responsible for securing private keys
Ease of Use	Beginner-friendly, requires minimal technical knowledge	More complex, requires understanding of key management
Backup and Recovery	The platform can help recover access if credentials are lost	No recovery option if private keys/seed phrase are lost
Trust Requirements	Requires trust in a third-party custodian	No need to trust a third party
Risk of Hacks	Funds are at risk if the platform is compromised	Funds are only at risk if the user mishandles private keys
Transaction Fees	Often lower for internal transfers	Standard blockchain network fees apply

Custodial VS Non Custodial Wallets

Let's dive a little deeper in the custodian and non custodial types of wallets, as differences, pros and risks are very different. The key difference between them lies in who controls the private keys, the crucial pieces of information required to access and manage the funds.

Custodial Wallets: *A custodial wallet is a type of cryptocurrency wallet where a third party, typically a centralized exchange or wallet provider, holds and manages the private keys on behalf of the user. This means that the user does not have full control over their funds but instead relies on the service provider to secure and manage access to the assets. When you create a custodial wallet, usually a centralized Exchange, the platform generates the private keys and holds them on your behalf. You* *can access your funds using your login credentials (username and password), but you do not directly control the private keys. The wallet provider manages the security, backup, and recovery of the keys, making it more user-friendly for people unfamiliar with private key management.*

Benefits:

Ease of Use: *Custodial wallets are user-friendly, as the service provider manages the private keys and security, making it simple for beginners to store and access their crypto without dealing with complex setups.*

Backup and Recovery: *Since the wallet provider holds the private keys, they can help recover funds if you lose access, unlike non-custodial wallets where you are solely responsible for your keys.*

Integration with Services: *Custodial wallets often integrate seamlessly with exchanges and financial services, allowing quick transactions, trading, and access to features like staking and lending.*

Risks:

Lack of Control: *The primary drawback of a custodial wallet is that you don't have control over your private keys. "Not your keys, not your coins" is a common saying in the crypto community, emphasizing the importance of self-custody.*

Counterparty Risk: *You must trust the custodian (the platform) to securely store and manage your funds. If the platform is hacked, goes bankrupt, or experiences a security breach, your assets may be at risk.*

Centralized Control: *Since custodial wallets are typically operated by centralized entities, they are subject to government regulations and may freeze your funds if compelled by authorities or due to internal policies.*

Non-Custodial Wallets: *A non-custodial wallet is a cryptocurrency wallet where the user has full control over their private keys and, therefore, their funds. In this setup, the user is solely responsible for the security and management of their private keys, with no third-party involvement. When you create a non-custodial wallet, such as through a hardware wallet or a software wallet like MetaMask or Trust Wallet, the private keys are generated and stored locally on your device. Only you have access to these private keys, often represented as a recovery seed phrase, a series of 12 or 24 words that can be used to restore access to your funds if needed. Non-custodial wallets give you complete autonomy over your funds, but they also place the responsibility for security and recovery entirely on you.*

Benefits:

Full Control: *Non-custodial wallets give users complete control over their private keys and, by extension, their funds. You are the only one who can access and manage your assets.*

Decentralization: *Non-custodial wallets align with the decentralized ethos of cryptocurrency, where there is no central authority controlling your assets. This means no one can freeze your funds or restrict your transactions.*

Security: *Since you control your private keys, your funds are immune to platform hacks, bankruptcy, or other risks associated with centralized services (as long as you manage your private keys securely).*

No Counterparty Risk: *You don't have to trust a third party to manage your funds, reducing the risk of loss due to the custodian's errors or malfeasance.*

Risks:

Responsibility for Security: *With great power comes great responsibility. If you lose access to your private keys or forget your recovery seed phrase, there is no way to recover your funds. This makes secure storage of keys essential.*

Complexity: *Managing private keys and using non-custodial wallets can be more technically demanding, especially for users who are new to cryptocurrency.*

Higher Risk of User Error: *The complexity of self-management increases the risk of mistakes, such as sending funds to the wrong address, mishandling private keys, or falling victim to phishing attacks.*

Multi-Signature Wallets: *A multi-signature (**multisig**) wallet is a type of wallet that requires multiple private keys to authorize a transaction. This is especially useful for organizations or joint accounts where more than one person must approve a transaction before it is processed. Multisig wallets are ideal for businesses or groups that need collective control over funds, such as decentralized autonomous organizations (DAOs). Examples of multisig: **Gnosis Safe**, Popular for managing crypto assets in organizations, **Electrum,** that offers multisig functionality for Bitcoin.*

Security:

Security is a major concern for cryptocurrency holders, as funds are often targeted by hackers. The level of security depends on how wallets are used and whether the user is diligent about protecting their private keys.

Backup and Recovery: *Most non-custodial wallets generate a recovery seed phrase, a series of 12 or 24 random words that can restore the wallet and its associated funds in case of device loss or damage. It is crucial to store this seed phrase securely, as losing it means losing access to the wallet forever.*

Two-Factor Authentication (2FA): *Many custodial wallets and exchanges offer two-factor authentication for added security. This requires users to verify their identity using a second method (such as a code from a mobile app) in addition to their password.*

Hardware Wallets for Long-Term Security. *For long-term storage of significant amounts of cryptocurrency, hardware wallets are considered one of the most secure options. Since they store private keys offline, they are virtually immune to online attacks like phishing, malware, and hacks.*

Avoiding Phishing and Malware: *Phishing, Attackers may try to trick users into giving up their private keys or recovery phrases via fake websites or emails. It is essential to verify the authenticity of any website or wallet provider before entering sensitive information, as malware can steal private keys or intercept transactions. Using a secure device and updated antivirus software is important when managing cryptocurrency wallets.*

The world of centralized finance, or CeFi, offers a promise of simplicity and ease, where even a beginner can feel confident navigating the intricate landscape of cryptocurrency. User-friendly interfaces make the journey smooth, thoughtfully designed to guide newcomers through the maze of trading and investment with ease. For those who might be daunted by the complexities, CeFi provides a comfortable entry point, where technology takes the hand of the user and leads them forward. In this centralized world, high liquidity reigns supreme. CeFi platforms, vast in scale and operating with the assurance of centralized control, offer users the ability to buy and sell large amounts of cryptocurrencies without causing waves. Transactions flow seamlessly, with minimal price slippage, making it feel like the markets themselves bend to accommodate the trader's will. For many, CeFi's greatest strength lies in regulation and trust. Knowing that these platforms operate within the bounds of local laws brings a sense of security, a comfort in trusting your funds to institutions that play by the rules. It's a relationship built on the understanding that the platform will uphold its end of the bargain.

And if things go wrong? Customer support is always there, a lifeline for users, especially those still finding their feet in the volatile world of crypto. Whether through live chat or email, help is just a click away, ready to resolve issues with accounts, transactions, or security, giving users peace of mind. But no system is without its cracks. The very thing that makes CeFi so powerful, centralization, also carries its greatest risk. Entrusting assets to a third party means handing over control of the private keys. In moments of crisis, be it a security breach or platform failure, users could find themselves cut off from their funds, powerless to reclaim them. And while regulation offers comfort, it's also a source of uncertainty. The shifting sands of cryptocurrency regulation mean that CeFi platforms are constantly at the mercy of new laws and rules. Governments may impose sudden restrictions, limiting services or closing off entire markets, leaving users and platforms alike scrambling to adapt. Then there's the ever-present shadow of security breaches. Despite the robust security measures most platforms now boast, history has shown that no system is infallible. High-profile hacks have struck in the past, wiping out fortunes in a single stroke. And though the walls are higher now, the risk still lingers, a reminder that even in this polished, user-friendly world, danger is never far away.

The DeFi Family

The rise of decentralized finance (DeFi) has revolutionized the way we think about financial services, offering a radically different approach from traditional, centralized financial systems. As cryptocurrencies become more integrated into the global economy, decentralized finance is leading a movement toward open, permissionless, and trustless systems. DeFi allows users to access financial services such as lending, borrowing, trading, and earning interest without relying on intermediaries like banks or financial institutions. Decentralized finance refers to the broad category of financial services built on blockchain technology, specifically on decentralized networks such as Ethereum, Binance Smart Chain, and Solana. DeFi aims to remove intermediaries in financial transactions, providing peer-to-peer services that allow for greater transparency, reduced fees, and enhanced control over one's assets. In traditional finance (CeFi), central entities like CEXs are required to facilitate transactions. In contrast, DeFi uses smart contracts, self-executing contracts, with the terms of the agreement directly written into code to automate these processes. The trust is placed in technology and code rather than third-party institutions. At the heart of the DeFi lies a suite of services. Among these, decentralized exchanges (DEXs) stand as the true pioneers.

Platforms like **Uniswap** and **PancakeSwap** don't just offer a marketplace, they offer freedom. Here, users trade tokens directly from their wallets, with no need for an intermediary, no gatekeeper standing between them and their assets. It's peer-to-peer trading in its purest form, where control and privacy remain firmly in the hands of the individual, and the flow of assets moves as smoothly as the code that runs the exchange.

What the Hell is a Decentralized Exchange?

Decentralized Exchanges (DEXs) are platforms that allow users to trade cryptocurrencies directly with one another without the need for a central authority or intermediary, such as a bank or a centralized exchange (CEX). They operate through blockchain technology, leveraging smart contracts to enable peer-to-peer transactions. DEXs are a key component of the decentralized finance (DeFi) movement, aiming to create a more open, permissionless, and transparent financial system. The concept of DEXs began gaining traction alongside the rise of cryptocurrencies, particularly Bitcoin and Ethereum, in the 2010s. Early cryptocurrency exchanges were centralized, operating much like traditional stock exchanges, where users had to trust the platform to hold their funds. These centralized platforms were vulnerable to hacking, fraud, and regulatory intervention, which led to the creation of DEXs. The first significant decentralized exchange was **EtherDelta**, launched in 2017, which allowed users to trade Ethereum-based tokens (ERC-20) directly through smart contracts. However, EtherDelta's user interface and performance were not user-friendly, and the platform faced several legal issues. It wasn't until 2018-2020 that DEXs began to see widespread adoption, with the launch of platforms like **Uniswap, SushiSwap, and Balancer**, which brought better usability and liquidity. DEXs operate on a blockchain, typically Ethereum, though newer platforms have expanded to other blockchains such as **Binance Smart Chain, Solana**, and **Avalanche**. The core technology behind DEXs involves:

Smart Contracts: These are self-executing contracts where the terms are written directly into code. In DEXs, smart contracts facilitate trades, manage liquidity pools, and execute other financial functions without requiring an intermediary.

Liquidity Pools: Users deposit pairs of cryptocurrencies into a pool to enable trading. These pools provide liquidity for the exchange and are essential for DEXs, as they eliminate the need for an order book like centralized exchanges.

Automated Market Makers (AMMs): DEXs commonly use AMMs, where liquidity pools are algorithmically managed to set the price of assets. Popular AMM models include the **Constant Product Market Maker** used by **Uniswap.** This contrasts with traditional exchanges, where prices are determined by buy and sell orders.

Cross-chain Bridges: Some DEXs have developed cross-chain capabilities, allowing users to trade assets across different blockchain networks (e.g., Binance Smart Chain to Ethereum).

Top 10 Popular Decentralized Exchanges:

Uniswap (Ethereum): The most popular DEX, known for its simplicity and extensive liquidity pools. It uses the AMM model and is a leader in Ethereum-based token swaps.

SushiSwap (Ethereum, Multiple Chains): Forked from Uniswap, SushiSwap adds features like staking and yield farming and supports multiple chains.

PancakeSwap (Binance Smart Chain): The largest DEX on Binance Smart Chain, PancakeSwap offers lower fees compared to Ethereum-based DEXs and includes yield farming and lotteries.

Balancer (Ethereum): A unique DEX where liquidity providers can create custom pools with multiple assets. Balancer also supports weighted pools.

Curve Finance (Ethereum, Multiple Chains): *Focused on stablecoin trading, Curve offers low slippage and fees for stablecoin pairs, making it ideal for stablecoin arbitrage.*

dYdX (Ethereum): *A DEX focused on derivatives and margin trading, offering perpetual contracts and advanced trading features not commonly found on other DEXs.*

Serum (Solana): *A high-speed DEX built on the Solana blockchain, known for low fees and fast transactions due to Solana's high throughput.*

QuickSwap (Polygon): *A DEX on the Polygon network, QuickSwap offers the advantages of low transaction fees and quick trades, leveraging the Ethereum Layer 2 solution.*

In the uncharted waters of decentralized exchanges, where privacy, censorship resistance, and complete control over funds are the defining features, there lies a shadow, regulatory challenges and risks that threaten the very freedom they offer. One of the greatest concerns is the lack of KYC/AML compliance. Most DEXs don't enforce the rigorous Know Your Customer (KYC) or Anti-Money Laundering (AML) rules that centralized exchanges are bound by. This freedom comes at a cost. As regulators across the globe, from the U.S. to the EU and China, tighten their grip on illicit financial activities, decentralized platforms find themselves walking a tightrope. Their very nature defies traditional oversight, yet they are increasingly under the watchful eyes of authorities. Beyond the regulatory landscape, security risks loom large. Decentralized exchanges are powered by smart contracts, brilliant in concept but vulnerable to flaws in execution. Poorly written code can become an open door for exploits, and there have been numerous instances where hackers have drained liquidity pools, leaving users reeling. For those who provide liquidity or trade on these platforms, the technical risks are ever-present, like a storm cloud on the horizon.

Then, there's the murky terrain of regulatory gray areas. Decentralization makes it difficult for governments to pinpoint a central authority, yet the law is catching up. In 2021, the **U.S. Securities and Exchange Commission (SEC)** signaled that even decentralized protocols might fall under securities laws if they facilitate the trading of regulated assets. The rules, once aimed at centralized exchanges, are slowly creeping into the decentralized realm. Sanction risks are another concern. DEXs, being free from central control, can be used to circumvent sanctions or trade in restricted assets, a scenario that raises alarms among governments. Developers and contributors to these protocols, though decentralized in nature, may find themselves in the crosshairs of the law if their platform becomes a haven for illegal activities. Despite the illusion of anonymity, legal accountability still haunts the minds of developers.

The story of **EtherDelta** stands as a cautionary tale, though decentralized, its creators were pursued by the SEC for facilitating unregistered trading. The message is clear: decentralization may not be an ironclad shield. Even within the platform, the lack of oversight makes DEXs fertile ground for market manipulation. The pseudonymous nature of trading on these exchanges leaves them vulnerable to practices like wash trading or front-running, where manipulators bend the rules in their favor, unchecked by the watchful eyes that govern centralized systems. But it's not just trading that thrives in these decentralized ecosystems. Platforms like **Aave** and **Compound** have redefined lending and borrowing, allowing users to lend out their cryptocurrencies and earn interest or borrow against their assets in a completely autonomous environment. And then there's **Yield Farming**, where protocols like **Yearn**. Finance dangle the promise of rewards, enticing users to provide liquidity to certain markets in exchange for the tantalizing opportunity to earn returns. It's an alluring dance of risk and reward, where the brave, and sometimes the reckless, seek fortune in the decentralized world. Yet, for all its promise, this new frontier remains fraught with uncertainty, a place where innovation and regulation wrestle for dominance. In the intricate world of DeFi a hidden universe operates behind the scenes. Decentralized applications, known as dApps, each one built on the solid foundation of blockchain technology.

What the Hell is a d'App?

Decentralized applications (dApps) are a key innovation in the crypto space, providing a new way to build applications that operate on blockchain networks without central control. dApps, or decentralized applications, are applications that run on a decentralized network of computers (blockchain) rather than being hosted on a centralized server. They often use smart contracts to function, ensuring operations are transparent, autonomous, and tamper-proof.

Key Components:

Backend on Blockchain: The code and data of dApps live on the blockchain, making them immutable and censorship-resistant.

Smart Contracts: These are self-executing contracts with the terms directly written into code, providing automation and security.

Frontend Interface: dApps still have a user-facing interface, typically accessed via a web or mobile app.

Characteristics:

Decentralized: *Operate on a peer-to-peer network or a blockchain, making them immune to control or shutdown by a single authority.*

Open-Source: *The source code is usually open, promoting transparency and allowing developers to contribute.*

Tokenized Economy: *Most dApps have their own native tokens used for transactions, incentivization, or governance.*

Trustless and Secure: *dApps rely on cryptographic security and consensus algorithms, eliminating the need for users to trust a third party.*

Types of dApps:

Financial dApps (DeFi): *Provide decentralized financial services like lending, borrowing, staking, and trading without intermediaries (banks, brokers). Example:* **Uniswap** *(decentralized exchange),* **Aave** *(lending/ borrowing platform).*

Gaming dApps: *Create play-to-earn environments where users can trade in-game assets or cryptocurrencies. Example:* **Axie Infinity, Decentraland.**

Social dApps: *Allow decentralized social networking, ensuring user control over data and preventing censorship. Example:* **Minds, Steemit.**

NFT dApps: *Facilitate the creation, trading, and showcasing of Non-Fungible Tokens (NFTs), which represent ownership of unique digital assets. Example:* **OpenSea, Rarible.**

Governance dApps: *Enable decentralized governance of protocols and communities through token-based voting. Example:* **MakerDAO, Compound** *(protocol governance).*

Utility dApps: *Provide services like decentralized storage, cloud computing, and identity management. Example:* **Filecoin** *(storage),* **Golem** *(computing).*

Popular Platforms for dApps:

Ethereum: *The largest and most popular platform for building dApps, known for its smart contract functionality and vibrant developer ecosystem.*

Binance Smart Chain (BSC): *A high-speed, low-cost alternative to Ethereum, gaining popularity due to its compatibility with Ethereum tools.*

Solana: *Offers fast transaction speeds and low fees, making it an emerging platform for dApps, particularly in DeFi and NFT spaces.*

Polkadot: *Allows interoperability between different blockchains and supports dApp development across chains.*

Cardano: *A platform focused on peer-reviewed research and security, growing in the dApp ecosystem.*

How dApps Work:

Smart Contracts: *A smart contract on the blockchain executes predefined rules autonomously. For example, a lending dApp might automatically distribute interest payments based on pre-set criteria.*

Blockchain Network: *Users interact with the blockchain via a dApp. When a user submits a transaction, it is sent to the blockchain, verified by the network's consensus mechanism, and recorded immutably.*

Wallet Integration: *Users access dApps through web browsers or mobile applications with wallet integration, such as* **MetaMask,** *to interact with the blockchain securely.*

Benefits:

Censorship Resistance: *No central authority controls the dApp, preventing censorship or shutdown by governments or corporations.*

Trustless Operation: *Users don't need to trust a third party, as dApps rely on blockchain's cryptographic security and consensus.*

Transparency: *All transactions are publicly recorded on the blockchain, ensuring accountability and traceability.*

Ownership of Data: *Users retain control over their data, unlike traditional applications where centralized services store and monetize user data.*

Interoperability: *Many dApps, especially in DeFi, can work together, allowing seamless interaction between different protocols and services.*

Challenges and Risks:

Scalability: *As blockchains grow in usage, network congestion can lead to high transaction fees and slower processing times (e.g., Ethereum's gas fees).*

User Experience: *dApps often require technical knowledge to use, which can be a barrier to mainstream adoption.*

Security Risks: *Smart contracts, if not properly audited, can be vulnerable to bugs and exploits, leading to loss of funds.*

Regulation: *The decentralized nature of dApps makes them hard to regulate, creating uncertainty for developers and users, especially in areas like DeFi.*

Dependence on Blockchain Performance: *The performance and usability of a dApp are dependent on the underlying blockchain's scalability and reliability.*

While there are several blockchains that support these applications, **Ethereum** stands as the primary backbone of most DeFi projects, revered for its groundbreaking smart contract functionality. But it's not alone—other networks, like **Binance Smart Chain** and **Solana**, have stepped into the spotlight, offering their own advantages, such as lower fees and lightning-fast transaction speeds. At the heart of this digital landscape lie smart contracts, the true workhorses of DeFi. These programmable contracts are like silent sentinels, poised to act the moment conditions are met. There's no need for a central authority to verify or enforce the terms; the code itself is the law. Transactions unfold seamlessly, as if orchestrated by an invisible hand. But none of this could exist without liquidity pools. These pools, governed by smart contracts, are vast reserves of tokens that allow platforms like Uniswap to facilitate instant token swaps. Users, known as liquidity providers, deposit their tokens into these pools and, in return, earn fees and rewards for their contributions. It's a system that relies on mutual trust, driven by code and incentivized by profit. Governance, too, takes on a unique form in the DeFi world. Many projects distribute governance tokens—tokens like **AAVE**, **UNI**, or **COMP** to users, giving them the power to steer the ship. These tokens grant voting rights, allowing users to influence the direction and decisions of the protocol itself, as if each token carried a voice of its own. To fuel this intricate ecosystem, DeFi relies on native tokens. These tokens power everything from transactions to staking to governance.

What the Hell is Staking?

Staking is a process in which cryptocurrency holders participate in the operation of a blockchain network by locking up (or "staking") their coins or tokens to support the network's security, operations, and consensus mechanism. Staking is central to Proof of Stake (PoS) and its variants, where participants (validators) are chosen to validate new transactions and secure the network based on the amount of cryptocurrency they hold and stake, rather than relying on energy-intensive mining, as seen in Proof of Work (PoW). Staking allows participants to earn rewards for securing the network, and it is seen as a more energy-efficient alternative to mining, particularly for modern blockchains.

Here are the current approximate annual yields (often called APY - **Annual Percentage Yield***) for staking on the five most popular Proof of Stake (PoS) blockchains. These rates can fluctuate based on network conditions, validator performance, and other factors. For final and confirmed conditions please check directly on the relevant Blockchain Explorer or platforms.*

Ethereum 2.0 (ETH)
Staking Yield: ~4% to 6% APY
Notes: The yield on Ethereum staking varies based on the total amount of ETH staked and the network's performance. Rewards come from newly minted ETH and transaction fees.

Cardano (ADA)
Staking Yield: ~4% to 5% APY

Notes: Cardano offers a consistent reward rate, with rewards distributed every epoch (around 5 days). **ADA** holders can delegate their stake to a pool without locking their tokens.

Polkadot (DOT)

Staking Yield: ~13% to 15% APY

Notes: Polkadot offers one of the higher staking yields among major blockchains. The rewards are influenced by the number of DOT staked and the network's inflationary model.

Solana (SOL)

Staking Yield: ~6% to 8% APY

Notes: Solana's staking rewards are relatively high due to the fast throughput of the network. Staking SOL typically requires choosing a reliable validator to maximize rewards.

Avalanche (AVAX)

Staking Yield: ~8% to 11% APY

Notes: Avalanche's staking rewards are based on the length of time tokens are staked and the performance of the validator. A minimum staking period of 2 weeks is required for validators.

These are approximate yields, and you should always verify the current rates with the respective networks or platforms you're staking with, as they can change over time.

Factors Affecting Staking Rewards:

Total Staked Supply: As more tokens are staked, yields tend to decrease due to a larger pool of stakers sharing the rewards.

Validator Performance: Poorly performing validators can lower your staking rewards or even result in slashing penalties (a penalty system used in Proof of Stake (PoS) networks to discourage misbehavior by val-idators)

Inflationary Models: Many blockchains mint new tokens as staking rewards, which can dilute the value of the tokens if inflation outpaces demand.

Unstaking (Unlocking): To withdraw your staked tokens, you must go through an unstaking process, which usually involves a delay known as an "unbonding" period (ranging from a few days to several weeks, depending on the network).

Risks of Staking:

Slashing: Validators can be penalized for misbehavior, such as going offline or trying to manipulate transactions. In such cases, a portion of the staked assets may be forfeited, a process known as "slashing."

Liquidity Risk: While staking, your tokens are locked up and cannot be easily sold. In case of price volatility, stakers may be unable to react quickly to market changes.

Validator Risk: If you delegate your stake to a validator, the reliability of that validator becomes crucial. Poorly performing validators (those who go offline or are slashed) can result in lower or no rewards for stakers.

Inflation Risk: Many PoS networks use inflationary rewards (i.e., new tokens being minted to reward stakers), which could devalue the token over time if demand doesn't keep pace with the increasing supply.

Staking vs. Yield Farming: Yield farming in crypto is a process where users lend or stake their cryptocurrencies in decentralized finance (DeFi) platforms to earn rewards, typically in the form of additional tokens. It *involves providing liquidity to pools, where users earn a share of transaction fees or interest. Yield farmers often move their funds between different platforms to maximize returns. Rewards can vary based on platform, token, and liquidity demand. It is a high-risk, high-reward strategy due to volatile markets and potential smart contract vulnerabilities. While both staking and yield farming (common in DeFi) involve locking up tokens to earn rewards, there are significant differences:*

Staking: *In PoS blockchains, staking secures the network and helps achieve consensus. Rewards come from block creation and transaction validation.*

Yield Farming: *In DeFi, yield farming involves providing liquidity to decentralized exchanges or lending protocols. The rewards are often much higher but come with higher risks, such as impermanent loss or smart contract vulnerabilities.*

Staking Platforms: *Several platforms have emerged to make staking more accessible to the average user. These platforms aggregate staking pools, making it easy for users to delegate their tokens and start earning rewards without running a validator node. Some popular platforms include:*

Binance Staking: *Binance offers staking services for several PoS blockchains, allowing users to earn rewards by simply holding coins on the platform.*

Coinbase Staking: *Coinbase supports staking for **Ethereum, Tezos,** and other blockchains, making it easy for users to participate.*

Kraken Staking: *Kraken provides staking services for a wide range of cryptocurrencies, including **Ethereum, Polkadot,** and **Cosmos.***

Users navigate this digital realm by connecting their crypto wallets, MetaMask being one of the most popular choices, and from there, they interact with smart contracts, executing transactions with a few simple clicks. The question then arises: how does one acquire DeFi tokens? Before entering the world of DeFi, users must first gather these tokens, the key to participation. Some tokens represent the native assets of specific platforms, AAVE for the Aave platform, for instance, while others are more general, designed to be used across the ecosystem. There are two main paths to acquiring these tokens. For beginners, centralized exchanges (CEXs) like Binance, Coinbase, or Kraken provide a familiar, user-friendly gateway. But for those already comfortable in the crypto landscape, the decentralized exchanges (DEXs) are where the true spirit of DeFi shines. On platforms like Uniswap, SushiSwap, or PancakeSwap, users can swap one token for another with ease. Here, no intermediaries stand between the user and their funds—just a direct connection to the blockchain.

Transactions on these DEXs are non-custodial, meaning the user retains full control of their assets from start to finish, no centralized entity in sight. In this world of code and contracts, DeFi operates like a self-sustaining machine, quietly reshaping the future of finance, one transaction at a time. But let's dive in how to Buy DeFi Tokens. The journey begins with a simple but crucial step: creating a wallet. In this world of decentralized finance, not just any wallet will do, you'll need one capable of storing tokens from the Ethereum or Binance Smart Chain ecosystems. **MetaMask** or **Trust Wallet** are two of the most popular choices, each acting as a digital safe where your future tokens will reside. Once you have your wallet, it's time to fund it. But this isn't as straightforward as pulling out cash. First, you must acquire Ethereum (ETH) or another base cryptocurrency from a centralized exchange, platforms like Binance, Coinbase, or Kraken. After purchasing your Ethereum, you'll transfer it to your new wallet. ETH will be your fuel, paying for gas fees as you navigate the DeFi landscape. Now, with your wallet funded and ready, it's time to venture to a decentralized exchange (DEX). Navigate to platforms like Uniswap or SushiSwap. You'll connect your wallet to the DEX, and once connected, ensure you have enough ETH to cover the transaction fees before moving forward. And then the moment arrives: swapping tokens. Here, you select the specific token you wish to purchase. Enter the amount, and with a single click, the transaction is executed. Behind the scenes, the blockchain verifies your trade, and before long, the tokens appear in your wallet, quietly awaiting your next move. Let's see now how to Store DeFi Tokens. Storing them securely is where the real responsibility begins.

Cryptocurrencies, particularly DeFi tokens, are frequent targets for hackers. Unlike centralized exchanges, decentralized platforms do not offer custodial services, so the safety of your tokens rests entirely in your hands. You're the custodian now. First, always enable Two-Factor Authentication (2FA) on any account or wallet that supports it. This extra layer of protection can be the difference between a secure wallet and a compromised one. Next, your private keys and seed phrases, the lifelines to your wallet, must be kept safe. Backup these keys, but never online. Instead, store them in a secure, offline location, whether it's within the encrypted walls of a password manager or tucked away in a physical vault. These are not to be shared with anyone, no matter what. Finally, phishing attacks lurk around every corner. Be vigilant when connecting your wallet to dApps, and always double-check URLs. One careless click could send your private keys straight into the hands of a thief. One of DeFi greatest gifts is permissionless access. Anyone, anywhere, with nothing more than an internet connection, can step into this world. There are no banks to contend with, no borders to cross, just you and the open doors of decentralized finance. With that access comes control and ownership. No middleman holds sway over your assets. In DeFi, the keys are yours, and with them, the power to navigate the market without the need for a centralized intermediary. It's a liberation from traditional systems, placing users firmly in the driver's seat. And the innovation! DeFi stands at the forefront of financial evolution, bringing forth concepts like yield farming, where users can earn returns by providing liquidity to pools, or automated market makers (AMMs) that ensure seamless trading.

What the Hell is an Automated Market Maker (AMM)?

An Automated Market Maker (AMM) is a type of decentralized exchange (DEX) protocol that enables the trading of digital assets without the need for a traditional order book. Instead, AMMs rely on mathematical formulas and liquidity pools to determine the price of assets and facilitate trades. AMMs are a core component of the decentralized finance (DeFi) ecosystem and have become popular due to their efficiency and ability to function without intermediaries. Here's a breakdown of how AMMs work and their key concepts:

Liquidity Pools

__Definition:__ A liquidity pool is a smart contract that holds reserves of two or more tokens. These tokens are deposited by liquidity providers (LPs) to enable trading between the assets in the pool.

__Mechanism:__ Instead of matching buyers and sellers, trades occur between users and the liquidity pool. When someone wants to swap tokens, they send one token to the pool and receive another token in return.

__Liquidity Providers (LPs):__ LPs deposit pairs of tokens (e.g., ETH/ USDC) into the liquidity pool. In exchange for providing liquidity, LPs earn a portion of the transaction fees generated by trades in the pool.

Incentives: LPs are incentivized to provide liquidity by earning fees and potentially earning additional rewards (like governance tokens).

Pricing Formula: AMMs like **Uniswap** use a mathematical formula to determine the price of assets. The most common formula is $x * y = k$, where:

x is the quantity of one token in the pool,

y is the quantity of the other token,

k is a constant, meaning the product of the two quantities must remain constant.

Price Impact: Large trades can significantly change the ratio of tokens in the pool, impacting the price due to slippage. This is a natural outcome of the AMM model.

Slippage: Slippage occurs when the price of an asset changes between the time a trade is initiated and executed. This is common in AMMs because large trades can shift the balance of tokens in the pool.

Mitigation: Traders can set slippage tolerance to minimize losses if the price changes too much during a trade.

Impermanent Loss: Impermanent loss occurs when the value of tokens in a liquidity pool changes relative to their value if they were held outside the pool. If the price of one token changes significantly, LPs may experience a loss compared to simply holding the tokens. The loss is called "impermanent" because it only becomes permanent if the LP withdraws their tokens from the pool. If the token prices return to their original ratio, the loss can disappear.

No Order Books: Traditional exchanges rely on order books to match buyers and sellers. AMMs, on the other hand, rely on liquidity pools, which means there is no need for an order book.

Gas Fees Impact: *Since AMMs operate on blockchains like Ethereum, transactions require gas fees. High gas fees can make small trades uneconomical, though layer-2 solutions (like Optimism or Arbitrum) are emerging to reduce costs.*

Popular AMMs:

Uniswap: *One of the first and most well-known AMMs, using the constant product formula.*

Curve Finance: *Specialized for stablecoins and uses a different formula that reduces slippage for assets with similar prices.*

Balancer: *Supports multiple tokens in a single pool (not just pairs), allowing for more complex portfolio management.*

Concentrated Liquidity (Uniswap V3): *In Uniswap V3, liquidity providers can choose specific price ranges in which to provide liquidity, concentrating their capital where it's most effective. This leads to more efficient use of capital and can increase rewards for LPs.*

Governance: *AMMs often use governance tokens (e.g., UNI for Uniswap, CRV for Curve) to allow users to participate in decisions about protocol upgrades, fee structures, and new features.*

Community Control: *Governance tokens enable decentralized control over the platform, giving the community power to shape its future.*

Key Advantages of AMMs:

Decentralized and Permissionless: *Anyone can provide liquidity or trade without needing to ask permission from a central authority.*

Efficiency: AMMs operate 24/7 and allow for fast, automated trading without the need for market makers or brokers.

Earn Fees: LPs earn passive income by providing liquidity, which can be attractive in markets with high trading volume.

Key Risks of AMMs:

Impermanent Loss: LPs risk losing value if asset prices fluctuate significantly.

Smart Contract Risk: Since AMMs are based on smart contracts, there's a risk of bugs or exploits in the code leading to losses.

High Gas Fees: On networks like Ethereum, gas fees can be prohibitively high during periods of congestion.

But with such power and innovation come risks. Smart contract vulnerabilities pose one of the most significant threats, tiny bugs or errors in the code can become gaping holes for hackers to exploit, siphoning off funds in the blink of an eye. Then there's regulatory uncertainty. DeFi operates in a shadowy space, often untouched by the laws that govern traditional finance. But this could change. As governments begin to tighten their grip, users may find themselves navigating new legal complexities, unsure of what the future holds. Finally, there are liquidity risks. Some DeFi projects may find themselves strapped for liquidity, especially in times of market volatility or during a security breach. In such moments, even the most promising projects can find themselves teetering on the edge of collapse. And so, DeFi is a landscape rich with opportunity but fraught with dangers. Those who dare to tread its paths must be both bold and cautious, ready for the rewards but ever aware of the risks. DeFi is poised to reshape the global financial landscape, offering unprecedented access to financial services. As decentralized governance and cross-chain solutions mature, DeFi could merge more seamlessly with traditional finance (TradFi), bridging the gap between decentralized innovation and real-world financial needs. The rise of layer 2 scaling solutions, increased interoperability across blockchains, and more user-friendly interfaces are likely to make DeFi accessible to a broader audience. However, the growth of DeFi will also depend on how global regulatory frameworks evolve, as governments and financial institutions grapple with how to regulate this decentralized and borderless ecosystem.

What the Hell are Decentralized Databases?

Decentralized databases in the crypto space are a critical component of decentralized systems like blockchain networks. A decentralized database is a distributed storage system where data is stored across a network of nodes, eliminating the need for a central authority. Each node holds a portion or the entirety of the data, and changes to the database must be validated and synchronized across all nodes. In the context of blockchain, decentralized databases complement the ledger system by offering efficient storage and retrieval, enabling decentralized applications (dApps) to manage data without relying on centralized servers.

Key Features of Decentralized Databases:

Immutability: Data, once written, cannot be altered or deleted without network consensus.

Trustless architecture: No central authority controls the database, instead, trust is established through cryptographic proofs and consensus mechanisms.

Fault tolerance: *Since the data is replicated across multiple nodes, the failure of one or more nodes does not compromise the entire system.*

Censorship-resistant: *No single entity can censor or block access to data, ensuring open and equal access.*

Security: *Data is cryptographically secured, and decentralization reduces the likelihood of single points of failure or breaches.*

How Decentralized Databases Work in Crypto:

In the crypto ecosystem, decentralized databases typically work in tandem with blockchain technology to handle data storage for decentralized applications. While blockchains manage the ledger of transactions, decentralized databases manage off-chain data like user information, files, or large-scale content. The blockchain layer ensures consensus and transaction integrity, while the decentralized database provides efficient and scalable storage, reducing blockchain bloat.

Popular Decentralized Databases in Crypto:

IPFS (InterPlanetary File System): *A peer-to-peer distributed file system. IPFS enables data to be stored in a decentralized manner, making it an ideal solution for file sharing and large-scale decentralized storage. IPFS is commonly used by dApps for managing files and data not directly on-chain.*

Filecoin: *Built on top of IPFS, Filecoin is a decentralized storage network where users can rent out their storage space to others. It incentivizes storage providers with FIL tokens, enabling a decentralized marketplace for data storage.*

Arweave: A blockchain-like storage solution that enables permanent data storage. Arweave focuses on archiving and storing data immutably, providing long-term decentralized storage solutions for dApps and users.

BigchainDB: A scalable blockchain database that combines blockchain's decentralization and immutability with traditional database functionality. It can handle high transaction volumes and provides a decentralized architecture for enterprise use cases.

Swarm: Originally developed as part of the Ethereum project, Swarm is a decentralized storage and communication system for the web3 ecosystem. It is designed to handle both data and messages, aiming to create a fully decentralized and incentivized network for storage and distribution.

Benefits of Decentralized Databases in Crypto:

Data Ownership: Users retain control over their data rather than handing it over to centralized entities.

Transparency: Decentralized databases are often public, allowing for greater transparency of how data is used and stored.

Security: Cryptographic techniques and consensus mechanisms help ensure the integrity and security of the data.

Cost-Effectiveness: Decentralized storage solutions like Filecoin and IPFS may reduce storage costs by tapping into unused global storage capacity.

Challenges of Decentralized Databases:

Scalability: Although decentralized databases are more scalable than traditional blockchains, they can still struggle with handling very large datasets or high-throughput applications.

Latency: Decentralized systems often have higher latency compared to centralized solutions due to the need for node synchronization and consensus.

Data Redundancy: To ensure availability and fault tolerance, data is often replicated across multiple nodes, which can lead to inefficient use of storage space.

Complexity: Managing and developing decentralized database solutions can be more complex compared to traditional centralized systems, requiring specific expertise in distributed systems and cryptography.

Use Cases in Crypto and Beyond:

Decentralized Applications (dApps): dApps need decentralized storage to operate effectively without relying on centralized servers. Decentralized databases store user data, transaction history, and files off-chain while interacting with the blockchain for verification and settlement.

NFT Storage: NFTs often reference metadata (like images, audio, or video files) stored off-chain in decentralized databases. IPFS is commonly used for this purpose, ensuring that NFT content is not controlled by any single entity.

Content Distribution: Platforms aiming to disrupt traditional content distribution models (e.g., video streaming, file sharing) can use decentralized databases to distribute data efficiently and securely.

Decentralized Social Networks: *These networks rely on decentralized databases to store user profiles, posts, and interactions in a way that's resistant to censorship.*

DeFi (Decentralized Finance): *Many DeFi platforms use decentralized databases to store non-transactional data such as market feeds, user profiles, and governance information, enhancing the decentralization of the entire ecosystem.*

The Future of Decentralized Databases:

As the crypto ecosystem continues to grow, the need for scalable and efficient decentralized databases will increase. Future advancements in decentralized storage technology may focus on improving scalability, reducing latency, and developing more user-friendly interfaces for developers and end-users. Layer 2 solutions, sidechains, and off-chain storage will likely evolve in parallel with decentralized databases, ensuring that decentralized applications can scale while remaining decentralized at their core. In conclusion, decentralized databases play a fundamental role in the crypto space by enabling data to be stored in a trustless, secure, and censorship-resistant manner. They are essential to the continued evolution of decentralized applications, DeFi, and the broader web3 movement, offering a solution that balances the need for security, transparency, and efficiency.

~ 8 ~

CRYPTOCURRENCIES

My favorite section of the book is finally here, a deep dive into the world of individual cryptocurrencies. We will take a closer look at some of the most important and influential digital currencies in the market today. Each cryptocurrency operates within a unique technological framework, using its own blockchain and underlying systems, making it essential to understand their key differences and functionalities. This exploration will cover in detail the first ten Cryptocurrencies by capitalization as per **CoinGecko** on the date of the writing of this book, along with the ecosystem of the first two, while we'll give a brief overview on the most important following coins.

We'll cover the technology behind them, and the specific blockchains they operate on. More importantly, we will analyze what sets each one apart, its unique value proposition and the role it plays within the broader digital economy. Some cryptocurrencies excel in providing decentralized financial services, while others are best suited for privacy, scalability, or as a stable store of value. By understanding their strengths, weaknesses, and best use cases, we can appreciate how each contributes to the rapidly evolving crypto landscape. As we dive deeper into this pool of digital assets, we'll highlight the factors that drive their adoption, the challenges they face, and what makes them stand out in an increasingly crowded space. But before you take the plunge and dive headfirst into this vast pool of coins, like **Scrooge McDuck** would, let me take a moment to clear up a few basic concepts. These will be your guide, helping you navigate how blockchain really works when it comes to cryptocurrencies and what it has to offer. From the role of blockchain explorers, to the the intricacies of the burning mechanism, a key player in the cutting-edge world of Tokenomics.

What the Hell is the Tokenomics?

Tokenomics (a blend of "token" and "economics") refers to the economic structure and system surrounding a cryptocurrency or blockchain-based token. It encompasses how a token functions within a particular ecosystem, its use cases, and the underlying factors that determine its value and distribution. Understanding tokenomics is essential for evaluating the sustainability, utility, and potential value of a project. Few basics:

Total Supply: The maximum number of tokens that will ever exist.

Circulating Supply: The number of tokens currently available in the market.

Token Distribution: How tokens are initially allocated, such as through an Initial Coin Offering (ICO), Initial Exchange Offering (IEO), or airdrop. Tokens might be allocated to early investors, developers, marketing efforts, or community rewards.

Governance: Some tokens give holders voting rights on project decisions or protocol changes (e.g., governance tokens like those in decentralized finance projects).

Access to Services: *Tokens may be used to pay for services or gain access to certain features within a blockchain platform or decentralized application (dApp).*

Incentives: *Tokens are often used to incentivize certain behaviors, such as staking, liquidity provision, or network participation. Tokens can be used to reward network participants, such as miners, stakers, or validators, for securing the network or providing liquidity in decentralized exchanges. Some projects have staking models where users lock up their tokens in return for rewards, further reducing the circulating supply.*

Token Governance and Economics:

Inflation/Deflation Models: *Whether the token has a fixed supply (deflationary) or if new tokens can be issued (inflationary). Deflationary models tend to increase scarcity over time, potentially driving up the value.*

Minting: *How new tokens are created and introduced into the ecosystem, often via mining, staking, or other consensus mechanisms.*

Burning: *Some projects periodically burn tokens, removing them from circulation, to control supply and affect price.*

Market Behavior:

Liquidity: *How easily the token can be traded on various platforms or exchanges. Higher liquidity typically results in less price volatility.*

Price Stability: *Some tokens (e.g., stablecoins) are designed to maintain a stable value, often pegged to another asset like the US dollar.*

Monetary Policy: Projects often define their own monetary policy, which can include rewards, vesting periods for founders or early investors, and how the project plans to sustain value over time.

For instance, in a decentralized finance (DeFi) project, tokenomics may involve:

Utility: Tokens are used to access platform features like yield farming or lending.

Governance: Token holders can vote on protocol upgrades or changes.

Rewards: Users are rewarded with tokens for staking, providing liquidity, or participating in governance.

Supply: The project may have a fixed supply, meaning no more tokens will be created, or it may introduce new tokens periodically to fund future developments.

The Burning Mechanism

A fundamental aspect of tokenomics planning is the burning mechanism. This process acts as a regulator of both liquidity and scarcity, directly influencing the inflation rate and the intrinsic value of any cryptocurrency. By reducing the total supply of tokens in circulation, burning helps maintain balance within the ecosystem, often driving up demand and price as tokens become more scarce. In many ways, this mechanism can be likened to the powerful tools used by central banks, like the Federal Reserve in the legacy economy, to manage money supply and inflation. However, in the decentralized world of crypto, burning is an automated and transparent process, giving projects greater control over their token's economic model while simultaneously enhancing its value proposition for holders and investors. It is a process where coins or tokens are permanently removed from circulation. A deliberate act, one that sends these tokens to a place from which they can never return, a burn address, a cryptic wallet no one can access. Once sent there, the tokens are lost to the void, making them unusable forever. It's a strategy, one with many faces, aimed at shaping the economy of the cryptocurrency itself. The burn address is a curious thing, visible for all to see on the blockchain, a string of random numbers and letters, like a vault with no key. One of the most notorious of these addresses on the Ethereum network is:

0x000000000000000000000000000000000000dead.

When tokens are sent here, their fate is sealed, they vanish from circulation, never to be touched again. The process begins with transaction initiation. A user, a project, or a protocol makes the decision to burn tokens. They prepare the transaction, sending the tokens to the designated burn address. The blockchain captures it all, recording the moment in its unchangeable ledger, where the burn is visible for anyone who cares to look. Once the transaction is complete, the tokens cease to exist in the ecosystem. And with them gone, the total supply updates, reflecting the new reality, a reality shaped by scarcity. One of the more notable examples of this came when Ethereum underwent its **EIP-1559 upgrade** in 2021. With this upgrade, a part of every transaction fee paid in ETH was burned. Each time a transaction was processed, a portion of the fee was sent to the burn address, reducing Ethereum's circulating supply bit by bit. By burning tokens, any project can curb inflation and maintain the value of the tokens that remain. **Binance Coin (BNB)** is a prime example of this strategy. The project regularly conducts burns, gradually shrinking the total supply. The goal? To cut the original supply of 200 million

BNB tokens in half, creating scarcity and potentially driving up value. In the realm of decentralized finance (DeFi), burning often plays a more dynamic role. Some protocols build burning into their reward systems or governance mechanisms. For instance, platforms like **Yearn.Finance** allow users to burn tokens in exchange for governance privileges, giving them a voice in how the protocol evolves. It's a form of participation, where burning becomes an entry ticket into the governance arena. Sometimes, burning tokens is about trust. Developers and project teams use it to show their long-term commitment. By burning a portion of their own tokens, they signal that they're here for the future, not just for short-term gains. In Initial Coin Offerings (ICOs), crucial projects may burn unsold tokens after the offering, showing investors they won't flood the market and drive down the token's value. Different projects employ different burning strategies. Some follow scheduled burns, tied to specific milestones or quarterly reports. Binance Coin is well-known for its regular, quarterly burns, based on the trading volume on the Binance exchange. Others, like **TRON (TRX)**, follow a more flexible path, conducting manual burns when market conditions or community sentiment call for it. And then there's the burn-on-transaction model, where a percentage of each transaction is automatically burned. This is common in deflationary tokens, where every movement of the token reduces the overall supply. **SafeMoon** is one such example, each transaction burns a percentage, shrinking the supply while redistributing rewards to holders. Some blockchains even use **Proof of Burn (PoB)** as a consensus mechanism. Here, participants burn their tokens to prove their commitment to the network, earning the right to create new blocks. It's a system where staking meets burning, with the added effect of reducing supply. **Slimcoin** uses this method, asking participants to sacrifice tokens in exchange for block creation rights. In other cases, projects perform token buybacks and burns. This is a model where a portion of profits is used to buy back tokens from the market, which are then burned.

The **PancakeSwap (CAKE)** platform employs this strategy, regularly buying and burning tokens to control supply and support token value. Burning isn't just a small-time mechanism, some of the biggest projects in crypto have used it. As we said above, Binance Coin (BNB) regularly burns tokens, with one of its largest burns to date in July 2021, when it burned over 1.29 million BNB, worth more than $390 million. Ethereum's EIP-1559 upgrade has turned ETH into a deflationary asset, burning ETH with every transaction. Even meme coins like **Shiba Inu (SHIB)** have embraced the concept, burning tokens to create scarcity within their massive supply. And sometimes, burning is a decisive move, as seen when the **Stellar Development Foundation (SDF)** burned 55 billion XLM tokens in 2019, cutting the total supply in half. The goal was to sharpen the foundation's focus and remove the excess from circulation, a bold move in an unpredictable market. The burning mechanism, in all its forms, is more than just a technical feature, it's a powerful strategy that shapes the supply and value of tokens across the cryptocurrency landscape.

Wrapped Coins

A wrapped coin, or a wrapped token, feels like a bridge between worlds, a way to carry one treasure into a land where it doesn't quite belong. It's a token that holds the essence of one cryptocurrency while existing on an entirely different blockchain. The term "wrapped" fits perfectly, as if the original asset is carefully placed inside a digital vault, then presented as a token on another blockchain. The beauty of it? This wrapped token carries the same value as the original, but now, it can travel through ecosystems and applications previously out of reach. Take **Wrapped Bitcoin (WBTC)** as an example. It's Bitcoin, but it lives on the Ethereum blockchain, allowing BTC holders to engage with Ethereum's decentralized apps, like DeFi protocols, all without having to part with their beloved Bitcoin. How does this magic happen? It starts with the issuance. You send your original cryptocurrency, say Bitcoin, to a custodian. This custodian, be it a smart contract, a decentralized entity, or even a centralized organization, holds your Bitcoin securely. In exchange, it issues an equivalent amount of wrapped tokens, ready to be used on the target blockchain. But the journey doesn't stop there. When you're ready to redeem your wrapped token and return to the safety of your original asset, you send it back to the custodian.

They release your Bitcoin, and the wrapped tokens are burned, disappearing from circulation as if they never existed. A delicate balance, the wrapped tokens always maintain a 1:1 peg with the original cryptocurrency. One WBTC always equals one BTC. Custodians ensure that the original asset remains securely locked up, mirroring the number of wrapped tokens in the wild. Much of this process is driven by smart contracts, handling the wrapping and unwrapping with automatic precision. Deposit the original crypto, and the wrapped tokens emerge. Redeem them, and they vanish, like a well-practiced magic trick. This tokenization isn't limited to cryptocurrencies alone. It opens doors to real-world assets like gold, fiat currencies, or even stocks. Take **Pax Gold (PAXG)**, for example—gold transformed into blockchain tokens, tradable and flexible in the world of digital assets. Popular wrapped coins have already made their mark. Wrapped Bitcoin (WBTC) reigns supreme, representing Bitcoin on Ethereum. It lets Bitcoin holders roam freely through Ethereum's decentralized platforms while their BTC value remains intact. **Wrapped Ethereum (WETH)** is another key player. Ethereum itself, reshaped to become ERC-20 compliant, so it can interact seamlessly with other tokens in the Ethereum ecosystem. **Wrapped Binance Coin (WBNB)** lets BNB users explore decentralized applications on Binance Smart Chain.

Even **Wrapped Filecoin (WFIL)** exists, allowing Filecoin holders to engage with Ethereum-based DeFi platforms, expanding the horizons of decentralized storage.

But with these opportunities come challenges. Interoperability is the key advantage, enabling assets from one blockchain to interact with another. It's a leap forward, allowing users and developers to build decentralized applications across multiple networks. And let's not forget the vast opportunities wrapped tokens bring to DeFi, giving users access to lending, borrowing, staking, and yield farming, services that might have been unavailable on their asset's native blockchain. Yet, it's not all smooth sailing. The process often relies on centralized custodians. Users have to trust that these custodians will hold their original assets securely, and that the 1:1 peg will hold. This introduces counterparty risk. WBTC, for instance, depends on centralized custodians to maintain its value. And then, there's the risk of smart contract vulnerabilities. The code that powers the wrapping and unwrapping could contain flaws, making it a potential target for hackers. A bug in the system, and funds could be lost. Liquidity issues are another concern. If there's not enough liquidity for a wrapped token on the target blockchain, it can become a challenge to trade or redeem it effectively. And if a custodian fails, whether due to hacking, insolvency, or fraud, the wrapped token could lose its value entirely, no longer backed by the original asset it once represented. Wrapped tokens stand at the crossroads of possibility and risk, offering users the chance to stretch their assets across blockchains while demanding trust and vigilance in return.

Blockchain Explorers

One of the most valuable tools you'll likely rely on frequently for verifying information on the blockchain is a Blockchain Explorer. These powerful platforms allow you to explore, track, and validate transactions, blocks, and addresses within a blockchain network. Whether you're checking the status of a transaction, viewing historical data, or verifying the legitimacy of an address, blockchain explorers provide transparent access to real-time information. For both newcomers and seasoned users, they serve as an essential resource, helping you navigate the often-complex world of blockchain with greater confidence. A blockchain explorer feels like a window into the heart of a blockchain network, a tool that lets users peer into the vast, interconnected web of records that make up the blockchain. With a few keystrokes, anyone can search and explore the endless rows of transactions, blocks, and addresses, all meticulously logged and available for viewing. It offers a user-friendly path into real-time information, from the details of a single transaction to the larger workings of the entire network. In the world of blockchain, where transparency is sacred, these explorers become indispensable for understanding the flow of data. Tracking a transaction becomes effortless with an explorer.

You simply enter a **Transaction Hash (TXID)** and suddenly, the screen lights up with every detail, who sent it, who received it, how much was transferred, and the fees paid to make it all happen. Each transaction, no matter how small, tells its own story, recorded permanently on the blockchain. For those curious about the building blocks of the chain itself, the explorer reveals the intricate details of every block added to the chain. It's all there, block height, timestamp, a list of the transactions held within, the miner or validator who earned the reward for securing it. The rewards themselves, freshly minted coins, shine as a sign of work done and effort rewarded. Wallets, too, open up under the explorer's gaze. Enter a wallet address and you can see everything, balance, the history of transactions, incoming and outgoing, all laid bare. Explorers offer a way to understand how funds flow, how tokens move across the network. And for those looking to submit transactions, explorers provide a snapshot of current transaction fees, a quick guide to avoid overpaying or getting caught in a bottleneck of delays. The explorer also serves as a mirror to the network's pulse, showing statistics in real-time. The hash rate, the difficulty, the total number of transactions—all available at a glance, a living portrait of the blockchain's ongoing work. For smart contracts, especially on networks like Ethereum, the explorer becomes even more important. It allows users to dig deeper into contract addresses, checking event logs and interactions with decentralized applications (dApps), giving insights into the mechanics of these coded agreements. Each blockchain often has its own dedicated explorer, tailored to its specific architecture.

For Bitcoin, platforms like **Blockchain.com** or **Blockchair** offer these insights, while Ethereum finds its records revealed on **Etherscan** or **Ethplorer**. Other blockchains, like Solana, Polkadot, and Cardano, have their own explorers: **Solscan**, **Polkascan**, and **Cardanoscan**, respectively, while **Tronscan** opens the world of Tron. For smart contracts, explorers provide access to source codes, interactions, and event logs, offering developers and users alike a window into the workings of blockchain applications. Explorers offer a range of possibilities, from transparency to research. It's a new level of insight, a way to see how all the pieces of the blockchain world fit together.

Atomic Swaps

An atomic swap unfolds like a delicate dance between two individuals, each holding the currency of their own world. They stand apart, separated by the invisible lines of blockchain networks, yet there is no need for a middleman. No third party will oversee the exchange. The process is direct, peer-to-peer, and, above all, trustless. The term "atomic" resonates in the air. It whispers a promise that this trade either happens fully or not at all, there is no halfway, no room for one to leave the other in the dark. Both will emerge with what they seek, or the exchange will unravel before it begins, protecting them both from fraud. Two users meet in this digital space. They do not rely on a centralized exchange but instead reach across their chains, their currencies. Bitcoin in one hand, Litecoin in the other, they prepare to swap. The magic of atomic swaps lies in their cross-chain nature. It matters not that their assets lie on different blockchain networks. A Bitcoin can be traded for a Litecoin, or perhaps for Ethereum, without the need to convert to a middle currency. The process flows naturally across these virtual borders. Trust is unnecessary here. The swap unfolds under the careful watch of smart contracts.

These contracts, powered by **Hash Time-Locked Contracts**, or **HTLCs**, bring order to the transaction. The cryptography that binds them ensures no step is skipped. Alice, the keeper of Bitcoin, and Bob, holding Litecoin, begin the process. First, they agree, on the amount, on the rate. It's simple. A quiet acknowledgment. Then, Alice takes the next step. From the shadows of her code, she conjures a secret. A long, cryptographic string, random and powerful. She hashes it, reducing it to a form only she knows. This secret is the key to the entire exchange. She locks her Bitcoin away, bound in an HTLC, and tied to that cryptographic hash. Bob can only touch it if he holds the key, the original secret. But Alice doesn't give him the key just yet. Now it's Bob's turn. He mirrors her movements, creating his own HTLC on the Litecoin network, locking his funds with the same cryptographic hash Alice provided. The secret is the key here as well. Alice can only claim the Litecoin if she reveals the original secret, the pre-image. Both coins, bound to each other, wait patiently, locked away by their contracts, for the reveal. The execution is flawless. When Alice claims Bob's Litecoin, she does so by revealing the secret, a whisper passed through the contract. The moment Bob sees it, he acts. With that same secret in hand, he reaches out and claims Alice's

Bitcoin. It's seamless, like watching two hands clasp and release in perfect harmony. If one of them hesitates, fails to meet the contract's demands within the time frame, the funds slip back into their original owners' accounts. No one is cheated. No one is left wanting. The process is either complete or it dissolves, leaving both parties whole, untouched by risk. There is no need for centralized exchanges. Alice and Bob don't trust a faceless entity with their hard-earned cryptocurrency. There are no hacks, no inflated fees.

Their swap happens between them, across the chains. Bitcoin and Litecoin, Ethereum and more—it doesn't matter which currency they trade. The swap is always secure, tied inextricably to the cryptographic promise of the HTLC. Neither party needs to share personal information. Their privacy is intact. But the process has its challenges. To dance this dance requires skill, an understanding of the technical complexity involved. Creating these HTLCs and interacting with blockchain networks isn't simple, not for everyone. And not all blockchains are ready to host these atomic swaps. Certain features must be in place, like support for HTLCs, which popular blockchains like Bitcoin and Litecoin possess. Others do not. The pace, too, is slower than the bustling centralized exchanges. Each step depends on the block times of the two currencies involved, a delay that can be frustrating. Still, for those who value security, privacy, and autonomy, the trade is more than worth it. Atomic swaps have begun to shape decentralized exchanges, integrating into their ecosystems and allowing users to trade without relying on middlemen. They unlock new possibilities for cross-chain payments, particularly in the realm of decentralized finance. Atomic swaps represent a new frontier in the world of cryptocurrency, a place where trust isn't required and fraud doesn't stand a chance.

$$\sim 9 \sim$$

BITCOIN

Bitcoin (BTC) is the first and most well-known cryptocurrency, often referred to as "digital gold." Created in 2008 by the pseudonymous Satoshi Nakamoto, Bitcoin introduced blockchain technology, setting the foundation for the entire cryptocurrency ecosystem. The release of its whitepaper, "Bitcoin: A Peer-to-Peer Electronic Cash System," outlined a revolutionary decentralized currency free from intermediaries like banks. This peer-to-peer system allowed individuals to trade directly, without the need for central authorities. On January 3, 2009, the first block, known as the Genesis Block, was mined, marking the official birth of Bitcoin. Embedded within it was a message reflecting the failing state of traditional economies, symbolizing a shift away from centralized financial systems.

Initially, Bitcoin was known only within cryptography circles, but it gained attention in May 2010 when 10,000 BTC was exchanged for two pizzas, a moment now celebrated as Bitcoin Pizza Day. Bitcoin's recognition grew rapidly as exchanges were established, enabling people to trade fiat currency for Bitcoin. By 2013, it had become a media sensation, with its value skyrocketing. In 2017, Bitcoin's price reached nearly $20,000, sparking widespread speculation. Over time, Bitcoin garnered the attention of institutional investors and corporations. Companies like **Tesla** and **MicroStrategy** added Bitcoin to their balance sheets, recognizing it as a store of value. In 2021, **El Salvador** became the first country to adopt Bitcoin as legal tender.

At Bitcoin's core is its blockchain, a decentralized ledger maintained by a global network of nodes that verifies transactions. This transparent, tamper-resistant system ensures that transactions are secure and immutable. Bitcoin uses a **Proof of Work (PoW)** consensus mechanism, where miners solve complex mathematical puzzles to add new blocks to the chain, earning newly minted Bitcoin as a reward. While energy-intensive, this process maintains the network's security and decentralization.

What the Hell is a Proof of Work (PoW)?

Proof of Work (PoW) is the original consensus mechanism used by blockchains to secure the network and validate transactions. It was first introduced with Bitcoin in 2009 and has since been adopted by many other cryptocurrencies. PoW requires network participants (miners) to solve complex cryptographic puzzles, consuming significant computational power and energy. In return, miners receive rewards in the form of new cryptocurrency and transaction fees. The basic concept of PoW revolves around the idea of requiring "work" (computation) to be done to produce new blocks of transactions on the blockchain. The "work" consists of finding a solution to a mathematical puzzle, which is computationally expensive to solve but easy to verify. The process is as follows:

Transaction Pool: *Pending transactions are collected into a pool (called a **mempool** in Bitcoin), awaiting validation and inclusion into a block.*

Puzzle Solving: *Miners compete to solve a cryptographic puzzle, typically by finding a hash that meets certain criteria. This hash is generated using the SHA-256 algorithm in Bitcoin's case. The goal is to find a hash value lower than a target set by the network's difficulty level. Miners* *achieve this by varying a value called the nonce and repeatedly hashing the block until they find a valid solution.*

Proof of Work: *Once a miner finds a valid hash, they broadcast the solution to the network as proof that they have completed the computational work. This is the "proof of work" that other nodes can easily verify by checking the solution.*

Block Creation: *The winning miner gets to add a new block to the blockchain, containing the validated transactions.*

Rewards: *The miner receives a reward consisting of newly minted cryptocurrency (called a block reward) and the transaction fees included in the block.*

Block Propagation: *The new block is shared with other nodes in the network, and the process repeats with miners competing to add the next block.*

Security: *PoW is highly secure because it requires significant computational effort to alter the blockchain. An attacker would need to control more than 50% of the network's total hashing power, which is extremely difficult and costly.*

Decentralization: *PoW encourages decentralization because anyone with the necessary hardware can participate in mining. However, the energy requirements can centralize mining in regions with cheap electricity or where large mining farms dominate.*

Resource Intensive: *PoW requires vast amounts of computational power and energy, making it environmentally costly. This is one of the main criticisms of PoW compared to other consensus mechanisms like Proof of Stake (PoS).*

Difficulty Adjustment: PoW blockchains like Bitcoin automatically adjust the difficulty of the cryptographic puzzle based on how quickly miners are adding new blocks. This ensures that blocks are added at a consistent rate, regardless of the total hashing power of the network.

Examples of Cryptocurrencies Using Proof of Work:

Bitcoin (BTC): Bitcoin is the original PoW cryptocurrency. Its mining process uses the SHA-256 hashing algorithm, and it's known for being energy-intensive, as more powerful mining hardware (**ASICs**) are required to compete for rewards.

Litecoin (LTC): A fork of Bitcoin, Litecoin uses the Scrypt hashing algorithm, which was initially designed to be less reliant on specialized hardware like ASICs, although ASICs now dominate Litecoin mining as well.

Ethereum (ETH) (until 2022): Ethereum used PoW up until its transition to Proof of Stake (PoS) with Ethereum 2.0. Ethereum's PoW used the Ethash algorithm, which was memory-intensive and ASIC-resistant to promote decentralization.

Monero (XMR): Monero uses the **RandomX PoW algorithm,** which is designed to be ASIC-resistant and more favorable for CPU mining. Monero's focus on privacy makes it a popular choice for those seeking anonymity in mining.

Bitcoin Cash (BCH): A fork of Bitcoin, Bitcoin Cash uses the same SHA-256 PoW mechanism but with different network parameters, such as larger block sizes, to support faster transaction times.

Bitcoin's primary function is to serve as a store of value, often compared to gold due to its finite supply of 21 million BTC. Investors see it as a hedge against inflation, preserving wealth over time. One of Bitcoin's key advantages is its first-mover status. As the original cryptocurrency, it has gained global recognition and trust that newer coins still pursue. Its extensive network of miners and nodes makes Bitcoin one of the most decentralized and secure cryptocurrencies. Unlike platforms such as Ethereum, which supports smart contracts, Bitcoin is designed for simplicity, focusing on secure payments and transfers, rather than complex programmable applications. Bitcoin's scarcity, capped at 21 million coins, is a significant differentiator, driving its narrative as "digital gold." In contrast to cryptocurrencies with inflationary models, Bitcoin's hard cap reinforces its value.

Its development is maintained by a decentralized community through **Bitcoin Core**, the original software behind the network. Changes to the code are carefully tested and agreed upon by the community, ensuring a consensus-driven approach that reflects Bitcoin's decentralized ethos. Though Bitcoin has faced challenges with scalability and transaction speed, solutions continue to evolve. Despite these hurdles, Bitcoin remains a trusted leader in the cryptocurrency space, providing a secure and decentralized means of transferring wealth globally, while shaping the future of finance.

What the Hell is Mining?

Crypto mining is the process by which transactions are verified, added to a blockchain, and new units of cryptocurrency are generated. Mining is fundamental to many blockchain networks, particularly those that use Proof of Work (PoW) consensus mechanisms.

Mining serves two main purposes:

Securing the Network: *Miners validate transactions and prevent double-spending by ensuring that the same coins aren't used more than once in a blockchain.*

Creating New Coins: *Mining is also the process through which new cryptocurrency coins are minted and introduced into circulation.*

Key Steps in Crypto Mining:

Transaction Verification: *Miners collect pending transactions from the network, verify their authenticity, and ensure the sender has sufficient funds.*

Cryptographic Puzzle: *To add a block to the blockchain, miners must solve a complex mathematical puzzle, often involving finding a hash (a cryptographic output) that meets specific criteria (such as having a certain number of leading zeros).*

Proof of Work (PoW): *The first miner to solve the puzzle provides "proof of work," showing they have done the necessary computational work. This proof is shared with the network for validation.*

Block Creation: *Once a valid solution is found, the miner adds the block containing the validated transactions to the blockchain.*

Rewards: *The miner receives the block reward, which is a certain number of new cryptocurrency coins, and transaction fees from the transactions they confirmed.*

Evolution of Crypto Mining:

CPU Mining: *In the early days of Bitcoin (2009-2010), mining could be done using ordinary* **CPUs (Central Processing Units).** *The difficulty of the puzzles was low, allowing anyone with a standard computer to mine Bitcoin.*

GPU Mining: *As the mining difficulty increased, miners switched to* **GPUs (Graphics Processing Units),** *which are much more efficient at solving the cryptographic puzzles. GPUs offered more processing power for mining cryptocurrencies like Bitcoin and Ethereum.*

ASIC Mining: *With further increases in difficulty, specialized hardware called* **ASICs (Application-Specific Integrated Circuits)** *was developed. ASICs are tailor-made for mining and are far more efficient than GPUs. ASICs dominate Bitcoin mining today due to their higher performance and energy efficiency.*

Mining Pools: *As the difficulty of mining increased and the rewards became harder to achieve individually, miners began to pool their resources to share computational power and rewards. Mining pools allow participants to work together to solve puzzles and distribute the rewards proportionally based on their contribution. The biggest mining pools are essential players in the crypto mining ecosystem, combining the resources of multiple miners to increase their chances of solving cryptographic puzzles and earning block rewards.*

Below is a list of the largest mining pools for Bitcoin (BTC) at the date of publication of this book, ranked by their current market share and geographic location.

Foundry USA:
Market Share: ~30-35%

Location: United States

Overview: Foundry USA is currently the largest Bitcoin mining pool by market share. The rise of Foundry reflects the growing influence of North American mining, particularly in response to China's crackdown on mining activities. Foundry is part of the **Digital Currency Group (DCG)**, a major player in the crypto space.

AntPool:

Market Share: ~13-20%

Location: China (now operates internationally)

Overview: Operated by **Bitmain**, the world's largest producer of Bitcoin mining hardware (ASICs), AntPool is one of the most established mining pools. Even after China's ban on crypto mining, AntPool continues to be a dominant force, as many of its operations have relocated to countries with favorable regulations.

F2Pool:

Market Share: ~9-14%

Location: China (now operates internationally)

Overview: F2Pool is one of the oldest Bitcoin mining pools, founded in 2013. Despite the crackdown on mining in China, F2Pool has maintained its dominance by expanding its operations globally, including to North America and Central Asia.

Binance Pool:

Market Share: ~10-12%

Location: International (Binance is based in the Cayman Islands, but operates globally)

Overview: Binance, the world's largest cryptocurrency exchange, launched its mining pool in 2020. It quickly became one of the largest mining pools due to the exchange's vast resources and access to a large user base.

ViaBTC:
Market Share: ~6-8%

Location: China (now operates internationally)

Overview: ViaBTC was founded in 2016 and has become one of the largest pools, especially after the decline of some other Chinese mining pools. ViaBTC offers mining services for a variety of cryptocurrencies and has a significant presence in the Bitcoin mining space.

Poolin:
Market Share: ~5-7%

Location: China (now operates internationally)

Overview: Poolin is a Chinese mining pool that has faced challenges due to regulatory changes in China. Despite these obstacles, Poolin remains a top mining pool and has continued operations by moving its infrastructure abroad.

Luxor Mining:
Market Share: ~3-5%

Location: United States

Overview: Luxor is a North American mining pool focused on providing miners with advanced financial services, including profit-switching algorithms and hashrate liquidity markets. Luxor has grown in prominence, particularly as mining in the U.S. has expanded.

Slush Pool (Braiin Pool):
Market Share: ~2-3%

Location: Czech Republic

*Overview: Slush Pool, now rebranded as **Braiin Pool**, is historically significant as it was the first Bitcoin mining pool, established in 2010. Although its market share is smaller compared to newer pools, it remains a trusted name in the industry, known for its stability and innovation in mining software.*

BTC.com:

Market Share: ~1-2%

Location: China (Bitmain-owned now operates internationally)

Overview: BTC.com is another major pool owned by Bitmain. Despite losing some ground in recent years due to regulatory changes in China, BTC.com continues to be a player in the Bitcoin mining industry with operations worldwide.

SBI Crypto:

Market Share: ~less then 1-1%

Location: Japan

*Overview: SBI Crypto is part of the financial giant **SBI Holdings**, a major player in Japan's financial services sector. SBI Crypto has built mining facilities in various locations, including Texas, as part of the global shift of mining away from China.*

Types of Mining:

Solo Mining: *In solo mining, an individual miner works alone to solve cryptographic puzzles and earn rewards. This is less common today because the computational power needed for solo mining is extremely high.*

Pool Mining: *In pool mining, multiple miners combine their computational power to solve cryptographic puzzles faster. The reward is shared proportionally based on each miner's contribution to the pool's total hash rate.*

Cloud Mining: *Cloud mining involves renting computational power from a mining service provider. Users pay to lease mining power, and the provider handles the hardware and operations. In return, users receive a share of the mining rewards. This method allows users to participate in mining without owning mining equipment.*

Popular Cryptocurrencies that Use Mining:

Bitcoin (BTC): *The most well-known cryptocurrency, Bitcoin mining uses the Proof of Work consensus algorithm. The current block reward for Bitcoin miners is 6.25 BTC, halving approximately every four years.*

Litecoin (LTC): *A Bitcoin fork, Litecoin is another cryptocurrency that uses PoW mining but with the Scrypthashing algorithm, making it less reliant on ASICs in its early stages.*

Ethereum Classic (ETC): *After Ethereum's switch to Proof of Stake, Ethereum Classic continues to use the PoW algorithm, allowing miners to validate transactions.*

Zcash (ZEC): *A privacy-focused cryptocurrency that uses the PoW consensus mechanism and a specialized hashing algorithm called Equihash, designed to be ASIC-resistant.*

Monero (XMR): *Known for its privacy features, Monero uses a PoW algorithm called **RandomX** that is designed to be ASIC-resistant, allowing more decentralization by favoring CPU mining.*

Bitcoin Halving: *Every 210,000 blocks (roughly every four years), the Bitcoin block reward is halved. This event, known as the halving, reduces the amount of new Bitcoin entering circulation, which historically has had a significant impact on the supply/demand dynamics of the market.*

Hash: *is the output of a cryptographic algorithm that converts input data of any size (like a transaction) into a fixed-size string of characters. In blockchain networks like Bitcoin, the SHA-256 (**Secure Hash Algorithm 256-bit**) is used to generate these hash values. For example, when miners process a Bitcoin block, they are tasked with finding a specific hash value that meets the network's difficulty criteria. This requires re-*

peatedly running transactions and a random number (called a nonce) through the SHA-256 algorithm until they find a hash that matches the target. The hash produced must meet a condition set by the network, and finding this valid hash is called solving the puzzle. This process requires significant computational effort, and the rate at which miners can perform these operations is their hashrate.

Hash Power (Hashrate): Hash power, also known as hashrate, refers to the computational power used by miners in blockchain networks (such as Bitcoin) to solve cryptographic puzzles in a Proof of Work (PoW) consensus mechanism. It measures the speed at which a miner or mining network can process hash functions and find the correct solution needed to add a new block to the blockchain. In simpler terms, hash power represents how much computing power a miner or mining pool is contributing to the network to secure transactions and create new blocks.

How Hash Power is Measured: Hash power is measured in hashes per second (H/s). It indicates how many hashing operations a miner or mining rig can perform each second. Since modern mining hardware can perform trillions of hash operations per second, common units used to describe hash power include:

Kilohash (KH/s): 1,000 hashes per second
Megahash (MH/s): 1 million hashes per second
Gigahash (GH/s): 1 billion hashes per second
Terahash (TH/s): 1 trillion hashes per second
Petahash (PH/s): 1 quadrillion hashes per second
Exahash (EH/s): 1 quintillion hashes per second

For example, if a miner has a hashrate of 100 TH/s, it means that their mining hardware can process 100 trillion hashes every second.

Regulatory and Compliance:

Energy Regulations: *Governments are increasingly looking at the environmental impact of mining. In places where energy consumption is heavily taxed or regulated, crypto mining can become unsustainable. Countries such as China have banned mining, while others are looking at ways to regulate it.*

Taxation: *Mining rewards are typically subject to taxation as income in many jurisdictions. Miners need to track the value of the cryptocurrency they earn and report it to tax authorities.*

Legalization and Bans: *Some countries have outright banned crypto mining due to its energy consumption or potential for illegal use cases, like money laundering. In contrast, other jurisdictions are adopting regulations to legalize and encourage mining.*

Environmental Concerns: *Given the significant energy consumption associated with PoW mining, some governments and regulatory bodies are calling for more environmentally friendly consensus mechanisms, such as Proof of Stake.*

As cryptocurrencies evolve, mining is also set to change. PoW-based blockchains may gradually phase out in favor of more energy-efficient consensus mechanisms like Proof of Stake (PoS) or Proof of Authority (PoA). However, mining will remain a core aspect of some major cryptocurrencies, especially Bitcoin. Meanwhile, environmental and regulatory pressures may drive miners to explore renewable energy options or find new ways to reduce their carbon footprint.

Bitcoin Layer 1, 2 and 3 interconnected solutions

As Bitcoin adoption has grown, so have the challenges, particularly around scalability and functionality. To address these limitations, Bitcoin's architecture has evolved through a layered approach. Layer 1, the foundational Bitcoin blockchain, is responsible for security and basic transaction processing, but its capacity is limited. To enhance speed and efficiency, Layer 2 solutions, have been developed by third parties to handle transactions off-chain, reducing congestion. Recently, Layer 3 innovations have emerged, building on top of these two layers to enable more advanced applications, such as smart contracts and cross-chain interoperability. But before diving into the core topic, allow me to clarify the definition of layers in blockchain

Layer 1, the foundation of every blockchain, serves as the bedrock upon which everything else is built. It is the base protocol, the core of networks like Bitcoin, Ethereum, Solana, or Cardano, where the most fundamental functions occur. This layer is where the consensus mechanism lives, the process that decides the fate of every transaction. For Bitcoin, this mechanism is Proof of Work (PoW). Ethereum, however, has evolved, shifting to Proof of Stake (PoS) with its Ethereum 2.0 upgrade, relying on validators who stake their assets to secure the network. Beneath these mechanisms lies the security of the system itself, driven by the decentralized nature of the blockchain and the cryptography that holds it together. Each transaction is scrutinized, verified, and then, through this decentralized consensus, added to the ledger for eternity. Of course, each of these blockchains has its own native currency that powers the entire system. For Bitcoin, it's the well-known BTC, the digital gold that moves across the network. Ethereum's ETH fuels everything from simple transactions to complex decentralized applications. But this layer, while powerful, has its limits. Scalability is a constant challenge. As the network grows, so does its strain, leading to slower transaction times and painfully high fees, especially in moments of heavy usage.

Layer 2 rises to meet these challenges, a bridge between efficiency and the unyielding security of Layer 1. These solutions don't replace the base blockchain but rather build atop it, enhancing scalability and reducing costs while still depending on the security of the underlying system. With off-chain transactions, Layer 2 takes much of the workload off the primary blockchain's shoulders, processing transactions elsewhere before settling them in batches on the main chain. It's like relieving traffic from a crowded highway by opening parallel routes, only bringing the cars back when necessary. In this realm, smart contract interaction flourishes. Complex operations that would bog down the base layer can now unfold on Layer 2, freeing Layer 1 from the burden and allowing more to happen faster. But, despite being processed off-chain, these transactions don't lose the security that blockchain promises. They are, after all, still tethered to Layer 1, where the final reckoning occurs. The examples of Layer 2 solutions are fascinating in their creativity. The **Lightning Network** for Bitcoin allows users to create payment channels off-chain, where transactions are instant and nearly free. Only when these channels close do they settle on the Bitcoin blockchain, reducing congestion. Ethereum, ever a hub of innovation, offers solutions like **Optimistic Rollups** and **zk-Rollups,** where countless transactions are bundled up and posted as a single entry on the Ethereum chain. **Plasma**, too, emerges as a framework for child blockchains attached to Ethereum, a clever way to boost throughput by delegating most transaction processing to smaller, specialized chains.

And then, there's **Layer 3,** the layer closest to the end-user, the bridge that connects complex blockchain systems to the practical world. Here is where dApps, or decentralized applications, come to life, built atop platforms like Ethereum, Solana, and Binance Smart Chain. These apps range from DeFi platforms to NFTs and gaming ecosystems, each offering a window into what blockchain can do for everyday people. Layer 3 also holds the key to interoperability, enabling the connection between different blockchains, allowing users to move assets and data across previously isolated systems. This interconnectedness is critical as the blockchain ecosystem grows, helping bring once-siloed technologies together into a seamless web of possibilities. It's not just about building on one blockchain but bridging many, opening up new realms of functionality. This layer also focuses on improving the user experience (UX), making blockchain applications more accessible through wallets, APIs, and development frameworks. Think of **MetaMask**, a simple yet powerful tool that allows users to interact with dApps across different blockchains. It's here, in Layer 3, where the magic becomes accessible, where developers can create and users can participate without needing to understand the deep complexities of the underlying technology. Yet, even here, off-chain systems play a role. **Oracles**, for example, bring real-world data into the blockchain, allowing smart contracts to access external information like weather reports or stock prices.

What the Hell are Oracles?

In the context of cryptocurrency and blockchain technology, an oracle is a service or system that connects blockchains to external, off-chain data sources. Blockchains are inherently closed systems, meaning they can't directly access data from the outside world. Oracles bridge this gap by feeding external data into smart contracts or blockchain systems. Smart contracts are self-executing contracts with the terms written directly into code. These contracts can be automated to execute certain actions based on predefined conditions. However, smart contracts are limited by the data they can access, they only know what exists within the blockchain. Oracles provide a way for smart contracts to obtain external data such as Weather reports, Stock prices, Exchange rates, Sports scores, Supply chain information. Without oracles, smart contracts would be unable to function properly for real-world applications.

Types of Oracles:

Oracles can be categorized into different types depending on how they function and where they get data from:

Software Oracles: These retrieve data from online sources (APIs, databases, or websites). For example, fetching cryptocurrency prices from an exchange.

Hardware Oracles: These collect real-world data from physical devices such as sensors or IoT devices. For example, a smart contract might need data from a temperature sensor in a warehouse.

Inbound Oracles: They bring external data into the blockchain (e.g., providing weather data to a smart contract).

Outbound Oracles: They send data from the blockchain to the outside world. For instance, after a smart contract's conditions are met, it could trigger a bank payment to a user.

Centralized Oracles: These oracles are controlled by a single entity. They are typically trusted, but pose a risk because a single point of failure could compromise the system.

Decentralized Oracles: These aggregate data from multiple sources to avoid relying on a single point of failure, making the data more trustworthy and resistant to manipulation.

How Oracles Work in Smart Contracts:

A smart contract may need to interact with real-world data to trigger its execution. For example, in a decentralized finance (DeFi) application, a smart contract might rely on an oracle to get the current price of a token or currency pair. Based on this price, the contract could automatically execute a trade, issue a loan, or settle a bet.

Challenges with Oracles:

Trust and Security: Since oracles introduce external data, they create a potential point of failure or manipulation. For example, if an oracle is compromised or delivers incorrect data, it could result in incorrect or malicious smart contract execution.

The Oracle Problem: This refers to the challenge of ensuring that the data provided by oracles is both reliable and tamper-proof. Blockchains are decentralized, but if oracles are centralized, they can undermine the system's trustworthiness. Decentralized oracles help to mitigate this issue.

Popular Oracle Solutions:

Some well-known decentralized oracle solutions in the crypto space include:

Chainlink: One of the most popular decentralized oracle networks, Chainlink allows smart contracts to securely interact with external data sources.

Band Protocol: Another decentralized oracle network that provides secure and scalable oracles for different blockchain applications.

__Augur:__ A decentralized prediction market platform that uses oracles to resolve events.

__Use Cases of Oracles:__

__DeFi (Decentralized Finance):__ Oracles provide price feeds for decentralized exchanges (DEXs), lending platforms, and synthetic assets.

__Insurance:__ In decentralized insurance, an oracle can provide real-time data such as flight delays or weather reports to automate claim processing.

__Prediction Markets:__ Oracles deliver results of real-world events (like election outcomes) to settle prediction market contracts.

This layer is the bridge between the blockchain world and reality, ensuring that blockchain applications can interact with the world beyond the ledger. The innovations of Layer 3 can be seen in projects like **Uniswap,** the decentralized exchange that allows users to trade tokens directly from their wallets without needing to trust a centralized intermediary. **Chainlink,** the oracle network, stands as another example, pulling data from the outside world into smart contracts, expanding their utility. And, of course, there are the wallets, tools like MetaMask and **Trust Wallet,** that allow users to store, manage, and interact with their assets easily, making the blockchain accessible to the average person. This layering of technology, from the base security and functionality of Layer 1, to the scaling and efficiency of Layer 2, and the accessibility and user-friendliness of Layer 3, creates a complex yet elegant system. It's the roadmap to a future where blockchain isn't just the foundation of digital currencies but an integral part of our daily lives.

In addition to Layer 2 and Layer 3 solutions, there is as well another protocol designed to facilitate interactions between multiple blockchains, the **Wormhole Protocol.**

What the Hell is the Wormhole Protocol?

The Wormhole Protocol is one of the leading interoperability solutions in the blockchain space, allowing for the transfer of assets and data between different blockchain networks. Its primary function is to facilitate cross-chain communication, connecting otherwise isolated Layer 1 blockchains like Ethereum, Solana, Binance Smart Chain, and others. It is a decentralized cross-chain messaging protocol that enables the transfer of digital assets and information across different blockchain networks. This includes tokens, NFTs, and other assets, making them interoperable between different ecosystems. By using the Wormhole Protocol, users can move their assets seamlessly between blockchains without the need for centralized exchanges or intermediaries. This enhances liquidity and allows projects to expand beyond their native chains. Wormhole acts as a bridge between different blockchains, using a network of nodes called **Guardians.** *These Guardians observe activities on connected chains and help validate the transfer of assets across chains. Here's how it works step by step:*

Token Transfer Process:

Locking Assets: *A user wants to transfer assets (e.g., ETH from Ethereum to SOL on Solana). The user deposits the token into a smart contract (often referred to as a* **"bridge contract"***) on the source chain (Ethereum).*

Guardian Network: *The Guardians (a decentralized group of validators) monitor the deposit on the source chain and verify that the transaction has occurred. Once confirmed, the Guardians sign a transaction that* *allows the Wormhole Protocol to mint an equivalent amount of wrapped assets (e.g., wrapped ETH) on the target chain (Solana).*

Minting on the Target Chain: *After verification by the Guardians, a token is minted on the target chain (e.g., wrapped ETH on Solana), representing the same value as the locked assets on the original chain.*

Redeeming Assets: *If the user wants to return the assets to the source chain, the process is reversed. The user burns the wrapped tokens on the target chain (Solana), and the corresponding amount of original assets is unlocked on the source chain (Ethereum).*

Cross-Chain Communication:

The Wormhole Protocol also enables the exchange of messages and data between blockchains. For example, decentralized finance (DeFi) protocols can use it to access liquidity from multiple chains or synchronize certain contract states across ecosystems.

Supported Blockchains:

Wormhole Protocol is designed to be a universal bridge, and it supports many of the major Layer 1 blockchain networks, including: Ethereum, Solana, Binance Smart Chain (BSC), Terra (now Terra 2.0 after the collapse of the original Terra network), Avalanche, Polygon, Fantom, and many others... As the ecosystem grows, more chains are expected to be integrated into Wormhole, making it one of the most expansive cross-chain bridges in the crypto world.

Types of Assets That Can Be Transferred:

Through Wormhole, users can transfer a wide range of digital assets, including:

Fungible tokens: *Such as cryptocurrencies like ETH, SOL, USDC, etc.*

Non-fungible tokens (NFTs): *Wormhole also supports NFT bridging between chains, allowing NFTs minted on one blockchain to be moved and traded on another.*

Other cross-chain data: *Wormhole can also facilitate the transfer of general messages or contract calls, not just assets.*

Key Use Cases:

DeFi Liquidity: *By bridging assets across multiple chains, Wormhole allows decentralized finance (DeFi) protocols to access liquidity from other blockchains, increasing capital efficiency and market depth.*

NFT Interoperability: *Wormhole enables NFTs to move across chains, allowing artists and creators to tap into different marketplaces.*

Cross-Chain dApps: *dApp developers can build applications that work across multiple blockchains, using Wormhole to manage data and assets across chains.*

Cross-Chain Yield Farming: *Users can move their assets between chains to access better yield opportunities across DeFi protocols on different chains.*

Wormhole and Layer 2:

While Wormhole primarily connects Layer 1 blockchains, it can also serve as a bridge between Layer 1 and Layer 2 solutions. For instance, Wormhole could allow assets to be moved between a Layer 1 like Ethereum and a Layer 2 solution like Arbitrum or Optimism, though this is not its primary function.

Security Considerations:

Decentralization: *The security of the Wormhole bridge is backed by the Guardian network, which is decentralized to avoid a single point of failure. However, the protocol has experienced vulnerabilities in the past, including a notable hack where the protocol lost funds but was later reimbursed.*

Audits: *Wormhole undergoes regular audits to enhance security, and the protocol's developers actively work to patch any identified issues.*

Future of Wormhole:

The Wormhole Protocol continues to expand its network of supported blockchains and services. The team is focused on increasing decentralization, adding more Guardian validators, and integrating new features to improve cross-chain compatibility.

Alternatives to Wormhole:

Other cross-chain protocols serve a similar function, including:

Polkadot: *A network built for cross-chain compatibility with its parachains system.*

Cosmos: *Another ecosystem designed to connect different blockchains via the Inter-Blockchain Communication (IBC) protocol.*

Synapse: *Another cross-chain bridge solution that enables liquidity and asset transfers across multiple blockchains.*

Lightning Network

The Lightning Network is a Layer 2 solution built on top of the Bitcoin blockchain, designed to address Bitcoin's scalability issues by enabling faster and cheaper transactions without compromising the security of the underlying network. It allows users to conduct transactions off-chain, reducing congestion on the main blockchain and making Bitcoin more efficient for everyday use. Bitcoin, while prioritizing decentralization and security, struggles with scalability. Each block is mined every 10 minutes and limited to 1 MB in size, allowing about 7 transactions per second (TPS). This limitation leads to delays and rising fees during periods of high demand, as users compete to have their transactions processed faster by offering higher fees. To solve these issues, the Lightning Network was proposed in 2015 by Joseph Poon and Thaddeus Dryja. It enables near-instant, low-cost transactions by allowing users to create payment channels between two parties. A channel is established when two users lock Bitcoin in a multi-signature wallet, enabling them to transact off-chain. Transactions are recorded between the parties without the need to broadcast them on the blockchain, with only the final balance being settled on-chain when the channel is closed. This system alleviates pressure on the main Bitcoin network while maintaining security and efficiency.

The Lightning Network also supports a network of payment channels, where transactions can be routed through multiple nodes. For example, if Alice has a channel with Bob, and Bob has one with Carol, Alice can send a payment to Carol through Bob without needing a direct channel. The network automatically finds the shortest path, ensuring fast, efficient payments. One of the key benefits of the Lightning Network is its ability to process transactions at lightning speed, free from the delays of Bitcoin's base layer. Fees are significantly lower, making it ideal for micropayments, small transactions like tips, digital downloads, or in-game purchases, that would otherwise be impractical due to high fees. By moving transactions off-chain, the Lightning Network enhances Bitcoin's scalability, theoretically allowing it to handle an infinite number of transactions per second. Additionally, the Lightning Network offers increased privacy. Since most transactions occur off-chain, only the final settlement is recorded on the Bitcoin blockchain, providing users with greater confidentiality. This is especially valuable in a world where privacy is becoming scarce. However, the Lightning Network has its challenges. Liquidity issues can arise if there isn't enough Bitcoin locked in the channels to facilitate transactions, and users must carefully manage their channels to maintain liquidity.

Opening and closing channels still require on-chain transactions, bringing associated fees and delays. Additionally, the complexity of managing payment channels and understanding the system can be daunting for average users, though wallets and services are improving to make the process more user-friendly. Security is also a consideration. While the Lightning Network is generally secure, leaving channels open for extended periods can pose risks. Proper management of channels is crucial to maintaining security. As of 2024, the Lightning Network has seen growing adoption, with wallets like **Strike**, **BlueWallet**, and **Wallet of Satoshi** offering Lightning integration. Major companies, including **X.com**, have implemented Lightning payments, allowing users to tip and pay easily via Bitcoin. The network remains decentralized, and anyone can run a Lightning node, contributing to its growth and liquidity. Looking forward, the Lightning Network is expected to play a critical role in Bitcoin's evolution, making it more practical for everyday transactions. Increased merchant adoption and improved user interfaces will help the network mature, while efforts to integrate Lightning with other cryptocurrencies could pave the way for seamless cross-chain transactions. The promise of fast, low-cost, and scalable payments is no longer a distant vision but an emerging reality in the world of Bitcoin.

Liquid Network

The Liquid Network is a Layer 2 sidechain solution for Bitcoin, designed to enhance Bitcoin's functionality by enabling faster transactions, greater privacy, and the issuance of digital assets. Developed by **Blockstream** and launched in 2018, Liquid primarily serves financial institutions, exchanges, and traders who require faster, more confidential transactions than Bitcoin's main chain allows. By settling large volumes of Bitcoin transactions off-chain, Liquid alleviates congestion on the Bitcoin blockchain, offering a solution tailored to institutional needs.

A sidechain is a separate blockchain that operates in tandem with the main chain, allowing assets to be transferred between the two via a process called pegging. In the Liquid Network, Bitcoin is "pegged" and becomes **L-BTC (Liquid Bitcoin)**, a 1:1 representation of Bitcoin. L-BTC can be used within the Liquid Network for faster, more private transactions and can be redeemed for Bitcoin on the main chain whenever needed. One of Liquid's standout features is its speed. While Bitcoin's block time is 10 minutes, Liquid reduces it to one minute, making it ideal for traders and exchanges that need fast settlement times. Additionally, the network offers enhanced privacy through **Confidential Transactions (CT)**, which hide transaction details like amounts and asset types, maintaining security without sacrificing confidentiality.

Another key feature is Liquid's ability to issue digital assets, such as stablecoins, tokenized fiat, security tokens, and commodities like gold. This capability is valuable for institutions looking to tokenize assets while leveraging Bitcoin's security. Liquid operates under a federation-based consensus model, where trusted entities called **Functionaries**, primarily exchanges, validate blocks and ensure network security. This differs from Bitcoin's decentralized proof-of-work system, offering faster finality for transactions while still maintaining security. The two-way peg between Bitcoin and Liquid allows seamless movement of assets between the chains. When users peg Bitcoin into Liquid, it is locked by the federation, and L-BTC is issued. When they want to return to Bitcoin, the L-BTC is sent back, and the original Bitcoin is unlocked. This process enables users to benefit from faster, more private transactions without leaving the Bitcoin ecosystem. Liquid's federation-based block signing ensures that transactions are confirmed within two minutes, offering rapid finality. This is especially useful for traders who need quick settlement times to take advantage of market opportunities.

Once a block is confirmed on Liquid, it is final, reducing the risk of chain reorganizations or double spending. The Liquid Network also caters to institutional traders, providing confidentiality for large transactions, which can be vulnerable to scrutiny on Bitcoin's transparent blockchain. Liquid's cryptographic privacy ensures that competitors and market watchers cannot monitor the flow of assets, offering a secure environment for sensitive financial movements. Liquid's utility extends beyond Bitcoin, with its ability to issue and manage digital assets. For example, stablecoins like **Tether (USDT)** exist on the Liquid Network, offering faster and more private transactions compared to Bitcoin's main chain. Additionally, Liquid facilitates cross-border payments and remittances with its fast confirmation times and low fees, making international transfers more efficient. For exchanges, Liquid is a crucial tool for speeding up fund transfers between platforms. Exchanges like **Bitfinex** use

Liquid to reduce congestion and streamline transactions, enhancing overall market efficiency. Its ability to tokenize real-world assets through **Liquid Securities** allows businesses to digitize assets like real estate and stocks, bringing traditional finance into the blockchain space. In summary, the Liquid Network enhances Bitcoin's capabilities by providing faster transactions, increased privacy, and flexibility. It serves a wide range of use cases, from institutional trading to digital asset issuance, all while maintaining the security of the Bitcoin ecosystem.

RSK (Rootstock)

RSK (Rootstock) is a smart contract platform functioning as a Bitcoin sidechain, enabling Ethereum-like smart contracts, decentralized applications (dApps), and tokenized assets on the Bitcoin blockchain. Its core objective is to expand Bitcoin's capabilities beyond a store of value, allowing it to become a fully programmable system while leveraging Bitcoin's robust security model. RSK integrates with Bitcoin through a two-way peg system, enabling the transfer of Bitcoin to the RSK sidechain as **Smart Bitcoin (RBTC)**, which powers smart contracts and dApps. RSK bridges Bitcoin's unmatched security with Ethereum's flexibility, creating a platform that offers the best of both worlds.

While Bitcoin excels at security and decentralization through Proof of Work mining, it lacks the ability to support more advanced functions like smart contracts and decentralized finance (DeFi). Ethereum, on the other hand, thrives in programmability but lacks Bitcoin's security strength. RSK's solution was to merge Bitcoin's security with Ethereum's programmability, enabling decentralized applications and financial services on Bitcoin. One of RSK's key features is its two-way peg system, where users lock their Bitcoin to create an equivalent amount of **RBTC on RSK**. RBTC is used to pay for gas fees and execute smart contracts, and can be converted back to Bitcoin at any time through the peg system. RSK also uses **Merge Mining**, allowing Bitcoin miners to secure both Bitcoin and RSK simultaneously, ensuring the network benefits from Bitcoin's vast security without additional costs.

RSK's native token, **RBTC**, is pegged 1:1 with Bitcoin, allowing users to interact with smart contracts, pay transaction fees, and engage with DeFi on Bitcoin. It opens a new frontier for Bitcoin-based DeFi applications, such as decentralized exchanges and lending platforms, making Bitcoin's ecosystem more versatile. Moreover, RSK provides interoperability with Ethereum, allowing developers to port their Ethereum dApps with minimal changes, leveraging Bitcoin's security while maintaining Ethereum's smart contract functionality. RSK's lower fees make it an attractive platform for decentralized applications, especially as Ethereum faces scalability challenges. Its merge-mining mechanism enhances security by leveraging Bitcoin's proof-of-work mining, while the federation of trusted nodes safeguards the two-way peg system, ensuring secure asset exchanges between Bitcoin and RBTC. RSK not only brings smart contracts to Bitcoin but also facilitates the tokenization of real-world assets, turning Bitcoin into a platform for financial innovation. Through token bridges, RSK allows assets to move seamlessly between different blockchains, creating a vibrant, cross-chain ecosystem. Projects like **Sovryn** and **Money on Chain** exemplify RSK's potential by enabling Bitcoin-backed DeFi applications, including stablecoins and decentralized lending. RSK's infrastructure is further strengthened by the RSK Infrastructure Framework (RIF), a suite of decentralized protocols designed to enhance scalability and offer solutions for identity, storage, and payments. While RSK brings smart contract functionality to Bitcoin, it faces challenges such as its reliance on a federation for the peg system, introducing a degree of centralization. Adoption remains another hurdle, as Ethereum continues to dominate the smart contract space. However, RSK's focus on Bitcoin's security could draw more users and developers over time, positioning it as a powerful platform for decentralized applications built on the most trusted blockchain.

Feature	RSK	Ethereum
Consensus Mechanism	Merge-mined with Bitcoin (PoW)	Proof of Stake (PoS) (after Ethereum 2.0)
Native Currency	RBTC (pegged to Bitcoin 1:1)	ETH
Gas Fees	Lower fees compared to Ethereum	Often higher fees
Security	Secured by Bitcoin's mining power	Independent PoS mining post-Ethereum 2.0
Interoperability	Bitcoin compatibility, Ethereum-like	Primarily Ethereum ecosystem
Smart Contract Language	Solidity (Ethereum-compatible)	Solidity
Target Market	Bitcoin-focused, financial services	Broader focus on DeFi and dApps

↓

Stacks (Formerly Blockstack)

Stacks is a Layer 1 blockchain that enables smart contracts and decentralized applications (dApps) on Bitcoin. Originally known as Blockstack, it rebranded to Stacks in 2020, aligning with the launch of its Stacks 2.0 blockchain. Unlike Ethereum, Stacks enhances Bitcoin's functionality by using Bitcoin as its base layer for security, allowing for decentralized applications and smart contracts. This is achieved through **Proof of Transfer (PoX)**, which anchors the Stacks blockchain to Bitcoin, making dApps on Stacks more secure, scalable, and efficient. Blockstack's original vision was to create a decentralized network where users, not corporations, controlled their data and identity.

Over time, it evolved into Stacks, focusing on a programmable layer atop Bitcoin. Stacks 2.0 harnesses Bitcoin's unmatched security while enabling smart contracts to function on the Bitcoin network. PoX allows Bitcoin to serve as the foundation for Stacks, where miners commit Bitcoin to mint new STX tokens. Bitcoin holders can participate in "stacking" by locking up their Bitcoin to earn STX rewards. Stacks' technology combines innovation with

Bitcoin's security. It uses **Clarity**, a custom smart contract language that is interpreted, ensuring greater precision and reducing vulnerabilities compared to compiled languages like Ethereum's Solidity. Clarity contracts are executed on the Stacks blockchain but settle on Bitcoin, leveraging the world's most secure blockchain. Stacks doesn't seek to replace Bitcoin but rather to augment it, enabling use cases such as DeFi, NFTs, and other blockchain services, all anchored to Bitcoin's security and immutability. One unique feature is that Stacks rewards users with Bitcoin itself through its stacking mechanism, unlike traditional staking systems that pay out in native tokens. The rebranding from Blockstack to Stacks signaled a shift in focus: from decentralized identity management to enabling smart contracts on Bitcoin. With this new direction, Stacks empowers developers to create dApps backed by Bitcoin's security, offering a programmable platform without requiring additional resources for network security. Another standout feature is NFTs on Stacks, which are anchored to Bitcoin's immutable blockchain. This gives digital assets, such as art and collectibles, an added layer of security and permanence compared to those on Ethereum. However, Stacks faces challenges. While it benefits from Bitcoin's stability, it also inherits some limitations, such as scalability and slower transaction times. Additionally, the Stacks ecosystem is still developing and doesn't yet match Ethereum's mature DeFi and dApp landscape. Despite these hurdles, Stacks is gaining traction and attracting developers, driven by its unique offering of smart contracts secured by Bitcoin.

Statechains

Statechains are a Layer 2 solution for Bitcoin that enables off-chain transfers of ownership without requiring participants to be online simultaneously or relying on a centralized entity. Introduced by Ruben Somsen in 2018, Statechains allow Bitcoin ownership transfers without moving coins on-chain, enhancing scalability, privacy, and reducing fees. Statechains achieve this by using multi-signature wallets, time-locked contracts, and blind signatures, which allow users to transfer control of private keys securely. The core idea is to make Bitcoin transfers more efficient and private by handling them off-chain. Instead of broadcasting every transaction to the Bitcoin network, Statechains facilitate the transfer of ownership by passing private keys to the new owner, keeping the Bitcoin in the same wallet. This off-chain process avoids transaction fees and blockchain congestion, enhancing scalability without compromising security. The system relies on multi-signature wallets where both the user and a Statechain entity hold keys, ensuring neither can move the Bitcoin independently. When ownership changes, the private key is handed off to the new owner, who collaborates with the Statechain entity to spend the Bitcoin, providing a secure and auditable way to transfer assets.

To ensure security, time-locked refunds allow users to reclaim their funds if the transfer process is interrupted. Blind signatures further enhance privacy by preventing the Statechain entity from knowing the details of transactions. When a transaction needs to be settled on-chain, collaborative spending occurs between the new owner and the Statechain entity, preserving privacy and security. **Watchtowers**, third-party auditors, monitor the network to prevent malicious behavior and double-spending. This system balances scalability, privacy, and security, allowing efficient Bitcoin transfers off-chain without network congestion. Statechains offer several advantages over other Layer 2 solutions, such as the Lightning Network and sidechains. Unlike the Lightning Network, Statechains don't require both parties to be online, and they are better suited for larger, less frequent transactions. Compared to sidechains, which rely on federated validators, Statechains use a simpler system with one trusted entity and robust safeguards like multisig wallets and time-locks. Despite their benefits, Statechains face challenges. Trust in the Statechain entity is critical, and users must carefully manage private keys to avoid theft. While the technology is promising, it remains in its early stages and requires further adoption and testing. **Mercury Wallet**, one of the first applications of Statechains, demonstrates the potential of this technology by enabling seamless off-chain Bitcoin transfers, offering a glimpse into a more scalable, private, and efficient future for Bitcoin.

OmniLayer (formerly Mastercoin)

OmniLayer, formerly Mastercoin, is a Layer 2 protocol built on Bitcoin, enabling the creation, issuance, and transfer of digital assets like tokens and smart contracts, while leveraging Bitcoin's security. Often described as a "**meta-layer**" or "**colored coin**" system, OmniLayer facilitates tokenization and smart contracts using Bitcoin's infrastructure. One of its most notable achievements is hosting **Tether (USDT)**, one of the first and most popular stablecoins, solidifying its role in the cryptocurrency space. Conceived by J.R. Willett in 2013, OmniLayer expanded Bitcoin's functionality to include custom tokens and smart contracts. Willett's vision was outlined in a whitepaper titled "The Second Bitcoin Whitepaper," and the platform, rebranded as OmniLayer in 2015, shifted its focus toward token issuance, decentralized exchanges, and basic smart contracts anchored to Bitcoin. This rebranding marked the beginning of OmniLayer's role in the growing digital finance ecosystem, with Tether as its most prominent use case. Operating as a meta-protocol, OmniLayer embeds additional data into Bitcoin transactions via the OP_RETURN field.

This method allows for token creation, transfer, and contract execution without altering Bitcoin's core functionality. Bitcoin continues to manage transaction data, while OmniLayer introduces new layers of functionality for digital assets, such as tokens and smart contracts. OmniLayer's tokens can represent digital currencies like Tether, assets, or commodities. While its smart contracts are more limited than Ethereum's, they enabled decentralized trading, token issuance, and even crowdfunding on Bitcoin. Token creation is straightforward, with rules embedded in smart contracts governing transfer and divisibility. Tether, initially built on OmniLayer, provided traders with a stable, USD-backed token on a decentralized platform. Although Tether has since expanded to other blockchains like Ethereum and Tron, OmniLayer remains crucial in its early foundation. Moreover, OmniLayer played a pioneering role in the initial coin offering (ICO) model, allowing projects to issue tokens in exchange for Bitcoin or other cryptocurrencies, directly on Bitcoin's blockchain. OmniLayer's security is rooted in Bitcoin's Proof of Work (PoW) mechanism, ensuring that every transaction inherits Bitcoin's immutability and resistance to attacks. This trustless, decentralized system eliminates the need for a central authority to mediate transactions, with all activity permanently recorded on Bitcoin's blockchain. However, OmniLayer has limitations. While it excels in token issuance and basic financial contracts, its smart contract functionality is less flexible than platforms like Ethereum.

Bitcoin's scalability issues, such as high fees and slower transaction times during network congestion, also affect OmniLayer's performance, making it less ideal for smaller, frequent transactions. Furthermore, competition from platforms like Ethereum, Binance Smart Chain, and even Bitcoin-based solutions like Liquid and RSK, offers more advanced features like confidential transactions and faster settlement times. In conclusion, OmniLayer is a foundational protocol that extends Bitcoin's functionality, enabling tokenization and decentralized trading. Though it faces challenges from more flexible platforms, its integration with Bitcoin's security and its contributions, particularly with Tether, make it a significant player in the digital asset ecosystem.

Drivechain

Drivechain is a concept in the Bitcoin ecosystem that enables integration of sidechains while maintaining Bitcoin's security. It aims to expand Bitcoin's capabilities without altering its core protocol, making it an appealing solution in the scaling debate. Sidechains, operating independently with their own rules and tokens, are connected to Bitcoin, allowing seamless value transfers between them. This is achieved through merged mining, where miners secure both Bitcoin and sidechains using the same computational resources, without extra hardware or effort. By leveraging Bitcoin's mining power, sidechains benefit from the same security as the main Bitcoin network. The core of Drivechain's proposal involves a soft fork to Bitcoin, introducing a two-way peg between Bitcoin and sidechains. Miners enforce this peg by mining both Bitcoin and sidechain blocks, ensuring locked BTC on the mainchain can be redeemed and moved back from the sidechain. Blind merged mining, a key feature, simplifies this process by allowing miners to mine sidechains without running a full sidechain node, reducing the technical complexity for participation. Drivechain offers several benefits.

First, it enhances scalability by offloading activities to sidechains, reducing the transaction load on Bitcoin's main chain. It also promotes experimentation, allowing developers to test new features, consensus algorithms, and smart contract capabilities on sidechains without risking Bitcoin's core security. Importantly, all these innovations remain within the Bitcoin ecosystem, avoiding the need for new tokens or separate blockchains. For miners, Drivechain provides additional revenue by enabling them to mine both Bitcoin and sidechains, making the process more profitable without the need for extra hardware. The mechanics are straight-forward: users lock BTC on the Bitcoin network, which is then represented on the sidechain. When users wish to return to Bitcoin, they burn the sidechain tokens, and miners unlock the corresponding BTC on the mainchain after a time delay, ensuring secure and seamless transfers. Despite its potential, Drivechain faces criticisms and challenges.

Critics argue that placing too much power in miners' hands, particularly in approving sidechain withdrawals, could lead to centralization or collusion. Security concerns arise from the risk of poorly designed sidechains affecting Bitcoin's reputation. Implementing Drivechain also demands significant changes to Bitcoin's infrastructure, which could face resistance from the decentralized Bitcoin community. Additionally, adoption requires both miners and developers to embrace the system, a potential hurdle if incentives are insufficient. Nonetheless, the use cases for Drivechain are compelling. It could bring smart contracts and decentralized finance (DeFi) to Bitcoin, similar to Ethereum's ecosystem, transforming Bitcoin from a store of value into a versatile platform. Sidechains could also enhance Bitcoin's privacy, enabling confidential transactions with technologies like **MimbleWimble** or **zk-SNARKs.**

Tokenization of assets on Bitcoin, currently dominated by platforms like Ethereum, would become possible, expanding Bitcoin's functionality. Drivechain also offers the opportunity to experiment with new consensus mechanisms, such as Proof of Stake (PoS), without compromising Bitcoin's Proof of Work (PoW) foundation. This innovation could allow Bitcoin to adapt to future demands while preserving its core security. In summary, Drivechain represents a middle ground in the Bitcoin scalability debate, offering innovation and experimentation without requiring drastic changes to Bitcoin itself. If successfully implemented, it could bring advanced features like smart contracts, privacy, and tokenization to Bitcoin, potentially solving its scaling and functionality issues. However, its success depends on widespread community support and adoption by miners and developers. While still in development and testing, Drivechain remains a promising topic of interest in the cryptocurrency space.

ARK

Ark is a blockchain platform designed to make blockchain technology accessible to everyone, regardless of technical expertise. It's often called a "Layer 3" solution because it builds on Layer 1 and Layer 2 technologies, offering scalability, customization, and user-friendliness. Ark aims to create an ecosystem of interconnected blockchains, called **"Bridgechains,"** facilitating interoperability and customization for developers, a solution to the longstanding challenge of cross-blockchain communication. Ark allows users to create independent blockchains, easing congestion and enhancing performance. Developers can build customized blockchains without needing to fork or start from scratch, giving them control over consensus mechanisms and tokenomics, while still being linked to the Ark ecosystem. This modular, scalable system makes Ark versatile for a variety of applications.

A key feature of Ark is **SmartBridge Technology**, enabling seamless interoperability between blockchains, whether Ark-based or not. By encoding data fields in transactions, Ark acts as an intermediary, allowing actions on one blockchain to trigger events on another without exchanges or third parties. This cross-chain functionality enhances decentralization.

Ark's security is powered by the **Delegated Proof of Stake (DPoS)** consensus mechanism, where **ARK** token holders vote for delegates who secure the network. The top 51 delegates are responsible for block production, maintaining a secure and decentralized network, and are incentivized through transaction fees and newly minted ARK tokens. For developers, Ark offers the **ARK Deployer**, a user-friendly tool that simplifies launching new blockchains. With APIs, SDKs, and a modular architecture, developers can build and integrate applications without needing advanced coding skills. Ark's flexibility allows users to select only the features they need, avoiding rigid frameworks. While Ark doesn't natively support smart contracts, the **ARK Virtual Machine (AVM)** facilitates smart contract interaction via SmartBridge technology, enabling cross-platform communication. With **WebAssembly (WASM) compatibility**, the AVM supports multiple programming languages, broadening the scope of applications built on Ark.

Ark's customization and scalability make it an ideal tool for enterprise blockchain solutions, enabling businesses to create private or permissioned blockchains tailored to their needs. In gaming, Ark enables decentralized applications (dApps) and cross-blockchain digital asset transfers. In finance, Ark supports DeFi projects, facilitating cross-chain asset transfers and decentralized exchanges while maintaining security and transparency. Through its innovative approach, Ark is shaping a more interconnected and accessible blockchain ecosystem, offering diverse possibilities across industries.

~ 10 ~

ALTCOINS

Ethereum Revolution has been built on four main pillars: Smart Contracts, Blockchain Technology, and the Future of Decentralization. Ethereum is a decentralized, open-source blockchain platform that has revolutionized the cryptocurrency space by introducing smart contracts.

What the Hell are Smart Contracts?

Smart contracts are self-executing contracts where the terms and conditions are written directly into lines of code. These contracts automatically enforce, verify, or execute the terms of a contract without requiring intermediaries. The code and the agreements contained within exist across a distributed, decentralized blockchain network, such as Ethereum. In essence, smart contracts enable trusted transactions and agreements to be carried out among anonymous parties without the need for a central authority, legal system, or external enforcement mechanism. The concept of smart contracts was first proposed by Nick Szabo, a computer scientist and cryptographer, in the 1990s. Szabo envisioned smart contracts as a tool to formalize and secure digital relationships. However, the technology to deploy them didn't exist until the creation of blockchain systems. It was the development of Ethereum, launched in 2015 by Vitalik Buterin, that popularized and enabled the widespread use of smart contracts. Ethereum's platform was designed from the ground up to support decentralized applications (dApps) and smart contracts, unlike Bitcoin, which was primarily designed for peer-to-peer financial transactions.

Key Features of Smart Contracts are:

Self-Execution: Once a condition is met, the contract automatically executes without human intervention.

Immutability: After being deployed, the smart contract cannot be altered. This ensures trust and security since no one can modify the contract's terms or back out of agreed conditions.

Transparency: Smart contracts run on public blockchains, allowing anyone to inspect the contract's logic and transactions, ensuring transparency.

Security: The decentralized nature of blockchain, combined with cryptographic encryption, ensures that the contract is tamper-proof.

Autonomy: Smart contracts remove the need for third parties such as notaries, lawyers, or banks to enforce or verify an agreement.

Cost-Efficiency: By automating contract execution, smart contracts reduce administrative overhead and costs.

How Do Smart Contracts Work?

Smart contracts operate in a "if-then" structure.

Setting the Terms: The parties agree to the contract terms, which are coded into the smart contract. For example, "If Party A delivers product X by date Y, Party B will release payment Z."

Deployment: *The smart contract is deployed on the blockchain, often on Ethereum or other compatible networks.*

Execution: *Once the conditions are met (verified by data or inputs), the smart contract self-executes the agreed-upon action. If the conditions aren't met, the contract remains inactive or can trigger an alternative outcome.*

A typical smart contract can manage financial transactions, real estate transfers, supply chain agreements, or voting mechanisms. With broad applications across industries, smart contracts automate processes, eliminate intermediaries, and reduce the need for trust. Some case uses:

Lending and Borrowing: *Platforms like Aave and Compound use smart contracts to automate lending and borrowing, where users can deposit assets and take out loans without banks.*

Insurance: *Smart contracts can automate insurance claims, automatically paying out when certain conditions are met (e.g., flight delays).*

Automated Market Makers (AMMs): *Decentralized exchanges like Uniswap use smart contracts to manage liquidity pools and enable automated, peer-to-peer trading.*

Supply Chain: *Smart contracts can improve transparency and efficiency in supply chains by automatically tracking and verifying the movement of goods, payments, and inventories. For example, payments can be triggered upon the delivery of goods or when certain milestones are achieved.*

Real Estate: *Smart contracts can facilitate property transfers by eliminating the need for traditional escrow services. They automate processes like payments and title transfers, reducing time and costs.*

Healthcare: *In healthcare, smart contracts can be used to manage patient records securely, ensure insurance claim validity, and even track medical supply chains.*

Voting and Governance: *Smart contracts ensure secure, transparent, and tamper-proof voting systems. Decentralized Autonomous Organizations (DAOs) often use smart contracts to manage decision-making and governance processes.*

Legal Agreements: *Smart contracts provide an automated way to manage agreements, contracts, and business deals without the need for manual enforcement.*

Benefits:

Efficiency: *Smart contracts streamline processes by automating manual tasks, which reduces the time needed to enforce agreements and minimizes delays.*

Trustless Transactions: *They eliminate the need for trust between parties by using code and cryptographic proofs to enforce terms.*

Cost-Reduction: *By removing intermediaries, such as legal teams and brokers, smart contracts drastically cut costs associated with transactions.*

Transparency and Trust: *Since they operate on public blockchains, the contract's terms are visible to all parties, ensuring fairness and reducing fraud.*

Security: *The decentralized and cryptographically secure nature of smart contracts makes them resistant to tampering, hacking, or manipulation.*

Challenges and Limitations:

Coding Bugs and Exploits: *Smart contracts are only as secure as the code they are written with. A poorly written contract can have vulnerabilities that hackers can exploit. This was notably seen in the 2016 DAO Hack, where a flaw in a smart contract led to the loss of $60 million in ETH.*

Oracles and Off-Chain Data: *Smart contracts often rely on external data, such as stock prices, weather reports, or event outcomes, to trigger certain actions. These are provided by "oracles," which act as bridges between the blockchain and real-world data. However, the reliance on third-party oracles can create points of vulnerability or manipulation.*

Legal and Regulatory Uncertainty: *Smart contracts exist in a regulatory grey area in many jurisdictions. Since they are code-based and self-enforcing, it's not always clear how legal systems should handle disputes or if a court of law can enforce a smart contract.*

Immutability: *While immutability ensures that the terms of a contract cannot be tampered with, it also means that mistakes or oversights in a contract cannot be easily corrected without deploying a new contract. This can lead to inefficiency or issues if bugs are found after deployment.*

Complexity in Negotiations: *Not all contracts can be easily translated into code. Certain human-based interpretations, such as intent or renegotiation, can be difficult to codify in a rigid, pre-programmed smart contract.*

Most common Platforms for Smart Contracts:

Ethereum: *The leading platform for smart contracts. It provides the Ethereum Virtual Machine (EVM) and a powerful developer toolkit (including Solidity) for writing and deploying smart contracts.*

Binance Smart Chain (BSC): *A more centralized alternative to Ethereum, providing lower transaction costs and faster speeds for deploying smart contracts.*

Solana: *Known for its high throughput and speed, Solana offers a scalable solution for smart contract-based applications.*

Cardano: *A research-driven blockchain platform that focuses on scalability and sustainability, with smart contract functionality enabled by its Plutus framework.*

Polkadot: *Enables interoperability between different blockchains, allowing smart contracts on Polkadot to interact with other networks and assets.*

The future of smart contracts is poised for exponential growth as more industries adopt blockchain technology. The ongoing development of Layer 2 scaling solutions, such as **Optimistic Rollups** *and* **zkRollups***, will help alleviate the high costs and slow transaction speeds on Layer 1 blockchains like Ethereum. These advancements will make smart contracts more accessible to everyday users and businesses. Additionally, cross-chain communication through projects like* **Polkadot** *and* **Cosmos** *will enable smart contracts to operate across multiple blockchains, increasing their utility and interoperability. This could lead to the widespread use of decentralized applications across finance, governance, and industry, while reducing reliance on single-blockchain ecosystems. Moreover, as artificial intelligence (AI) advances, we may see more complex* *smart contracts capable of handling intricate, nuanced decision-making processes, potentially automating industries in ways we can't yet fully envision.*

Ethereum's story begins with Vitalik Buterin, a Russian-Canadian programmer who recognized the limitations of Bitcoin and its scripting language. In late 2013, Buterin published the Ethereum whitepaper, outlining the concept of a decentralized platform that could handle much more than financial transactions. The idea was simple: allow developers to create decentralized applications that could run without downtime, fraud, or interference from third parties. Following a successful crowdfunding campaign in 2014, Ethereum officially launched on July 30, 2015, with its first iteration, "**Frontier.**

Ethereum was designed to go beyond Bitcoin's capabilities by providing a programmable blockchain that supports decentralized applications (dApps) and smart contracts. While Bitcoin serves primarily as a digital currency and store of value, Ethereum's innovation lies in its ability to execute code on a decentralized network, making it the foundation for many modern decentralized finance (DeFi) projects, NFTs, and decentralized organizations (DAOs). At its core, Ethereum's main function is to allow developers to create and deploy smart contracts and dApps, which automatically execute agreements or actions without requiring intermediaries. This innovation transformed Ethereum into a versatile platform for financial services, gaming, supply chains, and more. Over the years, Ethereum has undergone several upgrades, including "**Homestead**" (2016), "**Metropolis**" (2017-2019), and "**Ethereum 2.0,**" also known as "**The Merge,**" in 2022, which transitioned Ethereum from a Proof of Work (PoW) consensus mechanism to Proof of Stake (PoS).

Each stage has refined the platform's scalability, security, and functionality, cementing Ethereum's role as the go-to platform for decentralized innovation. Ethereum's blockchain is similar to Bitcoin's in that it records a public ledger of all transactions. However, Ethereum's blockchain is far more versatile, as it supports smart contracts and dApps. The blockchain operates through a network of nodes, each holding a copy of the blockchain. When a new transaction or contract is made, it is grouped with others into a "block," which is verified by nodes and added to the chain. This system ensures that no single entity controls the network, maintaining decentralization. Ethereum initially used a Proof of Work (PoW) system, where miners solved complex puzzles to add blocks to the chain, receiving **ETH** (Ethereum's native cryptocurrency) as a reward. However, PoW was energy-intensive and could not handle a large volume of transactions. This led to Ethereum 2.0, which introduced a Proof of Stake (PoS) model. In PoS, validators, who hold and lock up a certain amount of ETH, are chosen to validate transactions and create new blocks, consuming less energy and allowing for greater scalability.

What the Hell is the Proof of Stake (PoS)?

Proof of Stake (PoS) is a consensus mechanism used by many blockchain networks to secure transactions, validate new blocks, and maintain network integrity. It is an alternative to the energy-intensive Proof of Work (PoW) system used by blockchains like Bitcoin, and it aims to provide a more efficient, environmentally friendly way of achieving consensus. In PoS, instead of using computational power to solve cryptographic puzzles, participants (called validators) are selected based on the amount of cryptocurrency they hold and are willing to lock up (stake) as collateral.

***Energy Efficiency:** PoS significantly reduces the energy consumption compared to PoW, where miners need to expend massive computational resources to validate transactions. PoS validators are chosen based on the* amount of cryptocurrency they are staking, not by solving energy-intensive puzzles.

Validators: In PoS, validators replace miners. Validators are responsible for confirming transactions and creating new blocks. The more cryptocurrency a validator stakes, the higher their chances of being chosen to validate a block.

Staking: Validators must lock up a certain amount of cryptocurrency (called the stake) to participate in the block validation process. The size of the stake influences the probability of being selected to validate the next block. If validators act maliciously or fail to validate properly, their stake can be partially or fully "slashed" as a penalty.

Rewards: Validators earn rewards in the form of new cryptocurrency for validating blocks. These rewards can come from newly minted coins or transaction fees paid by users.

Security via Economic Incentives: PoS is secured by the financial interest of validators. Since they have staked their own assets, validators are motivated to act in the network's best interest to avoid penalties such as slashing.

How Proof of Stake Works:

Validator Selection: Validators are selected randomly or deterministically to propose new blocks. The probability of being chosen is proportional to the amount of cryptocurrency staked. This prevents wealth concentration because larger stakes only increase the probability but do not guarantee consistent block creation.

Block Validation: *When selected, a validator confirms the validity of the transactions in a block. Other validators then review and attest to the correctness of the block.*

Consensus: *Once enough validators approve the block, it is added to the blockchain. The validators are rewarded for their participation, and the network moves on to validate the next block.*

Slashing: *Validators who attempt to manipulate the network or fail to validate properly can be penalized by losing a portion of their staked assets. This is called "slashing," and it serves as a deterrent to malicious behavior.*

Variants of Proof of Stake:

Several variations of the PoS consensus mechanism have emerged to improve scalability, security, and governance:

Delegated Proof of Stake (DPoS): *In DPoS, token holders vote for a small number of delegates (also called witnesses) who are responsible for validating transactions and creating blocks. Delegates are elected by the community, making the system more democratic. DPoS networks are faster than traditional PoS due to a smaller number of validators.*
Example: **EOS, TRON.**

Nominated Proof of Stake (NPoS): *NPoS allows users to nominate validators by staking their coins. The system uses a combination of stake size and the number of nominations to choose the validators.*
Example: **Polkadot.**

Bonded Proof of Stake (BPoS): *Validators must bond or lock up a specific amount of cryptocurrency for a set period. Validators are then randomly selected to validate blocks.*

Example: **Cosmos.**

Liquid Proof of Stake (LPoS): *This variant allows stakers to delegate their staking power to a validator while retaining the ability to withdraw their stake at any time. It provides flexibility to stakers while keeping the network secure.*
Example: **Tezos.**

Hybrid PoS/PoW: *Some blockchains combine PoW and PoS to achieve a balance between decentralization and efficiency. For example, validators might be selected using PoS but confirmed through PoW mechanisms.*
Example: **Decred.**

Advantages:

Reduced Hardware Requirements: *PoS does not require specialized hardware (like ASICs used in PoW mining). Participants can use ordinary computers to run validator nodes, lowering the entry barrier for network participation.*

Faster Block Times: *PoS typically allows faster block creation because validators can be selected more quickly than PoW miners can solve cryptographic puzzles.*

Disadvantages:

Wealth Concentration: *PoS can sometimes lead to wealth concentration, where the more tokens a participant stakes, the more rewards they can potentially earn. This could theoretically lead to centralization, although PoS systems are designed to mitigate this risk.*

Initial Distribution Problem: *In PoS, the initial distribution of tokens can play a significant role in who becomes the dominant validator. If a* small group of individuals owns a large share of the cryptocurrency, they could have outsized influence over the network.

Slashing Risks: Validators face the risk of slashing, where they lose a portion of their staked assets for misbehavior or going offline. This can be risky for participants who are not experienced in running a validator node.

Security and Attacks: While PoS is secure under most conditions, it can be vulnerable to attacks such as long-range attacks or nothing-at-stake attacks, where validators try to create alternative blockchain histories. However, many PoS systems have built-in mechanisms to prevent such attacks.

Long-Range Attacks: PoS systems can be vulnerable to long-range attacks, where validators attempt to rewrite older blocks. Many PoS networks implement checkpoints and time-based finality to mitigate these risks.

Nothing-at-Stake Problem: In PoS, validators could theoretically support multiple competing chains (since staking requires less energy than PoW mining). To counter this, many PoS systems penalize validators who attempt to validate conflicting blocks.

Popular Blockchains Using Proof of Stake:

Ethereum 2.0 (ETH): Ethereum switched from PoW to PoS in 2022 to improve scalability, security, and energy efficiency. Validators in Ethereum 2.0 must stake at least 32 ETH to participate.

Cardano (ADA): Cardano uses a PoS protocol called Ouroboros, which selects validators randomly based on their stake and uses an epoch-based system to ensure fairness in block production.

Polkadot (DOT): *Polkadot employs Nominated Proof of Stake (NPoS), allowing users to nominate validators. Validators are then chosen based on stake size and number of nominations.*

Tezos (XTZ): *Tezos uses Liquid Proof of Stake (LPoS), where participants can delegate their staking power to validators without locking their tokens.*

Solana (SOL): *Solana uses a high-performance PoS mechanism combined with Proof of History (PoH), a time-stamping technique that improves scalability.*

Cosmos (ATOM): *Cosmos operates with a Bonded Proof of Stake (BPoS) system. Validators must bond a certain amount of ATOM, and token holders can delegate their stake to them.*

The heart of Ethereum is a remarkable piece of technology known as the **Ethereum Virtual Machine, or EVM.** It operates like a "world computer," one that stretches across countless nodes, tirelessly running smart contracts and decentralized applications, dApps. The EVM is what gives Ethereum its unparalleled flexibility and programmability, ensuring that these smart contracts are executed seamlessly and validated by every node in the network. It's this very system that makes smart contracts so powerful. These are self-executing agreements, capable of automating transactions with precision. Imagine decentralized finance, or DeFi. In this world, a smart contract might automatically issue a loan the moment collateral is provided, without the need for a traditional bank or human oversight. The contract simply performs its duty, efficiently and without question. At the core of these smart contracts is **Solidity**, Ethereum's primary programming language.

Designed specifically for this purpose, Solidity allows developers to code these contracts with ease, crafting intricate systems that the EVM will then bring to life. It's this unique combination, Ethereum's EVM and Solidity, that makes the platform a revolutionary space for developers, empowering them to build decentralized applications that push the boundaries of what's possible. Ethereum's vision, as outlined by Vitalik Buterin, is to be the "world computer," where decentralized applications can run without censorship, fraud, or third-party interference. Buterin saw Ethereum as a way to decentralize not just money, but entire industries. Ethereum's ability to host decentralized applications means that it has the potential to disrupt sectors ranging from finance and law to supply chain management and social media. This vision is deeply rooted in Ethereum's move to Proof of Stake with Ethereum 2.0.

The long-term goal is to make Ethereum scalable and secure enough to support millions of users while keeping it decentralized. Ethereum aims to reduce transaction costs (gas fees) and improve speed, paving the way for greater adoption. Ethereum's potential stretches across countless industries, its versatility giving rise to transformative use cases. Take smart contracts, for example. These self-executing agreements, mentioned before, eliminate the need for intermediaries, automating processes that once required human oversight. Whether in insurance, real estate, or law, smart contracts now breathe life into systems that were once cumbersome and slow, injecting them with speed and efficiency. But the possibilities don't stop there. Decentralized Finance, or DeFi, is perhaps one of Ethereum's most profound contributions. Imagine a world where lending, borrowing, and trading happen without the need for a traditional bank, no middleman, just peer-to-peer transactions powered by code. On platforms like **Aave**, Compound, and **Uniswap**, that world already exists. Financial freedom is at the fingertips of those willing to step into Ethereum's ecosystem. Then, there are Non-Fungible Tokens, or NFTs, digital tokens that represent ownership of something truly unique. Ethereum stands as the home of the largest NFT ecosystem, a place where artists, creators, and collectors can buy, sell, and trade digital assets, pieces of art, collectibles, anything that holds value in the digital realm. Each token tells a story, a one-of-a-kind creation stored on the blockchain. And finally, there are Decentralized Autonomous Organizations, or DAOs. Ethereum has made it possible for these organizations to exist, governed not by traditional leaders but by smart contracts.

What the Hell are DAOs?

A DAO (Decentralized Autonomous Organization) is an organization that operates based on rules encoded as smart contracts on a blockchain, with governance and decision-making typically distributed among token holders, rather than centralized leadership. DAOs aim to create decentralized, transparent, and community-driven entities that operate autonomously without the need for traditional hierarchical structures. A DAO is controlled by its members through a governance process, typically using voting mechanisms powered by blockchain technology. There's no central authority, and decisions are made by collective agreement. DAOs run based on smart contracts, which are self-executing contracts with terms directly written into code. Once a DAO is deployed, it can operate without human intervention, as the smart contract automates processes like fund allocation, governance decisions, or task executions.

Members of a DAO hold governance tokens, which give them the right to vote on decisions related to the organization, such as funding proposals, rule changes, or even future developments. The weight of a member's vote is often proportional to the amount of tokens they hold. Since DAOs operate on a blockchain, all actions and decisions are transparent and can be audited by anyone. This ensures that no central authority can act in secrecy, and every decision is visible to all members. DAOs operate in a trustless manner, meaning they do not rely on trusting individuals or central authorities. Instead, trust is placed in the code (smart contracts) that dictates how the DAO functions. This eliminates the risk of human error or manipulation.

How a DAO Works:

Smart Contracts: At the core of every DAO is a set of smart contracts deployed on a blockchain (typically Ethereum). These smart contracts define the rules and operating procedures for the DAO, such as how proposals are made, how funds are managed, and how decisions are implemented.

Token Distribution: Governance tokens are distributed to members, often through an initial coin offering (ICO), a token sale, or earned through participation in the organization. These tokens grant voting rights and decision-making power.

Proposal System: DAOs have a proposal system that allows members to suggest changes, request funding, or make decisions about the future of the organization. Proposals are typically created by members who stake tokens to put forth their ideas.

Voting Mechanism: Once a proposal is submitted, the community votes on it. The voting process can vary, but it is usually weighted by the number of tokens each participant holds. Some DAOs require a minimum number of votes or a specific threshold to pass a proposal. Execution: If a proposal is accepted, the DAO's smart contract automatically executes the decision. For example, if the proposal is to fund a new project, the smart contract will release funds according to the agreed-upon terms. This automation ensures that decisions are carried out without human intervention.

Types of DAOs:

Investment DAOs: *These DAOs pool funds from members and use collective decision-making to invest in various projects or assets, such as cryptocurrencies, NFTs, or startups. Example: The* **DAO** *(one of the first DAOs) was an investment fund.*

Protocol DAOs: *These DAOs govern decentralized protocols, such as decentralized finance (DeFi) platforms. They control key protocol parameters like interest rates, rewards, and governance upgrades. Example:* **MakerDAO**, *which governs the* **DAI stablecoin.**

Grant DAOs: *These DAOs are designed to allocate funds to developers or projects that contribute to the DAO's ecosystem. They offer grants based on community decisions. Example:* **Uniswap Grants Program.**

Service DAOs: *These DAOs provide decentralized services, such as development, marketing, or consulting, to other blockchain projects or communities. Members earn tokens for contributing their skills. Example:* **Raid Guild.**

Social DAOs: *These DAOs focus on building communities around shared interests or causes. Social DAOs may offer membership via token ownership, and they make decisions on how to manage community resources. Example:* **Friends with Benefits (FWB).**

Benefits of DAOs:

Decentralization: *Power is distributed among the members, removing the need for a central authority or leadership. Decisions are made collectively, ensuring that all voices are heard.*

Transparency: *All decisions, transactions, and governance actions are visible on the blockchain, ensuring full transparency and accountability.*

Global Access: *DAOs can operate across borders, allowing people from different regions to participate and collaborate in a decentralized manner.*

Autonomy and Efficiency: *DAOs can operate autonomously without human intervention, as smart contracts enforce the rules and execute decisions automatically. This can lead to more efficient operations compared to traditional organizations.*

Challenges and Risks of DAOs:

Smart Contract Risks: *Since DAOs rely heavily on smart contracts, any bugs or vulnerabilities in the contract code can be exploited. A famous example is The DAO hack in 2016, where a vulnerability in the smart contract led to the theft of a significant amount of funds.*

Governance Issues: *If governance tokens are distributed unevenly, a small group of large token holders could control the DAO, leading to centralization of power, which goes against the core principles of DAOs.*

Legal Uncertainty: *The legal status of DAOs is still uncertain in many jurisdictions. Since DAOs are not traditional legal entities, they may face difficulties with regulation, taxation, and legal protection.*

Coordination and Decision-Making: *DAOs often rely on large numbers of participants to make decisions, which can slow down the decision-making process. Reaching a consensus among many stakeholders can be time*

Ethereum continues to be the leader in blockchain innovation, with future developments focusing on further scalability and decentralization. Ethereum 2.0 and Layer 2 solutions are just the beginning of the platform's transformation. In the next few years, Ethereum aims to become a more sustainable and scalable network, enabling mass adoption of decentralized applications across various industries. The continued development of Ethereum's ecosystem, combined with its strong developer community, ensures that it will remain at the forefront of blockchain technology.

Ethereum Ecosystem

The Ethereum ecosystem is a vast and dynamic network of projects, applications, tools, and protocols built around the Ethereum blockchain, which serves as the foundation for decentralized applications (dApps) and smart contracts. Ethereum's ecosystem includes a wide range of actors, from developers and users to decentralized finance (DeFi) protocols, NFT platforms, Layer 2 scaling solutions, and more. At the core of Ethereum lies Layer 1, the very foundation where the main blockchain hums with activity. It is here that the true heartbeat of Ethereum can be felt, where every transaction is processed, every contract executed. But with this power comes its limitations. Layer 1 struggles with scalability, there's only so much it can handle at once. As more users flood in, the cracks begin to show, with transaction speeds slowing and costs rising, creating a challenge for those navigating this ever-growing network.

To meet these challenges, Layer 2 solutions emerge, rising like bridges above the foundation of Layer 1. These solutions work by taking transactions off the main chain, processing them elsewhere, and then settling the results back on Layer 1. By doing this, Layer 2 eases the burden on Ethereum's base layer, allowing it to breathe, to scale, and to thrive without the weight of every single transaction pulling it down. It is an elegant solution, a partnership between layers that keeps the system alive and efficient. And at the center of it all is **Ether (ETH)**, the native cryptocurrency of Ethereum, a currency with more than just financial value. ETH fuels the entire ecosystem, paying for the computational power needed to execute tasks, rewarding miners or validators for their efforts in maintaining the network's security and integrity. Every transaction within Ethereum's vast universe carries a cost, measured in gas fees. These fees, denominated in gas, reflect the computational effort required to process a transaction. The more complex the operation, the higher the gas required. Users pay in ETH to cover these costs, each transaction a subtle reminder of the unseen machinery that keeps Ethereum's world turning.

Feature	Layer 1 (Ethereum Mainnet)	Layer 2 (Optimistic Rollups, ZK-Rollups, Plasma)
Security	Secured directly by Ethereum PoS	Relies on Ethereum for final security guarantees
Transaction Speed	Slow (10-15 TPS)	Much faster (hundreds to thousands of TPS)
Cost	High gas fees	Lower fees due to batching of transactions
Use Cases	General-purpose, secure	Specific use cases (payments, DeFi, gaming)

Layer 1 vs Layer 2 solutions

Plasma

Plasma is one of Ethereum's early Layer 2 scaling solutions designed to address the scalability issues faced by the Ethereum blockchain. It was first proposed in August 2017 by Vitalik Buterin (Ethereum co-founder) and Joseph Poon (co-author of the Lightning Network), and it's a Layer 2 solution designed to increase the transaction throughput of Ethereum while maintaining the security of the underlying blockchain. Plasma works creating "**child chains**" that offload most of the computational work from the Ethereum mainnet (Layer 1). These child chains operate independently but are anchored to the Ethereum main chain, meaning they periodically report back to Layer 1 for final settlement and security. The architecture and design of Plasma stretch far beyond the main chain, reaching into a complex network of child chains, often called **Plasma Chains.**

These smaller blockchains operate off-chain, handling transactions with their own set of rules, governance, and consensus mechanisms. Yet, despite their independence, they are anchored to the security of Ethereum's main chain. Periodically, they submit data, known as "**State Commitments**," back to Ethereum, ensuring that the foundation beneath them remains solid, no matter how they operate. At the core of this communication is the power of smart contracts. Plasma relies on these contracts embedded in Ethereum's main chain to create a bridge between the child and root chains. Through these contracts, assets can be deposited or withdrawn, and the system guards against fraudulent activity. The Ethereum main chain remains the final arbiter, the ultimate authority that oversees the entire process, ensuring fairness and security. But to truly maintain this balance, fraud proofs come into play.

Plasma chains must ensure that the transactions processed off-chain are legitimate, and users are empowered to challenge any suspicious or malicious activity. Should an invalid transaction or block surface, a fraud proof can be submitted to the Ethereum mainnet. If the proof holds, the malicious data is reversed, preserving the integrity of the Plasma chain and securing the trust of those who operate within it. In the background of all this, the intricate cryptography of **Merkle Trees** (cryptographic data structures used to efficiently and securely verify large sets of data by hashing each piece of data and organizing them into a tree of hashes) works tirelessly. Plasma chains use this data structure to compress information, allowing only the root of the Merkle Tree, representing the entirety of the chain's state, to be submitted to Ethereum. Instead of every transaction clogging the main chain, just this compressed snapshot is enough to keep things running smoothly, reducing the load on Ethereum's mainnet while ensuring transparency.

It all begins with a simple deposit. Users move assets, whether it be Ether or other tokens, from Ethereum into the Plasma chain through a smart contract. Once inside, they can transact freely, free from the constraints of Ethereum's slower and more expensive processes. It's faster, more efficient, yet still tethered to the safety net of Ethereum's main chain. Within the Plasma chain itself, transactions flow like a river. Users can transfer assets, execute smart contracts, and interact with decentralized applications (dApps), all depending on the design of that specific chain. These transactions are handled off-chain, but they don't vanish into the ether, they're batched and, in time, committed to Ethereum, ensuring a periodic reckoning with the main chain. Of course, users don't stay in Plasma forever.

They have the option to exit, returning their assets to the Ethereum mainnet. This process involves submitting an exit request to the Plasma smart contract, but there's always a period of scrutiny. During this window, others can challenge the exit if they believe fraud is at play. If no valid challenge arises, the assets are released, safe and sound back on Ethereum. In the end, final settlement is what ties it all together. Periodically, the Plasma chain commits its state to Ethereum's main chain, ensuring that, even if something goes wrong within the Plasma chain itself, the assets and transactions are secured by Ethereum. It's a system built on layers of trust, speed, and efficiency, with Ethereum standing as the unshakable foundation beneath it all. The advantages of

Plasma chains are undeniable. With their ability to process thousands of transactions per second off-chain, they tackle Ethereum's biggest challenge: scalability. The vast majority of these transactions are handled away from the congested main chain, with only a small portion ever touching Ethereum.

This efficiency transforms the way things operate, allowing the system to breathe, where Ethereum's Layer 1 once gasped for air under the weight of its own popularity. And then there are the lower gas fees. Off-chain transactions mean that users barely feel the pinch of fees, an enormous relief compared to the high costs of Ethereum's mainnet. Gas fees only come into play when a user interacts directly with Ethereum for things like deposits, exits, or submitting fraud proofs. It's a small price to pay for the speed and efficiency Plasma offers. Despite their independence, Plasma chains are far from unprotected. Plasma also offers customizability, a playground for developers looking to experiment. Each child chain can be crafted with its own unique consensus mechanisms, governance models, and rules. It's a flexible design, allowing creators to shape their chains exactly how they see fit, without being tethered to the rigid structure of Ethereum's Layer 1.

As for use cases, Plasma opens doors to numerous possibilities. Payments, for one, are a natural fit. With high-frequency, low-value transactions like micropayments, Plasma excels. Users can move funds quickly and cheaply off-chain, making it ideal for systems where speed and cost are paramount. Similarly, token transfers benefit from Plasma's efficiency. In any scenario where fast, inexpensive transactions are needed, Plasma chains step in. Token-based applications, too, flourish in this environment, moving swiftly through the decentralized landscape. In the world of decentralized finance (DeFi), Plasma can be a game changer. Some DeFi applications don't require constant communication with Ethereum's mainnet, making Plasma an ideal staging ground. Gaming finds a perfect home within Plasma as well. Blockchain-based games often demand frequent interaction between users and in-game assets. Plasma allows players to trade and transact with minimal fees, while the true ownership of their assets is settled back on Ethereum, ensuring security. And finally, there's scalability for dApps. Developers seeking to build decentralized applications can use Plasma to offload the heavy computational work from Ethereum, transferring it to Plasma chains instead.

This frees up resources, allowing dApps to scale faster, cheaper, and more efficiently, creating a seamless experience for users. In this intricate web of off-chain activity, Plasma chains stand as a solution, not just to Ethereum's current limitations, but to the future of decentralized applications and economies. Plasma, while powerful, is not without its limitations. One of the most noticeable drawbacks is the delayed finality. Plasma chains don't offer the luxury of instant results. Instead, they rely on Ethereum to settle disputes and manage fraud proofs, and with that comes the inevitable waiting. Users must endure a **"Challenge Period,"** often stretching over a few days, before they can finalize their exits. For certain applications, those that thrive on immediacy and liquidity, this delay can feel like a frustrating pause in an otherwise fast-paced environment. Then there's the issue of smart contract limitations. Plasma was never intended to handle the intricacies of complex decentralized applications. It was built for the straightforward, payments and token transfers. While it's technically possible to implement smart contracts within Plasma's framework, the system is far more constrained than other Layer 2 solutions, such as **Optimistic Rollups** or **ZK-Rollups**. These alternatives offer broader support for dApps, allowing for more complex functionality that Plasma struggles to accommodate. Beyond the technical hurdles, complexity becomes another obstacle.

Plasma is intricate, its implementation demanding a deep understanding of both the child chains and their interaction with Ethereum's mainnet. Developers are tasked with navigating the fragile dance between chains, especially when it comes to handling fraud proofs and the often tricky exit mechanisms. It's a delicate balance, and one that requires careful oversight. This brings us to fraud proofs and user responsibility. Plasma's security hinges on the users themselves. Unlike other solutions where security is more automated, here the burden falls on the individuals. They must actively monitor the chain, ready to submit fraud proofs if something goes awry. For some, this added responsibility is empowering, but for others, it's an unwelcome chore, one that leaves the system vulnerable to human error or negligence. Despite these limitations, Plasma has seen notable implementations. **OmiseGO**, now known as **OMG Network**, was one of the first to embrace the Plasma model. It set out to build a decentralized exchange and payment platform, leveraging Plasma's scalability to handle a high volume of transactions.

It was a bold step into the future, a promise of what Plasma could achieve. And then there was Matic, which has since evolved into **Polygon**. Matic began with a hybrid model, blending Plasma with Proof of Stake to scale Ethereum. Its initial focus was on payments and simple token transfers, using Plasma to streamline the process. But like all things in the crypto world, Matic grew, transforming into Polygon, a broader multi-chain scaling solution, leaving behind the simplicity of its early Plasma days in favor of something far more expansive. Plasma's story is one of promise, challenge, and evolution. Its limitations are real, but so are its contributions to the ongoing quest for scalability in the Ethereum ecosystem.

Immutable X

In the world of Ethereum, where high gas fees and sluggish transaction times are the norm, something new emerges. It's called Immutable X, a Layer-2 scaling solution. Built to sit atop

Ethereum's vast blockchain, it's here with a purpose: to take non-fungible tokens, NFTs, and make them faster, easier to use, and cheaper to trade. Ethereum has always been powerful, but it stumbles when it comes to scalability. Immutable X changes that. It brings with it the promise of speed and efficiency, powered by something called **ZK-Rollups**. Imagine a marketplace where creators and collectors no longer dread gas fees. Immutable X removes this burden, allowing minting and trading without a single drop of Ethereum's usual costs. A user creates a digital masterpiece, and it's minted, just like that, without any extra fees.

They transfer it, sell it, and buy another, all without watching their balance disappear into gas. Immutable X handles up to 9,000 transactions per second, leaving Ethereum's own 15 TPS in the dust. And the magic lies in those ZK-Rollups. A technology that bundles up transactions, rolls them tight, and sends them to Ethereum's main chain, all while preserving the blockchain's cherished decentralization. Security and decentralization remain untouched. Immutable X clings to Ethereum's standards, using ZK-Rollups not just for speed, but to ensure every transaction is as secure as it gets. A user watches their trade close in an instant. No waiting. No hesitation. Whether it's in the middle of a fast-paced game or an art auction, Immutable X delivers finality in a heartbeat.

Developers step into the fold with ease, too. Immutable X extends its hand to them, offering APIs that cut through the complexity of blockchain integration. Building decentralized apps, dApps, is no longer a daunting task. It's simple, fast, and flexible. And for those concerned about the environment, there's more good news: Immutable X is carbon-neutral. Every step of the way, it offsets its footprint with verified carbon credits, quieting the whispers of blockchain's environmental impact. Behind this efficiency lies a technological marvel: Zero-Knowledge Rollups. ZK-Rollups, they call them. In a quiet way, they ensure that off-chain transactions stay valid without spilling any data to the blockchain. The details remain hidden, safe, and secure. Immutable X gathers these transactions, compresses them, and sends them off to Ethereum's mainnet in one neat package. This reduces Ethereum's workload, making scalability not just a promise, but a reality. The marketplace for NFTs shifts. Immutable X allows gas-free trading, minting, and transferring of digital assets. Platforms like **OpenSea** catch wind of it, integrating this new technology, allowing creators and collectors to breathe easier. For gamers, Immutable X offers something more, a chance to tokenize in-game items and trade them freely, without worrying about delays or costs. Games like **Gods Unchained** take full advantage, letting players manage their in-game economies with smooth transactions, all backed by Immutable X. Artists, too, find freedom here. They mint and trade their digital art without a second thought, knowing there are no gas fees to hold them back. It's a new world where creativity flourishes, unhindered by the limitations of the past. Immutable X partners with giants in the NFT space.

OpenSea, long loyal to Ethereum, makes the switch, allowing gas-free trading. Even **Illuvium**, a game where players earn and trade NFTs, steps into this new frontier. At the center of Immutable X's ecosystem sits a token, **IMX**. It serves more than one purpose. Those who hold it can stake their IMX, earning rewards for their loyalty, their participation in the network. Governance, too, is shaped by this token. IMX holders get a voice, a vote, on the upgrades, features, and changes that will define the platform's future. Every transaction on Immutable X pays a small tribute to this token, helping sustain the network's growth. Immutable X doesn't rest. Its goal is decentralization, where the community takes the reins, and token holders hold the power to shape the future. As more decisions are handed over, IMX tokens become keys to governance, unlocking the door to the platform's destiny. In a sea of Layer-2 solutions, Immutable X stands apart.

While others, like **Optimism** and **Arbitrum**, focus on scaling general blockchain functions, Immutable X hones in on NFTs, making it the premier choice for creators and collectors alike. Gas fees? Gone. The barrier to entry? Lowered, making the world of NFTs more accessible to everyone. And with its commitment to carbon neutrality, Immutable X silences the critics who decry blockchain's environmental toll. The future is clear. Immutable X isn't stopping. More features, more partnerships, more games, and more decentralized apps are on the horizon. Immutable X is poised to be the foundation of the next wave of NFT innovation, expanding its ecosystem and cementing its role as the go-to platform for anyone looking to explore the possibilities of NFTs, gaming, and beyond.

ZK-Rollups (Zero-Knowledge Rollups)

ZK-Rollups, a cutting-edge Layer 2 scaling solution, bring together two powerful concepts: **Rollups and Zero-Knowledge Proofs (ZKPs)**. The idea is simple yet revolutionary. Rollups bundle or "roll up" multiple transactions into a single batch, submitting it to the main blockchain, Ethereum's Layer 1. This technique significantly reduces the data load and computational strain on Layer 1, speeding things up and cutting costs. But the magic lies in the **Zero-Knowledge Proofs**, cryptographic tricks that allow one party to prove a transaction's validity without revealing anything about the transaction itself. The process begins with off-chain transactions, where ZK-Rollups handle the heavy lifting. Transactions take place on a separate Layer 2 network, far from the congestion of the main chain. As these transactions unfold, they're bundled into a single batch, ready for the next step. From here, the real innovation takes shape: proof generation.

For every batch of transactions, a Zero-Knowledge Proof, often in the form of a **SNARK (Succinct Non-Interactive Argument of**

Knowledge), is created. This proof ensures that all transactions in the batch are valid. Instead of sending every single detail to Ethereum's Layer 1, the ZK-Rollup submits only the compressed data, the SNARK proof and a state root, known as a **Merkle Root** (Merkle Trees are cryptographic data structures used to efficiently and securely verify large sets of data by hashing each piece of data and organizing them into a tree of hashes), back to the main blockchain. This step, known as the on-chain commitment, represents all the bundled transactions in one sleek package.

What makes ZK-Rollups truly remarkable is their instant finality. The ZK proof guarantees the validity of the transactions upfront, meaning that as soon as they're posted to Layer 1, they're considered final. No need for further checks or challenges—it's done. But who manages this intricate process? That role falls to the operator, a central figure responsible for bundling Layer 2 transactions, generating the proofs, and submitting everything to Layer 1. In return, the operator collects fees, ensuring the system runs smoothly. The backbone of ZK-Rollups is the rollup contract, a smart contract deployed on Ethereum's Layer 1. This contract doesn't just verify the proofs and store the compressed data, it maintains the state of the entire Layer 2 system. To make all of this possible, Merkle Trees play a critical role. These cryptographic data structures efficiently store and verify state changes, like balances, within the ZK-Rollup. Each state update is represented as a leaf in the tree, and only the root, the most concise representation of all those changes, needs to be posted on Layer 1. The benefits of ZK-Rollups are undeniable. The first is scalability. By processing transactions off-chain and sending only compressed data to Ethereum, ZK-Rollups dramatically increase transaction throughput. The blockchain becomes faster, smoother, and capable of handling far more than it ever could before. Security is another cornerstone. ZK-Rollups inherit Ethereum's security model, but with an added layer of cryptographic assurance through **Zero-**

Knowledge Proofs. Every transaction is guaranteed to be valid, with the proof committed to Layer 1, leaving little room for error or fraud. Cost efficiency is where ZK-Rollups shine. Since fewer transactions are posted to the main chain, users save on gas fees. And because ZK-Rollups deal in compressed transactions, those fees shrink even further, offering an economical solution for DeFi protocols and dApps. One of the most exciting advantages is instant withdrawal. Unlike other scaling solutions such as **Optimistic Rollups**, which require a lengthy challenge period before funds can be withdrawn, ZK-Rollups allow users to move their assets back to Layer 1 almost instantly. There's no need to wait, the cryptographic proof guarantees that everything is in order. Yet, even this promising technology comes with its own set of challenges.

Proof generation is a complex process, requiring significant computational power. Generating these ZK proofs, particularly **SNARKs, Zero-Knowledge Succinct Non-Interactive Arguments of Knowledge)**, is resource-intensive, often requiring specialized hardware. This makes it a more demanding task for operators. Then there's the issue of development costs. Building a ZK-Rollup system is not a simple endeavor. The cryptographic intricacies involved raise the bar for developers, making it a more expensive solution to implement compared to other Layer 2 options. Finally, ecosystem support is still catching up. While ZK-Rollups continue to grow in popularity, not all decentralized applications (dApps) or DeFi protocols support them yet. This limits their reach in certain use cases, though broader adoption seems only a matter of time. Several projects have already embraced ZK-Rollups. **ZkSync**, built on Ethereum, is one of the leading platforms. Known for its speed and low fees, zkSync focuses on payments and general-purpose smart contracts, offering a glimpse into the future of scalable dApps. Another notable player is **Loopring**, which uses ZK-Rollups to scale decentralized exchanges (DEXs). Loopring combines the advantages of ZK-Rollups with its own DEX protocol, creating a seamless and cost-effective trading experience. Then there's **StarkNet**, a scaling solution that employs STARKs, a different type of Zero-Knowledge Proof than SNARKs. StarkNet provides scalability for dApps on Ethereum, opening the door for even more complex applications. ZK-Rollups are widely regarded as one of the most promising scaling solutions for Ethereum and beyond. As the technology continues to evolve, proof generation times are likely to decrease, ecosystem support will broaden, and ZK-Rollups will be able to handle even more sophisticated smart contracts. Their robust security, instant finality, and potential for privacy-enhancing applications make them a crucial piece of the future blockchain landscape.

Optimistic Rollups

Optimistic Rollups are a Layer 2 scaling solution designed to significantly increase the scalability and transaction throughput of the Ethereum blockchain while preserving security and decentralization. Unlike some other Layer 2 solutions like Plasma or **State Channels**, Optimistic Rollups allow for more general-purpose smart contracts, making them ideal for decentralized finance (DeFi), decentralized applications (dApps), and other complex blockchain use cases. Let's break down how Optimistic Rollups work, why they are important, and how they fit into Ethereum's scaling strategy. Optimistic Rollups (ORUs) bundle transactions together and execute them off-chain, but unlike some other L2 solutions, they "optimistically" assume that transactions are valid without verifying each one immediately. This assumption is what gives them the term "optimistic." Only if someone challenges the validity of a transaction will a process of fraud proof verification take place.

This approach reduces the computational load on the Ethereum main chain (Layer 1), significantly lowering gas fees and increasing throughput. The security of Optimistic Rollups is anchored to Ethereum's main chain, meaning they still benefit from the same level of decentralization and security that Ethereum provides. Optimistic Rollups operate by shifting the majority of computation and transaction processing off-chain while committing data to Ethereum's Layer 1 for security. The process unfolds with precision, each step methodically building upon the last. It begins with batching transactions off-chain, where a multitude of actions are bundled together, far from the crowded lanes of the Ethereum mainnet. These transactions are executed in clusters by the Optimistic Rollup, their raw data compressed into a single unit. This batch, now reduced to its essential form, a **State Root** (a cryptographic hash that represents the entire state of a blockchain at a specific point in time) is posted to Ethereum's Layer 1.

The state root acts as a snapshot, representing the updated state after all those off-chain transactions have played out. But here's the catch, there's an optimistic assumption at the heart of it all. The system trusts that these transactions are valid, without verifying each one in real-time. It's a leap of faith. The rollup processes everything off-chain and sends the resulting state changes back to Ethereum, skipping the actual transactions themselves. The system, in essence, takes its chances that everything has gone smoothly. Of course, not everyone is so trusting. That's where **Fraud Proofs** come into play. If someone believes that something nefarious has slipped through, a fraudulent transaction or a malicious actor, they can submit a Fraud Proof, sounding the alarm. In response, a verification process begins.

The system checks the challenge, and if fraud is detected, the malicious transaction is swiftly undone. However, if no one raises a challenge within the designated window, typically one to two weeks, the transaction is locked in as valid, its fate sealed. With the challenge period behind them, transactions move to final settlement. The state change becomes a permanent part of the Ethereum blockchain. If fraud was uncovered along the way, the system punishes the guilty party, often through slashing mechanisms (a penalty system used in Proof of Stake (PoS) networks to discourage misbehavior by validators). It reduces a validator's staked tokens if they act maliciously or fail to meet network rules, enhancing security and network reliability, protecting the integrity of the system with swift justice. Behind the scenes, rollup contracts on Ethereum orchestrate the entire process. These smart contracts, deployed on Ethereum's Layer 1, manage the delicate interaction between the rollup and the blockchain. They safeguard the compressed data, the State Roots from the rollups, and stand ready to handle any fraud proofs or challenge processes that come their way. But none of this would be possible without the crucial challenge period, the window of time where disputes can be raised. This phase, though vital for security, brings with it a frustrating delay, often stretching to around a week before transactions can be fully finalized.

At the core of the security process is the fraud proof mechanism. Should a challenge arise, the rollup contract replays the disputed transaction on Ethereum, reenacting the events to determine if everything was as it seemed. It's a safety net, catching the lies before they can slip past, ensuring that the system remains both robust and fair. The benefits of Optimistic Rollups are clear and compelling. At the forefront is scalability. By shifting the bulk of transaction processing off-chain, Optimistic Rollups can handle thousands of interactions at once, all while reducing the strain on Ethereum's Layer 1. These off-chain transactions are bundled together, compressed into neat packages, and only the proofs are submitted to Ethereum.

Feature	Optimistic Rollups	ZK-Rollups	Plasma
Transaction Assumption	Assumes transactions are valid unless challenged	Proves every transaction with ZK-SNARKs	Uses child chains and relies on Ethereum for security
Smart Contracts	Supports general-purpose smart contracts	Limited smart contract functionality	Limited smart contracts
Finality Time	Delayed (due to challenge period)	Immediate finality	Delayed finality
Security Model	Fraud proofs	Zero-knowledge proofs	Fraud proofs
Gas Fees	Lower than Ethereum but higher than ZK-Rollups	Very low gas fees (due to compact proofs)	Medium gas fees
Complexity	Easier to implement, but slower finality	More complex but faster finality	Simple for token transfers

Layer 2 Solutions

What sets Optimistic Rollups apart from other scaling solutions like Plasma is their support for general-purpose smart contracts. This means they can handle complex dApps and DeFi use cases, functioning just like Ethereum's Layer 1, but with far less overhead. The doors to innovation remain wide open, and developers can build without the usual limitations imposed by other Layer 2 systems. Beneath it all, security inheritance stands as the cornerstone of trust. Optimistic Rollups derive their security from Ethereum's decentralization. Users know their funds and data are protected by the very foundation that makes Ethereum a powerhouse, adding another layer of confidence to this scaling solution. However, there are challenges lurking beneath the surface. Delayed finality is one such drawback. The challenge period, typically around a week, creates a frustrating delay for those needing immediate results. While this window is crucial for maintaining security, ensuring that any fraud is caught in time, it can slow down systems that thrive on speed, such as high-frequency trading or instant settlements. The need for fraud proofs introduces another layer of complexity. Optimistic Rollups rely on active participants to keep watch over the network, ready to step in and submit fraud proofs if something goes awry.

This requires vigilance from users and adds an extra layer of responsibility, one that not every participant may be prepared to take on. Compared to ZK-Rollups, Optimistic Rollups also face higher fees. Though they reduce costs significantly when compared to Ethereum's Layer 1, they still bear the overhead of maintaining the challenge window and resolving disputes. ZK-Rollups, with their more streamlined processes, often achieve even lower fees. Lastly, there's the issue of data availability. Despite inheriting Ethereum's security, Optimistic Rollups rely heavily on off-chain data for processing transactions. If that data is ever withheld or becomes unavailable, the entire system could be compromised. It's a vulnerability that, while not always at the forefront, lingers in the background as a reminder of the risks involved. In this intricate dance between scalability and security, Optimistic Rollups offer a promising solution, though not without its trade-offs.

We have several uses case, and at the forefront of this tale are platforms like **Optimism.** As one of the leading Optimistic Rollup solutions, Optimism is dedicated to scaling Ethereum without losing compatibility with existing Ethereum smart contracts. It's no wonder that many of the giants in decentralized finance, **Uniswap** and **Synthetix**, to name just two, have embraced it. For these projects, Optimism offers what they desperately need: lower fees and higher throughput, the lifeblood of decentralized exchanges (DEXs) and the financial applications that rely on them. In this new landscape, speed and affordability are no longer luxuries—they're necessities.

Arbitrum, another prominent player in this space, has followed a similar path. Supporting Ethereum-compatible smart contracts, Arbitrum provides the same crucial ingredients: lower fees and faster transactions. But it's not just the speed or the cost that draws developers, it's the flexibility. Arbitrum has quickly become one of the most widely adopted Layer 2 solutions, offering a developer-friendly environment that makes building and scaling projects smoother and more accessible. It's a platform that welcomes innovation, allowing DeFi protocols to thrive. Take **Synthetix**, for example. As a major DeFi protocol for synthetic assets, Synthetix needed a way to bring down the towering gas costs that often plagued users trading synthetic assets. The answer came in the form of Optimistic Rollups. By adopting this technology, Synthetix managed to keep trading affordable without sacrificing the security that Ethereum provides. It's a delicate balance, one that allowed users to trade freely, without the constant worry of high fees draining their profits. And then there's Uniswap, a titan in the world of decentralized exchanges. Uniswap's integration with Optimism marked a significant shift for its users. Suddenly, the platform that had been known for its revolutionary approach to trading was offering even more, faster and cheaper transactions. With Optimistic Rollups, Uniswap maintained its position at the top of the decentralized exchange world while enhancing the user experience, freeing traders from the burden of Ethereum's high gas fees. Layer 2 solutions like Optimistic Rollups remain essential. They're the key to achieving the kind of mass adoption that will bring Ethereum, and the decentralized world it supports, into the mainstream. The journey is far from over, but with platforms like Optimism and Arbitrum leading the way, the future looks promising.

State Channels

State Channels, a Layer 2 scaling solution, offer a way to make transactions faster and more efficient by taking most of the action off-chain. In this technique, two or more parties can execute numerous transactions between themselves without burdening the main blockchain, except for the opening and closing of the channel. It's a clever workaround to Ethereum's scalability problem, allowing participants to move freely without the usual congestion. It all begins with opening the channel. To set things in motion, the parties lock an initial state, this could be funds or specific contract conditions, into a smart contract on the Ethereum blockchain. This initial state is like laying the foundation for a building, recorded on-chain to keep everything official. Once that's done, the real magic begins. The bulk of the interactions happen in off-chain transactions.

The participants can now transact as much as they like, exchanging signed messages that reflect the changing state, be it updated balances or contract outcomes. But none of this touches the blockchain. These messages are kept off-chain, allowing for quick and seamless exchanges without the weight of on-chain verification slowing things down. Once the parties are done, it's time to close the channel. At this point, they submit the final state, the last record of their transactions or balances, back to Ethereum. The blockchain takes these signed messages, verifies the final state, and settles everything on-chain, bringing the off-chain interactions to a close with one final act. State Channels come in different forms. The most straightforward are Payment Channels.

These allow participants to make off-chain payments, only settling the final balance on the main chain. It's the same principle behind Bitcoin's **Lightning Network**, and Ethereum supports similar mechanisms for faster, cheaper payments. More advanced are **Generalized State Channels**, which can handle more than just payments. These channels allow for any kind of smart contract logic to take place off-chain. Whether it's a dApp's functionality or complex contract execution, everything can unfold off-chain until the final result is brought back to the blockchain. Despite their benefits, challenges lurk within State Channels. One major issue is the online requirement. Both parties need to stay connected throughout the channel's lifetime. If one becomes unresponsive, they run the risk of losing their funds, especially if the other party tries to close the channel unfairly. Thankfully, the use of **Watchtowers**, third-party services, can help mitigate this risk by monitoring the channel and defending against malicious closures. Another limitation is the number of participants. State Channels work best with small groups, usually no more than four people. Scaling beyond that can be cumbersome and is better suited to other Layer 2 solutions, like rollups. Then there's the risk of inactivity. If no one takes the initiative to close the channel, the funds or states locked inside could remain stuck indefinitely. A time limit can be set, but adding such a condition introduces additional complexity, something that needs to be managed carefully. And in the event of a force closure dispute, things can get tricky. If there's a disagreement over the final state, either party can submit what they claim is the latest version to the blockchain.

But here's the catch, the other party must be online to challenge it with an even newer version. If not, disputes can drag on, leading to delays or complications. Despite these challenges, State Channels offer compelling use cases. In gaming, for instance, players can make rapid off-chain interactions, only sending the final game results to the blockchain when necessary, reducing latency and slashing gas fees. For recurring services, such as subscriptions, State Channels make regular payments smooth and efficient. The service provider can collect fees off-chain, without having to execute every transaction on Ethereum. Several notable projects have emerged to make State Channels a reality. The **Raiden Network** an Ethereum's answer to Bitcoin's Lightning Network, offering a fast, low-cost way to transfer ERC-20 tokens off-chain. There's also **Connext**, a framework that allows for not just off-chain payments, but contract interactions as well. From gaming to financial services, Connext opens the door for a wide array of applications. Similarly, the **Celer Network** offers another State Channel solution, designed to provide secure, fast, and low-cost scaling for Ethereum. And then there's Polygon, another key player in the world of Layer 2 solutions, though its role in this story is one we'll explore more deeply later on. For now, State Channels remain a crucial tool in the ever-evolving quest to make Ethereum faster, cheaper, and more accessible.

Arbitrum Orbit

Arbitrum Orbit is an intricate part of the ever-expanding Arbitrum ecosystem, a world built on layers, each with its own purpose. At the heart of it lies **Arbitrum One**, a popular Layer 2 chain built on Ethereum, designed specifically to optimize smart contract execution through the power of Optimistic Rollups. Then, there's **Arbitrum Nova**, another Layer 2 chain, but this one is finely tuned for ultra-low-cost transactions, the kind that are essential for gaming and social media applications. But Arbitrum Orbit reaches further. It creates a Layer 3 scaling framework, a step beyond, where developers can carve out their own custom blockchain environments. Known as **Rollups**, these environments sit on top of Arbitrum One or Nova, allowing decentralized applications (dApps) and protocols to scale in a way that fits their unique needs.

Built on the foundation of Optimistic Rollups, **Orbit** takes the assumptions that make these rollups work: that all transactions are valid unless proven otherwise. Only when someone raises a challenge does verification step in, which saves time, increases throughput, and lowers costs. While Arbitrum itself operates as a Layer 2 solution to Ethereum, Orbit adds another layer, creating a dynamic Layer 3. Here, developers have the freedom to deploy independent blockchains, rollups that inherit the security and efficiency of Arbitrum but with more flexibility to tailor their systems to specific needs. The benefits of Orbit are clear. First, there's lower transaction costs. By shifting computation off-chain and onto Layer 3, the strain on both Ethereum's mainnet and Arbitrum Layer 2 is reduced. This leads to even more affordable transactions, making it a haven for applications that demand low fees. Then there's the matter of higher throughput. Orbit's architecture processes far more transactions per second than running directly on Ethereum or even Arbitrum.

For applications that depend on high-frequency interactions, this scalability is crucial. Another compelling feature is the ability to create application-specific rollups. Developers can fine-tune their Layer 3 rollups to cater to the specific needs of their dApp or protocol. This could mean custom token economics, governance models that fit their vision, or security mechanisms crafted just for them. Interoperability is also at the core of Orbit's design. Rollups built on Orbit can interact seamlessly with one another, as well as with the broader Arbitrum ecosystem. This means that assets and functionality can flow between different rollups, unlocking a network of possibilities. Orbit, though its Layer 3 solution, benefits from Ethereum's security. Every transaction on Orbit can be traced back to Ethereum's Layer 1, ensuring that while developers enjoy flexibility, they aren't compromising on the strong security guarantees that Ethereum provides. The applications of Arbitrum Orbit are vast. DeFi protocols can thrive here, using custom rollups to process financial transactions, lending, and trading at scale, all without clogging the main Ethereum or Arbitrum network. In the world of gaming, Orbit opens doors to a whole new level of speed and efficiency. Developers can process in-game transactions without delay and at minimal cost, giving players smooth, uninterrupted experiences.

NFT platforms, too, find a natural home in Orbit. Minting, trading, and transferring NFTs can happen at a fraction of the cost compared to Layer 2 or Ethereum, making the world of digital assets more accessible to a broader audience. For **social networks,** where interactions like posts, likes, and comments happen constantly, Orbit's Layer 3 rollups are a perfect fit. These platforms can reduce the costs of recording such frequent actions, all while keeping the experience smooth for users. In comparing Arbitrum Orbit to other Layer 3 solutions, such as ZK-Rollup-based Layer 3s, the differences are clear. ZK-Rollups, with their **Zero-Knowledge Proofs**, offer faster finality, but they come at a cost—literally. They're more computationally expensive. Orbit, with its reliance on Optimistic Rollups, offers a simpler and cheaper alternative, though it does come with a challenge period for fraud detection. And then there's **Polygon Supernets**, another option for developers to build custom blockchains on Layer 2. While Polygon offers its own trade-offs in terms of security, speed, and ease of deployment, Orbit's tight integration with the Arbitrum ecosystem and its focus on Optimistic Rollups sets it apart, offering unique advantages for those looking to scale.

At the helm of all this is the **Arbitrum DAO**, a decentralized body governing key decisions related to the Arbitrum ecosystem, including Orbit. The DAO gives power to the community, allowing members to propose and vote on changes or upgrades, ensuring that the entire network remains decentralized, transparent, and aligned with the needs of its users. Orbit is more than just another layer in the blockchain space. It's an invitation to developers, a call to create, scale, and innovate in ways that were once beyond reach. In the Arbitrum ecosystem, the future is being built, one layer at a time.

Tether

Tether (USDT) is one of the most prominent stablecoins in the cryptocurrency ecosystem.

What the Hell are Stablecoins?

Stablecoins are a type of cryptocurrency designed to maintain a stable value by pegging their price to a more stable asset, typically a fiat currency like the U.S. dollar, the euro, or commodities like gold. The primary goal of stablecoins is to combine the benefits of blockchain technology, such as decentralization, security, and efficiency, with the price stability of traditional assets. Stablecoins are vital to the cryptocurrency ecosystem because they provide a reliable medium of exchange, store of value, and unit of account, addressing the volatility that affects most cryptocurrencies like Bitcoin and Ethereum.

Use:

Medium of Exchange: Stablecoins are used in everyday transactions, enabling users to make payments or remittances without worrying about the volatility associated with traditional cryptocurrencies.

Unit of Account: By maintaining a stable value, stablecoins provide a standard for pricing goods and services in the cryptocurrency ecosystem.

Store of Value: Investors and traders can use stablecoins to store value, especially during times of market volatility when other cryptocurrencies experience significant price fluctuations.

DeFi Applications: In decentralized finance (DeFi), stablecoins are used in lending, borrowing, yield farming, and other financial activities that require stable, predictable pricing.

Types of Stablecoins:

Stablecoins are generally classified into three main categories based on how they maintain their stability:

First, Fiat-Collateralized Stablecoins: Are backed by traditional fiat currencies, such as the U.S. dollar or Euro, held in reserve by a central issuer. For every stablecoin issued, an equivalent amount of fiat currency is held in a bank account or other trusted financial institution. The value of these stablecoins is directly tied to the fiat currency, maintaining a 1:1 peg.

Examples are:

Tether (USDT): One of the earliest and most popular stablecoins, Tether is pegged to the U.S. dollar. It operates on multiple blockchains and is widely used across cryptocurrency exchanges.

USD Coin (USDC): Issued by **Circle** and **Coinbase**, USDC is a fully collateralized stablecoin that is audited regularly to ensure transparency and the 1:1 peg to the U.S. dollar.

TrueUSD (TUSD): A stablecoin that is also fully backed by U.S. dollars and designed to provide a transparent and compliant asset for use in the cryptocurrency market.

Pros:

Stability: Fiat-collateralized stablecoins offer the most straightforward form of stability since they are backed by actual fiat reserves.

Widespread Use: They are the most widely accepted stablecoins across exchanges and DeFi platforms.

Cons:

Centralization: Fiat-collateralized stablecoins rely on a centralized entity to manage the reserves, which may pose trust and regulatory risks.

Regulatory Concerns: Regulatory scrutiny of reserve management and transparency has been an issue for some fiat-collateralized stablecoins like Tether.

Second, Crypto-Collateralized Stablecoins: are backed by other cryptocurrencies rather than fiat. To account for the volatility of cryptocurrencies, these stablecoins are often over-collateralized—meaning more cryptocurrency is held in reserve than the value of the stablecoins issued. This approach ensures the stablecoin maintains its peg even during times of price fluctuations in the underlying collateral.

Examples are:

DAI: Issued by **MakerDAO**, DAI is one of the most well-known crypto-collateralized stablecoins. It is pegged to the U.S. dollar and backed by cryptocurrencies like Ethereum (ETH) or Wrapped Bitcoin (WBTC). DAI is decentralized, governed by smart contracts, and controlled by the MakerDAO community.

Pros:

Decentralization: Crypto-collateralized stablecoins often rely on smart contracts for issuance and redemption, eliminating the need for a centralized authority.

Transparency: The collateral backing the stablecoin is on-chain, meaning anyone can verify the reserves.

Cons:

Complexity: *Over-collateralization and liquidation mechanisms add complexity and may limit scalability.*

Volatility Risks: *The value of the collateral (cryptocurrency) can fluctuate, which may require frequent adjustments to maintain the stablecoin's peg.*

Third, Algorithmic Stablecoins: *do not rely on fiat or cryptocurrency reserves for their stability. Instead, they use algorithms and smart contracts to control the supply of the stablecoin, adjusting it dynamically to maintain a stable price. When the price of the stablecoin rises above its peg, the algorithm increases the supply, and when it falls below the peg, it reduces the supply.*

Examples are:

Ampleforth (AMPL): *Ampleforth adjusts its circulating supply based on demand, but unlike most algorithmic stablecoins, it does not maintain a constant price of $1. Instead, it adjusts the supply while allowing the price to fluctuate.*

TerraUSD (UST): *An algorithmic stablecoin that uses Terra's LUNA token to stabilize its price. UST has been widely used in the Terra ecosystem but faced significant issues in 2022,* **leading to a total collapse.**

Pros:

No Collateral Required: *These stablecoins do not require fiat or cryptocurrency reserves, making them highly scalable.*

Decentralization: They operate using algorithms and smart contracts, which can be entirely decentralized.

Cons:

Stability Concerns: Maintaining a stable peg without collateral can be challenging, especially during times of market stress. Algorithmic stablecoins have historically been prone to collapse.

Complexity and Trust Issues: Users need to trust the algorithm's ability to maintain the peg, which can be opaque and difficult to understand.

Use Cases for Stablecoins:

Trading and Hedging: Traders use stablecoins to hedge against volatility in cryptocurrency markets. Instead of converting to fiat, which may involve delays and fees, traders can hold stablecoins during market downturns and quickly re-enter the market when conditions improve.

Remittances: Stablecoins are increasingly used for cross-border payments and remittances due to their fast transaction times and low fees compared to traditional payment systems.

DeFi (Decentralized Finance): Stablecoins play a critical role in DeFi protocols. They are used for lending, borrowing, and providing liquidity in decentralized exchanges (DEXs). DeFi protocols like Aave, Compound, and MakerDAO rely heavily on stablecoins for collateral, interest payments, and liquidity pools.

Payments: Merchants and users are adopting stablecoins for online and peer-to-peer payments, as they offer fast settlement and lower fees than traditional payment processors.

The Regulatory Landscape:

Stablecoins have attracted significant attention from regulators due to their potential to impact the broader financial system. Issues related to transparency, reserve management, and the potential for systemic risks have led to discussions about how to regulate stablecoins. Regulators are concerned about whether fiat-backed stablecoins like Tether (USDT) have adequate reserves to back all issued tokens. This has led to calls for audits and greater transparency. On top of that, Stablecoins, especially those pegged to the U.S. dollar, could impact monetary policy if they become widely used in countries with weaker currencies. In this light, many governments are exploring ways to regulate stablecoins to ensure financial stability and protect consumers. In the U.S., there have been proposals to treat stablecoin issuers as banks, requiring them to hold reserves similar to traditional financial institutions.

Challenges and Risks of Stablecoins

Centralization: *Many stablecoins are issued by centralized entities, which goes against the decentralized ethos of blockchain technology. Centralized stablecoins also pose risks related to trust and regulatory intervention.*

Regulatory Risks: *As governments worldwide grapple with stablecoins' implications for the traditional financial system, stricter regulations could affect their usage and availability.*

Depegging: *Stablecoins that lose their peg to the underlying asset (e.g., a U.S. dollar-backed stablecoin dropping below $1) can face significant issues, particularly in times of market stress or when reserves are called into question.*

Security Risks: *Smart contract vulnerabilities in crypto-collateralized or algorithmic stablecoins could lead to hacks or exploits, potentially destabilizing the token.*

Stablecoins are expected to continue playing a crucial role in the cryptocurrency ecosystem, especially as the world moves toward more digital assets and central bank digital currencies (CBDCs). Their continued growth in adoption across DeFi, global payments, and remittances

Launched in 2014, Tether it is pegged to traditional fiat currencies, most notably the U.S. dollar, maintaining a 1:1 value. The vision behind Tether was to create a bridge between the fiat and crypto worlds, making it easier to move between the two without the instability often associated with other cryptocurrencies. The founders believed that the future of finance lies in the ability to transact in a decentralized, borderless manner but recognized the need for a stable unit of account to facilitate these transactions. The core idea was to integrate the benefits of blockchain with the stability of traditional currencies, addressing the challenges of volatility in the cryptocurrency market. Over time, the founders also emphasized Tether's role in providing liquidity to the broader cryptocurrency ecosystem, allowing traders to enter and exit positions without converting back to fiat. Tether was originally launched as **Realcoin** by Brock Pierce, Reeve Collins, and Craig Sellars in 2014. It was later rebranded to Tether in November of that year. The goal was to create a cryptocurrency that had the stability of the U.S. dollar but could leverage the decentralization and security of blockchain technology. Tether's adoption grew rapidly due to its perceived stability, but over the years, it has faced numerous controversies. Questions around its reserves and audits have often put Tether under regulatory scrutiny.

Despite these challenges, it remains the most widely used stablecoin and is essential to many cryptocurrency exchanges and platforms. Tether's primary innovation is its use of blockchain technology to provide the stability of fiat currencies within a decentralized, global digital economy, offering both the security and efficiency of blockchain transactions. This is particularly valuable in an ecosystem characterized by the volatility of other digital assets like Bitcoin and Ethereum. A critical function that Tether introduced was the integration of smart contracts, which automates transactions in a decentralized and secure manner. Tether operates on multiple blockchain platforms, including **Bitcoin** (via the Omni Layer, a protocol built on top of the Bitcoin blockchain that enables the creation, transfer, and trading of digital assets), **Ethereum** (as an ERC-20 token), **Tron**, and more. The Omni Layer allows for the creation and transfer of digital tokens, which is how Tether originally began. However, Tether's presence on Ethereum, which introduced the integration of smart contracts, further solidified its utility and adoption. Tether tokens are issued when a user deposits fiat currency into Tether Limited's reserves. An equivalent amount of USDT is minted and sent to the user, maintaining the 1:1 peg to the fiat currency. Users can then trade or hold these tokens on the blockchain. When a user wants to redeem USDT for fiat, the process reverses: the tokens are burned, and the fiat equivalent is transferred to the user's bank account. Because Tether operates on multiple blockchains, users can transfer Tether between different networks, making it a highly flexible asset. This cross-blockchain compatibility has been key to its adoption across different exchanges and platforms. While Tether operates on multiple blockchains, it typically adopts the consensus mechanisms of those platforms.

For example, Ethereum uses a Proof of Stake (PoS) mechanism, while Bitcoin (via Omni Layer) uses Proof of Work (PoW). Tether relies on these platforms' consensus mechanisms to verify transactions and secure the network. Across both centralized and decentralized exchanges, Tether has become one of the most traded assets. It serves a critical purpose, acting as a stable trading pair. When the market's winds shift unpredictably, traders turn to Tether as a safe harbor, hedging against the wild swings that define the space. In the realm of decentralized finance (DeFi), Tether takes on an equally vital role. Its stability, tethered to the U.S. dollar, makes it an appealing collateral asset for lending, borrowing, and yield farming. Remittances, too, have found new life through Tether. In regions where fiat currencies are unreliable, prone to inflation or devaluation, Tether has emerged as a reliable alternative. Its 1:1 peg to the U.S. dollar provides a steady store of value, making it increasingly popular for cross-border payments. People can transfer funds quickly and securely, without worrying about the value disappearing along the way. Yet, Tether's journey has not been without its challenges. Over the years, it has faced significant legal scrutiny, particularly surrounding its claims of full backing by reserves.

Questions arose: Was every Tether truly backed by a corresponding U.S. dollar, as promised? The stakes were high, and in 2021, Tether Limited found itself in the crosshairs of the New York Attorney General's Office. The result was a settlement, a fine and an agreement to provide regular reports on its reserves. It was a pivotal moment for Tether and for the broader stablecoin market, signaling the increasing importance of transparency and accountability. Despite these hurdles, Tether has proven resilient. It has taken strides toward increased transparency, publishing audits and reserve attestations to rebuild trust. These efforts have helped Tether maintain its dominant position in the market, where it continues to play a foundational role, a beacon of stability in an ecosystem always on the move.

Binance and BNB

Binance emerged on the scene in 2017, a bold newcomer in the fast-growing world of cryptocurrency exchanges. Behind it stood Changpeng Zhao, or "CZ" as he's known to the community, a visionary who quickly transformed Binance into the largest cryptocurrency exchange by trading volume. What began as a simple platform for buying, selling, and trading digital assets rapidly grew into something much larger, a vast ecosystem that stretched beyond trading to encompass its own blockchain, **Binance Smart Chain (BSC),** and its native cryptocurrency, **BNB.** Binance's influence now extended across decentralized finance (DeFi), staking, blockchain project launches, and much more. Binance's story began with a spark. In the midst of a cryptocurrency boom, the company raised $15 million through an Initial Coin Offering (ICO), issuing BNB as its native token. Launched during a period of rapid expansion in the industry, Binance distinguished itself with a user-friendly platform that supported a wide range of coins, low trading fees, and the ability to process vast numbers of transactions quickly. It wasn't long before Binance was the name on everyone's lips. By 2017, Binance had established itself as a go-to exchange, celebrated for its intuitive interface and high liquidity. But the real shift came in 2018. Facing regulatory pressure in China, Binance moved its operations to Malta, signaling the beginning of a global expansion that would cement its place as a dominant player in the crypto world. The next year, 2019, saw Binance take things a step further. It launched **Binance Chain,** a blockchain designed for decentralized trading with BNB as its native coin. Yet the true innovation lay in the introduction of **Binance Smart Chain (BSC),** a scalable and smart contract-compatible chain. BSC wasn't just about trading, it opened the door to decentralized applications and a world of automated financial services, all built on Binance's rapidly growing ecosystem. In 2020 and 2021, Binance diversified its offerings even further. **Binance Launchpad** provided a platform for new crypto projects to find their footing, while **Binance Academy** offered educational resources for those eager to learn. And **Binance Labs**, an incubator for blockchain startups, became a breeding ground for innovation. Throughout this expansion, BNB evolved from its original purpose as a token for trading fee discounts to a multi-purpose utility coin, central to the Binance Smart Chain ecosystem. Whether it was DeFi, staking, or governance, BNB found itself at the heart of it all. The evolution of BNB from its humble beginnings on Ethereum's blockchain to its migration to Binance's own chain is a testament to the coin's growing importance. Initially launched as an ERC-20 token, BNB was created to offer Binance users discounts on trading fees. But over time, it grew into much more than that.

Today, it powers everything from transaction fees on Binance Smart Chain to staking, where users can earn rewards while supporting network security. At the core of Binance's success is its exchange, the foundation upon which everything else was built. Here, users can trade a vast array of cryptocurrencies, with options for spot trading, margin trading, futures trading, and even peer-to-peer (P2P) trading. It's a robust platform, designed to cater to every level of trader, from the casual user to the institutional investor. But Binance's ambitions didn't stop there. Binance Chain became the first blockchain it developed, designed for fast and low-cost trading. Yet as Binance Smart Chain (BSC) gained prominence, it became clear that BSC would be the future of Binance's blockchain endeavors. Launched in 2020, BSC was built for the world of smart contracts, fully compatible with the Ethereum Virtual Machine (EVM). This meant that developers could easily port their decentralized applications (dApps) from Ethereum to BSC, taking advantage of lower fees and faster transaction times. Binance Smart Chain operates on a consensus model known as **Proof of Staked Authority (PoSA)**, blending the efficiency of

Proof of Stake (PoS) with the reliability of Proof of Authority (PoA). This hybrid approach allows for faster and cheaper transactions compared to Ethereum, making it an attractive option for developers looking to build decentralized applications or DeFi services. Through all of this, BNB remained the thread that tied everything together. Whether providing trading fee discounts on Binance's exchange or being used to pay transaction fees on Binance Smart Chain, BNB has become central to the entire Binance ecosystem.

Users can even stake their BNB, earning rewards while helping to secure the network. What began as a simple exchange has transformed into an ecosystem that touches every corner of the cryptocurrency world. From retail traders to institutional investors, developers to blockchain startups, Binance has created platforms and services that cater to all. And with BNB at the heart of its ecosystem, the company shows no signs of slowing down. The story of Binance is one of innovation, ambition, and the relentless pursuit of creating something bigger than anyone could have imagined in 2017. The burn mechanism at Binance was a quiet but powerful force, shaping the future of BNB. Periodically, Binance would buy back BNB tokens, not to hold or redistribute them, but to burn them, reducing the overall supply, making each remaining token more scarce. It was a deflationary tactic, a way to slowly increase the value of BNB over time, a strategy designed for the long game. But the utility of BNB went far beyond this subtle economic maneuver. It was also the gateway to new opportunities on Binance Launchpad, a platform for token sales of emerging blockchain projects. Holding BNB meant more than just a discount on trading, it was a ticket to participate in these token sales, where new ideas and innovations were born.

Many projects had risen through this platform, their tokens launched into the market after rigorous vetting by Binance. Some of the names, like **Fetch.AI**, **Band Protocol**, and **Axie Infinity**, would go on to make waves in the wider crypto world. Then there was DeFi, the decentralized finance landscape that had bloomed across Binance Smart Chain (BSC). BNB became the lifeblood of these protocols, flowing through yield farms, lending platforms, and liquidity pools. It wasn't just a token, it was a force driving decentralized systems forward, facilitating lending, borrowing, and earning across a rapidly growing ecosystem. For those looking to learn more, **Binance Academy** stood as a beacon of knowledge. Free educational resources were available, covering everything from blockchain fundamentals to advanced trading strategies. Whether someone was just beginning their journey into crypto or an experienced trader looking to sharpen their edge, Binance Academy offered a place to deepen their understanding. While Binance educated the masses, **Binance Labs** was at the forefront of nurturing new talent. As the venture capital and incubation arm of Binance, it poured resources into early-stage blockchain startups, offering funding, mentorship, and access to Binance's expansive ecosystem. Projects in DeFi, NFTs, and infrastructure found a home here, with Terra, **CertiK**, and Injective Protocol standing out among the success stories. On the other side of Binance's ecosystem, DeFi projects thrived. On **PancakeSwap**, a decentralized exchange, users traded tokens, farmed yields, and staked in liquidity pools, enjoying low fees and high rewards.

Venus offered a decentralized platform for lending and borrowing, where users could mint synthetic stablecoins. And then there was **Autofarm**, a yield aggregator designed to help users maximize returns from the various liquidity pools scattered across BSC. But Binance wasn't content with just DeFi. In 2021, it launched its own **NFT Marketplace**, an arena where users could mint, buy, and sell non-fungible tokens. Art, collectibles, gaming assets, everything could be found here, and all at a fraction of the cost that Ethereum-based platforms charged. The marketplace thrived, opening up new possibilities for creators and collectors alike. Several key projects anchored the Binance ecosystem.

PancakeSwap, the leading decentralized exchange on BSC, became known for its low fees, extensive yield farming options, and a wide variety of tokens. **Trust Wallet**, which Binance acquired in 2018, provided users with a secure, decentralized wallet supporting multiple cryptocurrencies. It integrated seamlessly with Binance DEX and BSC, making it an indispensable tool for traders. **Venus Protocol** emerged as a decentralized money market and synthetic stablecoin platform, allowing users to lend, borrow, and trade crypto assets. Finally, **Binance USD** (BUSD), Binance's stablecoin, became a core piece of the ecosystem. Pegged 1:1 with the U.S. dollar, BUSD was a reliable store of value across Binance's trading platforms and DeFi protocols. It anchored trades, lending, and even NFT purchases, offering a stable foundation in a world defined by volatility. The Binance ecosystem was vast, and with each passing year, it continued to grow, evolve, and innovate. Whether through cutting-edge technology, financial services, or education, Binance had built something far greater than an exchange—it had crafted a world.

Solana

Solana is a high-performance blockchain platform designed for decentralized applications (dApps) and cryptocurrencies. It aims to solve the scalability problems that have limited the growth of other blockchain networks by providing fast transaction speeds, low fees, and high throughput. Solana's ability to process tens of thousands of transactions per second (TPS) has made it a popular choice for decentralized finance (DeFi) applications, non-fungible tokens (NFTs), metaverse-based gamings and other dApps. Solana was founded in 2017 by Anatoly Yakovenko, a former Qualcomm engineer, with the goal of creating a blockchain that could scale without relying on Layer 2 solutions or sharding. The Solana mainnet launched in March 2020, and since then, it has rapidly gained adoption due to its unique architecture and performance. **Solana Labs**, the company behind Solana, and the non-profit **Solana Foundation** work together to support the development and growth of the ecosystem. Solana's world unfolded like a finely crafted piece of engineering, each component fitting together with precision.

At its heart was the enigmatic **Proof of History (PoH)**, a feature unlike any other in the vast expanse of blockchain. Anatoly Yakovenko had devised a cryptographic clock that worked like magic, allowing the network's nodes to agree on the order and time of events without needing the age-old systems of Proof of Work or Proof of Stake. It wasn't just a clock, it was the heartbeat of Solana, rhythmically stamping each event and transaction, ensuring smooth and efficient communication. The chatter between nodes became minimal, the network swifter, more agile. Yet, PoH was not alone. The familiar presence of Proof of Stake (PoS) lingered beside it. In Solana's realm, validators, guardians of the network, staked their **SOL**, Solana's native currency, as a pledge of trust. Their task? To process transactions, add blocks to the ever-growing blockchain, and in return, receive a reward, tokens of SOL for their diligence. In the background, Solana hummed with an energy rarely seen in the blockchain world. **High Throughput** was its defining trait, its ability to manage a staggering 50,000 to 65,000 transactions each second like a conductor leading a grand symphony. The notes of transactions played effortlessly, with no need for extra layers or sharding to ease the weight of the performance. It was seamless, fluid. The magic didn't end there. Each transaction came with low costs. Low Transaction Fees became a hallmark, a mere $0.00025 per transaction, enticing the world of decentralized finance and NFT marketplaces.

It was a world where speed met affordability, and developers flocked to build their dreams on Solana's shoulders. Beneath this intricate dance was **Sealevel**, the parallel runtime that allowed

Solana to perform the seemingly impossible: running multiple smart contracts side by side. Efficiency was the name of the game, and Sealevel gave the network the tools it needed to scale, to grow, and to welcome more contracts without missing a beat. But for Solana, speed was more than just a technical achievement, it was a way of life. The **Turbine Protocol** broke data into small packets, distributing them across the network's nodes, ensuring that communication flowed fast, without burdening bandwidth. It was like sending whispers on the wind, each packet finding its way swiftly, aiding Solana's pursuit of speed. And then there was **Gulf Stream**, pushing transactions toward validators before a block had even formed.

The traditional mempool, a place where transactions often waited their turn, was no longer needed. Gulf Stream gave Solana its edge, its signature fast confirmation times. The network's consensus, though, rested in the hands of **Tower BFT**, a clever variation of the **Byzantine Fault Tolerance algorithm**. It allowed the network to find agreement, to reach consensus quickly and with efficiency, keeping latency low and the system's performance sharp. Solana's journey was not just about technology, it was about building an entire world. Its Ecosystem grew with rapid momentum, drawing in developers and projects, particularly in the realms of decentralized finance, NFTs, and Web3 applications. In the burgeoning world of DeFi, protocols sprouted like wildflowers, each one a testament to Solana's prowess. There is **Serum**, a decentralized exchange that thrive on Solana's infrastructure, offering fast, cost-effective trades, while **Raydium** acts as an automated market maker, weaving its liquidity into Serum's market. On the side, Solend stepped in, a lending and borrowing protocol reminiscent of Aave on Ethereum, but powered by Solana's speed. Then there was the world of NFTs.

Magic Eden and **Solanart** became the go-to marketplaces, their platforms bustling with the trade of digital art, collectibles, and more. Solana's low fees and quick transaction times made it the perfect home for artists and traders alike. In the Web3 domain, applications like Audius emerged, offering decentralized music streaming, giving power back to artists, and rewriting the rules of content ownership. All of this revolved around SOL, the native cryptocurrency, the lifeblood of the Solana network. It flowed through every transaction, paid as fees, staked by validators, and used in the intricate mechanics of decentralized finance. SOL was also the key to Solana's governance, a future where decisions would likely rest in the hands of its holders, guiding the network's path forward. Yet, even in this dazzling world, challenges loomed. Network Outages cast shadows over Solana's glowing reputation, moments when the network fell silent, sometimes for hours, raising questions about its reliability. Validator centralization also stirred whispers of concern, despite its claims of decentralization, a small group of validators wielded much of the power, a potential vulnerability in Solana's otherwise robust armor.

The network's demand for high-performance hardware further narrowed the field of those who could participate in validation, a challenge that cut off smaller players from securing the network. Competition added to the stakes, other Layer 1 blockchains like Ethereum, Binance Smart Chain, and **Avalanche** raced toward the same goals of scalability and speed, each bringing its own strengths to the table. In many ways, Solana was destined to be compared to Ethereum, the giant of decentralized applications. Ethereum had the legacy, the vast ecosystem, but Solana had the speed, the promise of solving the very scalability issues that Ethereum wrestled with. As Ethereum evolved with Proof of Stake and Layer 2 solutions, it created a rivalry that would shape the future of blockchain itself. And yet, in this vast, competitive landscape, Solana stood tall, a top-tier Layer 1 blockchain, its ecosystem growing with the rhythm of decentralized finance, NFTs, and Web3 innovation. The world of developers and users was taking notice, each one seeking alternatives, each one watching Solana closely as it carved its place in the future of technology.

USDC

USD Coin (USDC) is a stablecoin that is pegged to the U.S. dollar, designed to maintain a 1:1 value with the USD. This means that each USDC token is backed by a corresponding U.S. dollar or dollar-equivalent asset held in reserve. USDC is a key player in the stablecoin ecosystem, providing stability and liquidity in the cryptocurrency market. It was launched in 2018 by **Circle** in partnership with **Coinbase** as part of the Centre Consortium. USDC stands tall in the ever-shifting landscape of digital currencies, a beacon of stability in a world often ruled by volatility. Its foundation rests on a promise of Transparency. Every USDC token in circulation has a dollar backing it, a quiet guarantee that builds trust. Issuers like ensure this by providing regular audits of their reserves, showing the world that each token is fully backed. It's not just about numbers, it's about faith, about building something solid in an environment where doubt often reigns. Regulation guides USDC every move, like a compass pointing toward compliance. The issuers must follow Know Your Customer (KYC) and Anti-Money Laundering (AML) regulations. This gives institutions assurance, making USDC a stable choice. USDC's reach extends beyond a single blockchain.

It embraces **Multi-Chain Support**, operating on networks like **Ethereum, Solana, Algorand,** and **Avalanche,** among others. It moves through various ecosystems, appearing on decentralized finance platforms and ensuring users have the flexibility they need. Wherever USDC goes, it delivers Fast and Low-Cost Transfers, offering speed to those using it for payments, remittances, or navigating DeFi. USDC offers liquidity as well. In Liquidity Pools, it pairs with other tokens on automated market makers like

Uniswap and **SushiSwap**. The trades happen quickly, seamlessly, allowing users to exchange their tokens against USDC with ease. For traders, USDC serves as a Safe Harbor during volatile times. When market prices plummet, they rush to convert their assets into USDC, finding stability amidst the chaos. It's not just individuals who rely on USDC, Corporate and Institutional Use continues to grow around it like vines around a sturdy pillar. Businesses and institutions, often cautious of the crypto world, turn to USDC for its compliance and regulatory backing. It becomes a trusted tool for payments, treasury management, and decentralized financial services, offering a way to engage with the digital world without sacrificing security.

The mechanics of USDC operate with simplicity and elegance. Issuance occurs when a user sends U.S. dollars to an issuer, and in return, USDC is minted, one token for each dollar, always equal, always backed. When a user wants to return to fiat, Redemption happens. They send USDC back, and the issuer transfers U.S. dollars to their account, burning the tokens in the process, keeping the supply balanced. USDC's reserves sit in cash and cash-equivalents like U.S. Treasury bonds, each one carefully monitored. Third-party auditors regularly inspect these reserves, ensuring transparency and confirming that everything is in place. A brief comparison of USDC with other stablecoins highlights the unique strengths and challenges of each within the broader cryptocurrency ecosystem. While all stablecoins aim to provide price stability, their approaches to transparency, regulation, and usage vary significantly. Lets start with USDT. Tether (USDT) is the most widely used stablecoin by volume, often serving as a default option for trading across both centralized and decentralized exchanges. However, Tether has faced ongoing scrutiny regarding the transparency of its reserves and whether it is fully backed by equivalent assets. Audits of USDT have been less frequent and less detailed compared to USDC's monthly, third-party audits. This gives USDC an edge in trustworthiness, particularly among institutional users. Furthermore, USDC operates in a stricter regulatory environment, making it more appealing for those who prioritize compliance and transparency.

However, Tether's ubiquity and multi-chain support make it highly liquid, which can be an advantage in certain markets. **DAI**, unlike USDC, is a decentralized stablecoin issued by the **Maker-DAO** protocol. It is algorithmically pegged to the U.S. dollar but backed by a variety of crypto assets rather than fiat currency. This decentralized nature appeals to those who seek stability without reliance on centralized issuers like Circle or Coinbase. However, DAI's stability can be more volatile during extreme market conditions, as its collateral is subject to the fluctuations of cryptocurrencies. In contrast, USDC offers a more predictable and reliable peg due to its direct 1:1 backing with U.S. dollars. While DAI is favored in decentralized finance (DeFi) for its decentralized structure, USDC's full collateralization and regulatory compliance provide greater reassurance for institutional users and those seeking more stable collateral in financial applications. **BUSD**, issued by **Binance** in partnership with **Paxos**, is another fiat-backed stablecoin that operates under similar regulatory frameworks as USDC. Both are fully audited, transparent, and compliant with U.S. regulations, making them comparably secure and trustworthy for users. However, BUSD is more closely tied to Binance's ecosystem, and its use is more prevalent on Binance's trading platforms. USDC, in contrast, benefits from broader adoption across multiple blockchains and ecosystems, making it more versatile for cross-platform use. In summary, each stablecoin presents unique strengths depending on the user's needs, whether prioritizing decentralization, transparency, liquidity, or regulatory compliance.

Ripple

Ripple is both a digital payment protocol and a cryptocurrency. The protocol, often referred to as **RippleNet**, is designed to enable real-time, cross-border payment settlements and remittances. Ripple's native cryptocurrency is called **XRP**, which is used as a bridge currency for facilitating transactions on the Ripple network. Ripple aims to provide a faster, more efficient, and cost-effective alternative to traditional banking and financial systems, especially for international transfers. Ripple was founded in 2012 by Chris Larsen and Jed McCaleb.

The company behind Ripple, **Ripple Labs**, focuses on working with financial institutions, banks, and payment providers to improve cross-border payment systems. Ripple was originally founded as **OpenCoin** in 2012, with the goal of creating a decentralized payment network that could offer a fast, scalable, and cost-effective way to transfer money. The project quickly gained traction, and by 2013, Ripple Labs was working with financial institutions to integrate the protocol into their existing systems. Ripple stands at the crossroads of finance and technology, forging partnerships with some of the world's most powerful financial institutions. Banks like **Santander, Standard Chartered**, and **American Express** explored Ripple's technology, recognizing its potential to revolutionize cross-border transactions. Ripple offers real-time gross settlement (**RTGS**) capabilities, making it an attractive option for global players seeking efficiency in payment systems. At the heart of this transformation lies **XRP,** Ripple's cryptocurrency. XRP is adopted by exchanges, liquidity providers, and financial institutions alike. Its speed and low transaction fees turn it into a favorite for remittances and institutional use cases. XRP soon become a bridge currency, allowing transactions between different fiat currencies without the usual intermediaries, offering a streamlined solution.

Ripple's innovation takes shape within **RippleNet**, a decentralized network of banks and payment providers. RippleNet offers real-time, secure, and low-cost international payments, cutting through the complexities of traditional systems like SWIFT. But unlike SWIFT, RippleNet delivers faster, more affordable solutions, positioning itself as a new force in global payments. Ripple Labs pre-mined 100 billion XRP tokens at launch, reserving a portion for itself while distributing the rest among users and institutions. Instead of relying on Proof of Work or Proof of Stake, Ripple operates on its own **Ripple Protocol Consensus Algorithm (RPCA)**. Through this consensus process, independent validators confirm transactions swiftly and with energy efficiency, bypassing the need for mining and staking. Ripple's technology doesn't stop at its consensus protocol. Its ability to process transactions in just 3 to 5 seconds and at a fraction of a cent in fees makes it highly effective for cross-border payments. Traditional banking systems struggle to keep up with such speed, and even many cryptocurrencies can't match Ripple's efficiency. The magic of Ripple lies as well in its interoperability. It isn't just a solution for crypto transactions but also bridges the gap between fiat currencies and cryptocurrencies. Financial institutions use XRP as a bridge, converting currencies seamlessly without multiple layers of conversions.

Ripple stands out for this feature, offering a unique advantage in a world where cross-border currency exchanges often require costly intermediaries. The inner workings of Ripple's system are as intricate as they are effective. RippleNet serves as the backbone, functioning like a next-generation version of SWIFT. But unlike its traditional counterpart, RippleNet handles the settlement of payments as well as the messaging process. RippleNet's design consists of three main components:

xCurrent, a payment processing system for real-time cross-border transactions.

xRapid, which leverages XRP as a bridge currency, enabling fast and affordable currency exchanges.

xVia, a platform that businesses and payment providers use to connect and send payments across RippleNet.

At the core of Ripple's efficiency is its system of **Validators**, a group of independent actors that confirm transactions using the RPCA protocol. Unlike Bitcoin's energy-intensive mining process, Ripple's validators ensure the network remains fast and accurate, preventing double-spending and maintaining security. Ripple explores new possibilities with its **Interledger Protocol (ILP)**. This protocol allows payments to flow seamlessly across different networks, whether they are traditional financial systems or decentralized blockchains. However, not all is perfect in Ripple's world. Centralization concerns remain a major criticism. Ripple Labs controls a significant portion of XRP—55 billion tokens were originally placed in escrow, allowing the company to release more tokens into circulation over time. Some argue this centralization makes Ripple less decentralized than networks like Bitcoin and Ethereum. Ripple's ongoing legal battle with the SEC adds another layer of regulatory risks.

In December 2020, the **U.S. Securities and Exchange Commission (SEC)** filed a lawsuit against Ripple, claiming that XRP was sold as an unregistered security. The legal battles started, sending Ripples down through the industry. Some exchanges delist XRP, and uncertainty shrouds Ripple's future in the U.S. market. If XRP is ruled as a security, it may face substantial hurdles in the U.S. market, affecting its liquidity and usability. Concentration of Validators also raises eyebrows. While Ripple boasts a decentralized network of validators, the number is far smaller than those of other blockchain networks. This raises questions about Ripple Labs' influence on network governance. Ripple doesn't stand alone in its mission. It faces competition from other blockchain projects, including **Stellar**, which was founded by Ripple's own co-founder, Jed McCaleb. Stellar offers a more decentralized solution for cross-border payments, further adding to the competitive pressures Ripple faces. And through it all, Ripple continues to build, driven by its vision of a more connected and efficient financial world.

Lido Staked Ether

Lido Staked Ether (stETH) is a token that represents staked Ethereum (ETH) in the Lido network. When you stake ETH using Lido, you receive **stETH** in return. This token represents your staked ETH plus any accrued staking rewards. Ethereum 2.0 introduces a proof-of-stake (PoS) mechanism, where validators need to stake ETH to secure the network. Staking directly requires a minimum of 32 ETH and involves running a validator node, which can be complex and resource-intensive. Lido's Role is to allow users to stake ETH without needing to run their own validator nodes.

Instead, Lido pools users' ETH and manages the staking process on their behalf. When you deposit ETH into Lido you receive an equivalent amount of stETH. This isn't just a token, it's a reflection of your staked ETH, growing steadily over time as staking rewards accrue. The value of stETH quietly appreciates, a mirror of the expanding ETH balance that sits behind it, each moment a little richer than the last. But unlike traditional staking, where your funds might feel like they've been locked in a vault, stETH provides liquidity. It's not confined, not tethered. You can freely trade it or use it in decentralized finance (DeFi) applications, giving you flexibility while your ETH keeps earning rewards. If you wish to turn it back into ETH, Lido's platform or secondary markets await you, though you may encounter slight delays or shifts in value due to market conditions. In this transparent world, Lido offers a clear view of the stakes, how much ETH is currently staked, the rewards earned, and other vital metrics. Nothing hides in shadows here. The Benefits of Using stETH unfold like a map to ease and opportunity.

There's no need to worry about the complexities of managing validator nodes or diving into the intricacies of Ethereum 2.0 staking. The liquidity and flexibility of stETH means you can leverage it in various DeFi protocols while still enjoying staking rewards, a balance of earning and freedom. And with diversification, users find themselves staking ETH without sacrificing the chance to explore other DeFi opportunities. But every opportunity comes with its Risks and Considerations. There's the ever-present specter of Smart Contract Risk, lurking in the underlying technology of DeFi services. Market Risk casts its shadow too, as the value of stETH may not always perfectly match ETH due to market forces. And of course, the evolving Regulatory Risk hovers, a reminder that the rules surrounding DeFi and staking services are still being written. Lido, however, stands firm with its governance and security. A decentralized autonomous organization (DAO) leads its decisions, with LDO token holders guiding the protocol's future. Security measures are always in place, from audits to bug bounty programs, fortifying Lido against threats and keeping user funds safe.

Dogecoin

Meanwhile, in the world of Dogecoin, the atmosphere is playful yet unexpectedly impactful. Born from a joke in December 2013, Dogecoin enters the scene as a "fun" and "light-hearted" alternative to Bitcoin. Crafted by software engineers Billy Markus and Jackson Palmer, it draws inspiration from the viral Doge meme, featuring the ever-charming Shiba Inu. What begins as a joke quickly evolves into something more. Dogecoin grows into a widely recognized digital asset, with a community that radiates creativity and warmth. Known for its charitable spirit, the Dogecoin community organizes donation initiatives, tipping content creators online, and even sponsoring high-profile events like a **NASCAR** driver and the 2014 Winter Olympics. Humor mixes with genuine impact as the community leaves its mark. Social Media Influence breathes life into Dogecoin's price and popularity. Influencers and celebrities, most notably **Elon Musk**, bring their weight to the coin, causing waves of attention and, with it, inevitable price fluctuations. Behind Dogecoin's lighthearted surface, serious technology drives it. Like Bitcoin, Dogecoin operates on a blockchain, using the Proof-of-Work (PoW) consensus mechanism. Miners solve complex mathematical problems, verifying transactions and keeping the network secure.

But unlike Bitcoin, Dogecoin's Supply knows no limit. Initially capped, the decision to remove the maximum supply unleashes an infinite flow of Dogecoins, over 140 billion of which are already in circulation. Dogecoin's pace is quicker too, with a Block Time of roughly one minute, far faster than Bitcoin's ten-minute block time. This speed allows for rapid transaction confirmation, giving Dogecoin an edge in day-to-day usability. It runs on the Scrypt hashing algorithm, designed to be more memory-intensive and resistant to specialized mining hardware, though over time, ASICs (Application-Specific Integrated Circuits) have found their way into Dogecoin mining. Use Cases and Adoption of Dogecoin might surprise those who see it as just a meme. It's used for tipping and donations, with users showing appreciation for content creators or supporting charitable causes through Dogecoin. Some retailers and online services even accept it as payment, and while Dogecoin rides the wave of being a memecoin, its influence stretches into real-world use, beyond the volatile ups and downs driven by social media trends. But Dogecoin's development isn't as robust as some other cryptocurrencies.

The Development Team largely relies on volunteers, with the original creators having stepped back. Governance is informal, shaped by community discussions and proposals rather than any formal structure. It's a digital democracy of sorts, powered by those who care enough to keep it alive. Yet, as with all things in the crypto world, Dogecoin comes with Risks and Considerations. Volatility is a constant companion—prices soar and plummet on the whims of market sentiment and internet trends. Its limited development raises concerns too, without steady innovation, Dogecoin lags behind other, more advanced projects. And then there's the speculative nature of Dogecoin. Its price is often driven by speculation rather than tangible value, creating opportunities for rapid gains but also for devastating losses.

Toncoin

Toncoin (TON) is the native cryptocurrency of the **Telegram Open Network (TON),** a blockchain platform developed by Telegram, a popular messaging app, to create a high-performance blockchain platform. The project aimed to offer fast and scalable blockchain solutions with a focus on user-friendly applications and integration with Telegram's ecosystem. Telegram's involvement in the blockchain space started with the announcement of TON in 2018. The project gained significant attention and raised substantial funds through a private token sale. Toncoin's story begins in the shadow of regulatory challenges. In 2020, Telegram, the original architect behind the TON blockchain, makes a fateful decision. Pressured by the U.S. Securities and Exchange Commission (SEC), the company halts the development of the TON blockchain and its ambitious token sale. The project's future seems uncertain, yet the heartbeat of TON continues to pulse through the efforts of others. Toncoin (TON), the native cryptocurrency of the TON blockchain, emerges from these trials, designed to carry the weight of its ecosystem. It becomes the lifeblood for facilitating transactions, paying for network services, and providing incentives to those who choose to participate in the sprawling TON network.

Within this digital landscape, Toncoin's functions come to life. It's not just a token, it's the currency for transaction fees, moving value across the TON network. Stakers, those who believe in the future of TON, lock up their Toncoin, placing their trust in the network's consensus process. Their reward? The chance to earn more, a return for their participation. And governance, the possibility that one day, Toncoin holders will have a voice in shaping the network's future, voting on decisions that could alter its course. Key features of TON make it stand apart from its competitors. It's a platform that thrives on scalability, its multi-layered architecture and sharding technology ensuring it can handle an ever-growing number of transactions without breaking a sweat.

Speed is a defining trait, transactions happen quickly, with low latency, positioning TON as a prime candidate for a variety of applications, from finance to decentralized services. The power of smart contracts also hums beneath the surface, enabling developers to craft decentralized applications (dApps) that can run on the platform, giving it a dynamic and adaptive edge. Though Telegram officially steps away, there remains a lingering connection. Once, there was a vision to integrate TON with Telegram's messaging platform, promising enhanced functionality and a seamless user experience. Now, that dream drifts further from reality, yet it still colors the way TON is perceived. The technical aspects of the TON blockchain reveal a carefully crafted system. It employs proof-of-stake (PoS) as its consensus mechanism, where validators stake their Toncoin to secure the network and validate transactions. The architecture, with its clever use of sharding and the masterchain structure, allows the blockchain to process multiple transactions in parallel, achieving efficiency and scalability that few can rival. The system is modular, designed with flexibility in mind, supporting a wide range of applications and services that extend the blockchain's reach far beyond its initial purpose. As the blockchain grows, so do its use cases. For those who believe in the future of TON, staking and governance present the opportunity to participate directly in the network's growth and governance, a chance to steer the ship and reap the rewards. Yet, despite its potential, TON's current status is shaped by its past.

After Telegram steps away, the project finds new life under the guidance of the **TON Foundation** and a community of independent developers. They continue the work, evolving the blockchain, separated now from its original creators. The vision remains, but it's in different hands, growing within the framework of a community-driven ecosystem. But adoption and ecosystem development are key to its success. For Toncoin and the TON blockchain to thrive, the ecosystem must grow. Developers need to build, partnerships need to form, and the community must engage. Only through these steps will TON's full potential be realized. However, with any innovation comes risks and considerations. Regulatory risk looms large, casting a shadow over the future. The legal landscape for cryptocurrencies is in constant flux, and scrutiny from regulators could impact the blockchain's progress. There's also the inherent market volatility that Toncoin faces, its value can rise or fall, dictated by market conditions and the whims of adoption. And development risks remain. The blockchain's future depends on attracting developers and users alike, growing its community, and continuously evolving to meet the needs of a fast-changing digital world. Toncoin's journey is still unfolding, a story of resilience, innovation, and the ever-present dance with regulatory forces. Its path may be uncertain, but the potential remains, shimmering just beyond the horizon.

Tron

TRON is a blockchain-based decentralized platform founded by Justin Sun in 2017. It aims to create a free, global digital content entertainment system with distributed storage technology. TRON enables content creators to cut out intermediaries, allowing them to directly connect with consumers and receive rewards in the form of TRX (its native cryptocurrency). The TRON network supports decentralized applications (dApps) and smart contracts, making it comparable to Ethereum, though it boasts higher transaction throughput and lower fees. It utilizes a **Delegated Proof of Stake (DPoS)** consensus mechanism for faster and more efficient processing. TRON acquired **BitTorrent** in 2018, further integrating its platform with peer-to-peer file-sharing capabilities. It also supports cross-chain interoperability with other blockchains. The network has expanded its ecosystem with DeFi, NFTs, and stablecoins, including its own algorithmic stablecoin, USDD. Its vision is to decentralize the web and disrupt the traditional entertainment and data-sharing industries.

Cardano

Cardano is a third-generation blockchain platform focused on creating a more secure, scalable, and sustainable environment for decentralized applications (dApps) and smart contracts. Developed by IOHK and founded by Charles Hoskinson, it aims to improve upon the inefficiencies of earlier blockchains like Bitcoin (first gen) and Ethereum (second gen). Cardano uses a unique proof-of-stake consensus mechanism called **Ouroboros**, which is designed to be energy-efficient and highly secure. Its layered architecture separates the settlement and computation layers, providing enhanced flexibility and functionality. The platform emphasizes peer-reviewed academic research and a scientific approach to development. Cardano's native cryptocurrency is **ADA,** used for transactions and staking. The platform is particularly focused on real-world applications, including financial inclusion in developing countries. Cardano aims to balance decentralization, security, and scalability while maintaining a sustainable blockchain ecosystem.

Avalanche

Avalanche is a decentralized blockchain platform designed for high scalability, low fees, and customizable blockchain networks. Launched in 2020 by **Ava Labs**, it aims to offer an alternative to traditional blockchains by supporting thousands of transactions per second (TPS) without sacrificing decentralization. Avalanche uses a consensus protocol known as Avalanche Consensus, which allows for quick finality in under two seconds. It is composed of three interconnected blockchains, **X-Chain**, **C-Chain**, and **P-Chain,** each serving distinct purposes such as asset transfers, smart contracts, and validator coordination. Avalanche supports Ethereum-compatible decentralized applications (dApps) through the C-Chain, allowing seamless integration with the Ethereum ecosystem. It uses a Proof of Stake (PoS) model for security, incentivizing validators to secure the network. The native token, **AVAX,** is used for transaction fees, staking, and governance. Its flexible architecture also enables the creation of custom subnetworks tailored for specific use cases. Avalanche is known for its energy efficiency compared to Proof of Work (PoW) networks.

Shiba Inu

Shiba Inu (SHIB) is a decentralized cryptocurrency launched in August 2020 as an Ethereum-based token. Originally created as a meme coin inspired by the Shiba Inu dog breed, it has grown into a prominent player in the crypto space. SHIB is part of a larger ecosystem, including other tokens like **LEASH** and **BONE**. Unlike traditional cryptocurrencies, Shiba Inu gained popularity through its community-driven approach and widespread social media attention. The **ShibaSwap** decentralized exchange allows users to trade SHIB and stake their assets for rewards. Its total supply started at one quadrillion, with a large portion sent to Ethereum co-founder Vitalik Buterin, who burned a significant amount. Shiba Inu aims to rival Dogecoin, and its passionate community, known as the "Shiba Army," supports its growth. It has become more than a meme, seeking to expand into utility-focused ventures like NFTs and decentralized finance (DeFi). Despite its humble beginnings, Shiba Inu continues to evolve in the crypto ecosystem.

Chailink

Chainlink is a decentralized oracle network that enables smart contracts on various blockchains to securely interact with real-world data, APIs, and external systems. It acts as a bridge between blockchain environments and external data sources, making it possible for smart contracts to execute based on real-time information like prices, weather, or events. Chainlink's decentralized nature ensures the accuracy, reliability, and tamper-resistance of the data it provides. The network uses a system of independent node operators who retrieve and verify data from multiple sources, reducing single points of failure. Chainlink's flexibility allows it to be integrated across different blockchain platforms and is widely used in DeFi (Decentralized Finance) for secure price feeds. The project has become a cornerstone of smart contract applications, enabling more complex and trustworthy automation.

Bitcoin Cash

Bitcoin Cash (BCH) is a cryptocurrency created in 2017 as a fork of Bitcoin (BTC) to address issues of scalability and transaction speed. Its primary goal is to offer faster, cheaper transactions compared to Bitcoin by increasing the block size from 1 MB to 8 MB (and later to 32 MB). This allows Bitcoin Cash to handle more transactions per second, making it more suitable for everyday payments and commerce. While it shares the same underlying technology as Bitcoin, Bitcoin Cash emphasizes being a peer-to-peer electronic cash system. BCH supporters view it as a true representation of Satoshi Nakamoto's original vision. However, the fork led to ideological divides within the Bitcoin community, with some preferring Bitcoin's focus on security and decentralization over BCH's approach to scalability. Despite this, Bitcoin Cash has grown to become a prominent cryptocurrency, accepted by various merchants and platforms worldwide.

Polkadot

Polkadot is a next-generation blockchain platform designed to enable multiple blockchains to operate together seamlessly. Founded by Gavin Wood, co-founder of Ethereum, Polkadot aims to solve interoperability challenges by connecting various blockchains into one unified network. Its unique relay chain coordinates and secures the network, while **Individual Parachains** can operate independently, each with its own features and use cases. This setup allows for scalability and specialization, letting developers create chains optimized for specific tasks. Polkadot uses a **Nominated proof-of-stake (NPoS)** consensus mechanism, which enhances security and energy efficiency. Through its cross-chain messaging, it facilitates data exchange between blockchains. The ecosystem also supports governance, allowing DOT token holders to vote on network upgrades and protocol changes. With substrate technology, developers can easily create custom blockchains. Polkadot envisions a decentralized web where multiple blockchains interact, share value, and unlock new possibilities.

DAI

DAI is a decentralized stablecoin on the Ethereum blockchain, pegged to the U.S. dollar. Unlike centralized stablecoins, DAI is not backed by fiat reserves but by over-collateralized crypto assets, such as Ethereum (ETH). It is created through the **MakerDAO** protocol, where users lock up collateral in smart contracts to mint DAI. DAI maintains its peg via a system of smart contracts and governance by MKR token holders. This stablecoin allows for decentralized lending, borrowing, and payments within the DeFi ecosystem. DAI is widely used for its stability, transparency, and resistance to censorship. It operates independently of traditional banking systems.

Uniswap

Uniswap is a decentralized exchange (DEX) built on the Ethereum blockchain, allowing users to trade cryptocurrencies directly without relying on intermediaries. Launched in 2018, it revolutionized decentralized finance (DeFi) by introducing an **Automated Market Maker (AMM)** model instead of traditional order books. Uniswap platform is open-source and governed by a decentralized community through its governance token, UNI. Uniswap is also compatible with ERC-20 tokens, making it a key player in Ethereum's DeFi ecosystem. Uniswap has undergone several upgrades, with Uniswap V3 introducing concentrated liquidity, enabling LPs to allocate capital more efficiently and improve returns. As a decentralized exchange, Uniswap eliminates the need for KYC/AML, providing privacy and autonomy for users.

Litecoin

Litecoin (LTC) is a decentralized cryptocurrency created by Charlie Lee in 2011 as a lighter, faster version of Bitcoin. It operates on a peer-to-peer network using a modified Bitcoin codebase, aiming to enable faster transaction times and lower fees. Litecoin uses the **Scrypt hashing algorithm**, which is less resource-intensive than Bitcoin's SHA-256, allowing for easier mining by individuals without specialized hardware. The total supply of Litecoin is capped at 84 million, four times that of Bitcoin. It shares many technical similarities with Bitcoin, such as its proof-of-work consensus mechanism, but processes blocks every 2.5 minutes, compared to Bitcoin's 10 minutes, making transactions quicker. Litecoin is often considered a "silver to Bitcoin's gold" due to its complementary role in the cryptocurrency space.

It has gained adoption for micropayments and everyday transactions, thanks to its lower fees and faster speeds. While it doesn't have the same market dominance as Bitcoin, Litecoin remains a significant player in the crypto ecosystem. The network is secured through decentralized nodes, and Litecoin also adopted technologies like **SegWit** and the Lightning Network for scalability. Though it lacks the extensive ecosystem of Ethereum or Bitcoin, it has maintained a stable presence as a reliable medium of exchange in the crypto market.

Monero

Monero emerges in 2014, carving out a space in the vast world of cryptocurrencies, one that prioritizes privacy above all else. Its decentralized blockchain hums with activity, ensuring that every transaction remains secure, private, and untraceable, far from the prying eyes of outsiders. At the heart of Monero lies privacy, its defining feature. Advanced cryptographic techniques form the bedrock of this secrecy. **Ring Signatures**, **Stealth Addresses**, and **RingCT (Confidential Transactions)** blur the lines, hiding details that would otherwise be visible on most blockchains. The sender, the receiver, the transaction amount, all of it shrouded in mystery, known only to those involved. It's a cloak of invisibility for digital transactions. With this level of anonymity comes fungibility. Every Monero coin, indistinguishable from the next, moves through the network free from any past associations. Unlike other cryptocurrencies that can be tainted by their transaction history, Monero coins are always clean, always equal. Monero's foundation is rooted in decentralization. There's no central figure pulling the strings, no authority to dictate its direction. It belongs to no one and everyone all at once. It begins without pre-mining, without any unfair advantage given to early adopters, allowing all users to stand on equal ground from the very beginning. Mining Monero isn't a task reserved for those with specialized equipment. Instead, its Proof-of-Work (PoW) consensus algorithm, enhanced by RandomX, favors the average user.

CPU mining reigns here, as Monero stays true to its vision of decentralization, making the process accessible and resisting the dominance of ASIC miners. The soul of Monero is open-source. Developers from across the world contribute to its evolution, driven not by profit but by a shared belief in privacy and freedom. The community, global and resilient, keeps Monero alive, pushing updates and improvements forward. Unlike Bitcoin's transparent ledger, where addresses and amounts are visible to all, Monero hides everything. The sender's address disappears into the ether, the amount traded veiled from view. It's a stark contrast to the openness of other blockchains, creating a delicate dance between privacy and transparency. For Monero, privacy is paramount. Scalability is another strength. As the network grows, Monero adapts, its dynamic block size expanding and contracting based on demand. The network flows with ease, meeting the needs of its users without clogging or delay. The essence of Monero is control, user control. Only the parties involved in a transaction know its details. There are no third parties, no intermediaries. Monero places the power squarely in the hands of its users, a silent promise that no one else will ever know. But with this power comes challenges. Monero's focus on privacy hasn't gone unnoticed. Regulators eye it warily, its anonymity linked to the darker corners of the internet. Associations with illicit activities cast a long shadow, and some exchanges, fearing backlash, have chosen to step away, delisting the coin. Still, the demand persists. Privacy-conscious users, undeterred by scrutiny, continue to turn to Monero. Behind Monero stands a community, strong and global, a network of developers and users who believe fiercely in its mission. They maintain it, nurture it, push it forward. Updates are constant, each one sharpening Monero's edges, improving its privacy, security, and performance. Despite the challenges, adoption grows. Merchants, valuing the anonymity it provides, begin accepting Monero for payments. Donations flow in, drawn by the privacy that Monero promises.

It's becoming a trusted method for those who want to give, without the world knowing. The costs of using Monero are low. Its transaction fees, thanks to the adaptive block size, remain modest. No exorbitant fees here—just a quiet, efficient network that keeps churning out secure transactions. For those on the go, **Monerujo** becomes a companion. A popular mobile wallet for Monero, it allows users to send and receive their private coins with ease, keeping the spirit of Monero close at hand. Monero continues to evolve, embracing **Atomic Swaps**, a technology that allows for seamless cross-chain swaps. No middlemen needed—Monero moves easily between chains, opening doors to other cryptocurrencies, enhancing its interoperability in a world that values connections. Its deflationary supply adds another layer of intrigue. Monero, like a treasure chest with a fixed number of gold coins, will one day stop growing. Its capped supply ensures that as demand rises, so too will its value, each coin becoming a little more precious over time. Regulatory pressure never leaves Monero's side. As governments tighten their grip on cryptocurrency regulation, Monero's anonymity remains a sticking point. Some exchanges have backed away, bowing to the pressure, but Monero stays the course. For those who value privacy, it remains a beacon, popular and enduring despite the forces arrayed against it.

Stellar

Stellar, a decentralized, open-source blockchain, rises into the world of digital finance in 2014, with a clear purpose etched into its core. It is designed not just as another cryptocurrency, but as a bridge, a way to connect the vast and often inaccessible world of traditional banking with the fluid, rapidly evolving world of blockchain technology. Behind it all stands Jed McCaleb, who once helped birth Ripple, now turning his focus toward something new: financial access for those who have long been underbanked, left out of the global economy's digital revolution.

The **Stellar Development Foundation (SDF)**, the driving force behind Stellar's creation, sets out with a mission. They want to tear down the walls that separate people from financial services, creating a system where sending money across borders is as easy as sending a text. At the heart of this system lies **Lumens (XLM)**, Stellar's native token, designed to pay transaction fees and ensure the network's smooth operation. The primary use of Stellar is clear from the start: fast, low-cost international transfers. Here, institutions find a way to tokenize fiat and other assets, allowing for the seamless movement of value across the globe. Transaction speed becomes one of Stellar's trademarks. Thousands of transactions move through the network every second, each one settling in the blink of an eye, usually within 2 to 5 seconds. But speed isn't everything. Low fees define the experience on Stellar. Transactions cost mere fractions of a cent, making it not only ideal for large transfers but also for the micro-transactions that other systems struggle to handle. Behind the scenes, Stellar's unique Consensus Mechanism sets it apart. Instead of relying on the power-hungry mining systems of Bitcoin or Ethereum, Stellar operates using the **Stellar Consensus Protocol (SCP)**. With SCP, quorum slices come into play, validating transactions in a more energy-efficient and decentralized way. There is no need for traditional mining here, Stellar moves at the pace of consensus. Stellar's reach extends beyond just crypto. It boldly supports fiat integration, opening the door for the issuance of stablecoins and digital versions of fiat currencies. The line between traditional money and digital assets blurs, as Stellar makes it easier than ever to convert between the two worlds. Its partnerships only fuel this mission.

IBM becomes a powerful ally, teaming up with Stellar to launch **World Wire,** a cross-border payment system aimed at revolutionizing how money moves across nations. Other financial institutions soon follow, recognizing the potential Stellar holds in transforming global finance. Though the Stellar Development Foundation guides much of its growth, Stellar remains decentralized. Validators, scattered across the globe, work to keep the network secure and running smoothly. These decentralized nodes, along with anchors, trusted entities on the network that issue fiat tokens, provide the essential link between fiat and crypto, ensuring that the network never loses its connection to the real world. While smart contracts on Stellar aren't as complex as those found on platforms like Ethereum, they serve their purpose well. Asset issuance and transfers become easy, smooth processes, allowing developers to create and manage custom tokens with a few simple commands. It's a system designed for efficiency, one that prioritizes ease of use and accessibility. But Stellar never loses sight of the need for compliance. In a world where regulators watch every move, Stellar builds in Know Your Customer (KYC) and Anti-Money Laundering (AML) features, ensuring that it can stand tall in the face of scrutiny. It's a blockchain that isn't just fast and decentralized but one that works hand-in-hand with the laws of the world. A moment of transformation comes when the community takes a bold step: Stellar votes to burn 55 billion XLM, removing them from circulation forever.

It's a move that shifts the network's dynamics, ensuring that the supply of **Lumens** remains limited, adding a layer of value and scarcity to the native token. In its ecosystem, Stellar is not just a payment network. It houses decentralized exchanges (DEX), allowing users to trade assets directly on the network without needing to leave the Stellar environment. Use cases stretch far beyond remittances, they include microfinance, mobile payments, and the tokenization of assets, with Stellar positioning itself as a versatile platform for all types of financial applications. Governance decisions remain largely in the hands of the Stellar Development Foundation, but the community's voice is always welcomed. Stellar fosters an environment where users can contribute ideas, shaping the future of the network. Through it all, Stellar's vision never wavers. It seeks to create a financial system that includes everyone, one that makes money transfers seamless and accessible to anyone, anywhere. Whether it's through fast international transfers, micro-payments, or creating a digital representation of real-world assets, Stellar's mission remains clear: to break down barriers and bring the world closer together, one transaction at a time.

Pol (ex Matic)

POL (formerly known as MATIC) is the native token of Polygon, a Layer 2 scaling solution for Ethereum that enhances its performance by increasing transaction speed and reducing costs. Originally launched in 2017 as MATIC, the rebranding to POL reflects Polygon's expanded ambitions beyond simply being an Ethereum scaling solution. Polygon operates as a Layer 2 network, working alongside Ethereum to offer faster and cheaper transactions while maintaining compatibility with Ethereum's security. POL is secured through a Proof of Stake (PoS) consensus mechanism, where users stake their tokens to validate transactions. The token itself is used to pay transaction fees, for staking, and for governance decisions on the Polygon network. What sets Polygon apart is its aim to become a multi-chain network, often referred to as "Ethereum's internet of blockchains." This vision allows Polygon to be interoperable with various blockchains, positioning it as a central player in the broader blockchain ecosystem. Polygon initially relied on Plasma, the framework that allows for fast and cheap transactions on Ethereum, by offloading some of the transaction load. Today, Polygon offers developers a **Software Development Kit (SDK)** to build their own custom blockchains, which can interact seamlessly with Ethereum. This flexibility, combined with high throughput, thousands of transactions per second, and low fees, has made Polygon a preferred platform for many decentralized finance (DeFi) projects. In addition to its technical strengths, Polygon also leverages Ethereum's security while offering faster and more independent transaction processing. This balance has made it a hub for DeFi projects like **Aave, Sushiswap,** and **Uniswap,** all of which have integrated with Polygon to take advantage of its scalability. POL token holders have governance rights on the network, allowing them to vote on protocol upgrades and other key decisions. As the Polygon ecosystem continues to grow, its vision remains focused on providing scalable, interoperable blockchain solutions that are compatible across multiple networks. This approach has made Polygon one of the most important projects in the blockchain space, not just for Ethereum, but for the broader adoption of decentralized technologies.

Ethereum Classic

Ethereum Classic (ETC) is a decentralized, open-source blockchain that emerged from a hard fork of Ethereum in 2016. It maintains the original Ethereum code after the controversial DAO hack, which led to a split in the community. The core philosophy of Ethereum Classic is "code is law," meaning smart contracts should be immutable, even in the event of exploits. ETC runs on the same Proof of Work (PoW) consensus mechanism as the original Ethereum, ensuring decentralization and security through mining. It supports smart contracts and decentralized applications (dApps) like Ethereum, but its development and upgrades are slower due to its smaller community. While Ethereum has moved to Proof of Stake (PoS), Ethereum Classic continues to adhere to PoW, preserving its original structure. ETC has a fixed supply, unlike Ethereum, which has no maximum cap. This makes ETC a more deflationary asset. Despite its smaller ecosystem, Ethereum Classic remains an option for developers who favor immutability and decentralized principles.

Stacks

Stacks (STX) is a blockchain solution designed to bring smart contracts and decentralized applications (dApps) to Bitcoin without modifying its core protocol. It operates as a Layer 1 blockchain that connects to Bitcoin, leveraging Bitcoin's security and stability while adding advanced functionality. STX is the native token of the

Stacks network, used for transaction fees and staking. Stacks introduces a unique consensus mechanism called **Proof of Transfer (PoX)**, where miners use Bitcoin to mine Stacks, creating a direct link between the two blockchains. Unlike Ethereum or other platforms, Stacks allows developers to build on Bitcoin's blockchain by adding smart contracts and dApps, making Bitcoin programmable. It also supports **Clarity**, a predictable and secure programming language for smart contracts. The Stacks ecosystem aims to enhance Bitcoin's utility beyond being a store of value, providing decentralized finance (DeFi) and non-fungible tokens (NFTs) to Bitcoin users. With its innovative approach, Stacks brings additional layers of functionality to Bitcoin without compromising its security.

Aave

Aave (AAVE) is a decentralized finance (DeFi) protocol that allows users to lend and borrow cryptocurrencies without the need for a traditional intermediary. It operates on the Ethereum blockchain and is considered one of the largest and most widely used DeFi platforms. The AAVE token is the native governance and utility token of the Aave platform. The platform enables users to deposit their assets into liquidity pools, which can then be borrowed by others. Lenders earn interest on their deposits, while borrowers provide collateral to secure their loans. Aave introduced flash loans, a unique feature that allows users to borrow assets without providing collateral, as long as the loan is repaid within the same transaction. AAVE token holders participate in governance decisions, such as proposing and voting on protocol upgrades. The token is also used as a safety mechanism in the protocol, where stakers backstop the system in the event of a shortfall. One of Aave's standout features is its support for a wide range of assets, offering users the flexibility to borrow and lend in various cryptocurrencies. It also provides variable and stable interest rates, giving borrowers the option to switch between rates based on market conditions. Aave's protocol is non-custodial, meaning users maintain control of their assets throughout the lending and borrowing process. Its security and transparency have made it a popular choice in the DeFi ecosystem, and it is continually expanding with features like layer 2 scaling solutions. The AAVE token has a limited supply, contributing to its deflationary nature, and it is used to incentivize participation in governance and staking. The protocol's long-term vision is to create a decentralized, permissionless financial system where individuals can earn, borrow, and lend without intermediaries.

Filecoin

Filecoin (FIL) is a decentralized storage network that allows users to rent out spare storage space and others to store their files securely. Launched in 2020 by **Protocol Labs**, it operates on a blockchain, with **FIL** as its native token, used to pay for storage services and reward participants. Filecoin aims to create a global, decentralized marketplace for data storage, addressing issues like data centralization and high costs in traditional cloud storage. The network incentivizes storage providers, who compete to offer the best price and reliability, making it a cost-efficient alternative to centralized platforms like AWS. Filecoin uses a **Proof of Replication (PoRep)** and **Proof of Space-Time (PoSt)** consensus mechanism to ensure data is stored securely and over time. This creates a more trustless environment, with the blockchain ensuring that files are available and retrievable when needed. Storage providers are rewarded with FIL tokens, and the network is designed to grow as more participants join, creating a decentralized and scalable storage ecosystem. Filecoin is widely used for archival storage,

NFTs, and Web3 projects, leveraging its decentralized architecture to ensure privacy and security.

Immutable

Immutable (IMX) is the native token of Immutable X, a Layer 2 scaling solution for NFTs on Ethereum, designed to enable fast, gas-free trading while maintaining security and decentralization. Launched by **Immutable**, a company focused on blockchain gaming and digital asset ownership, IMX powers the ecosystem's transaction fees, staking, and governance. Immutable X leverages zk-rollups, a Layer 2 technology that bundles transactions off-chain, reducing costs and congestion on Ethereum's main chain. The platform is built specifically for NFTs, enabling the minting and trading of digital assets without the high gas fees typically associated with Ethereum. IMX token holders can participate in the governance of the platform by voting on key protocol upgrades and improvements. Additionally, users can stake IMX to earn rewards for supporting network security. The platform has been widely adopted in the gaming and collectibles sectors, offering a seamless way to integrate NFTs into decentralized applications. With partnerships in the gaming industry and a focus on environmental sustainability by being carbon neutral, Immutable X aims to revolutionize NFT trading by making it more accessible, efficient, and eco-friendly.

Vechain

VeChain (VET) is a blockchain platform designed to improve supply chain management and business processes. Launched in 2015, it aims to provide enhanced transparency, traceability, and efficiency in global supply chains by leveraging blockchain technology. **VET** is the native cryptocurrency of the VeChain ecosystem and is used to transfer value across the network. Additionally, the platform operates with a dual-token system, where VET is used for staking and governance, while another token, **VTHO**, is used to pay for transaction fees. VeChain's primary focus is on providing enterprise solutions, and it has established partnerships with major companies like **Walmart** China, **BMW**, and **PwC**. The blockchain allows businesses to track products from manufacturing to delivery, ensuring authenticity and reducing counterfeiting. The network utilizes **Proof of Authority (PoA)**, which enables faster and more efficient transaction validation compared to Proof of Work or Proof of Stake systems. VeChain's goal is to enhance business operations by integrating blockchain into real-world applications, making it a popular choice for industries like logistics, healthcare, and luxury goods.

Cosmos Hub

Cosmos Hub (**ATOM**) is the native cryptocurrency of the Cosmos network, designed to solve the problem of blockchain interoperability. Launched in 2019, Cosmos Hub is a key part of the broader Cosmos ecosystem, often called the "**Internet of Blockchains.**" Its main goal is to enable different blockchains to communicate, share data, and transact with each other through its **Inter-Blockchain Communication (IBC) Protocol**. ATOM is used for staking, securing the network via the Proof of Stake (PoS) consensus mechanism, and as a governance token for voting on network upgrades. Validators and delegators stake ATOM to validate transactions and earn rewards. The Cosmos Hub does not issue smart contracts itself but serves as a central ledger for different blockchains, facilitating their interoperability. One of its unique features is the **Tendermint Consensus Engine**, which enables high-speed, scalable transactions. Cosmos Hub promotes a modular architecture where developers can create and connect customized blockchains called "zones," improving scalability and flexibility. Cosmos Hub's vision is to create a decentralized network of interconnected blockchains, moving away from siloed systems toward a more interoperable future.

Polygon Matic

Polygon (previously Matic Network) is a Layer 2 scaling solution designed to enhance Ethereum's capabilities by offering faster and cheaper transactions. Launched in 2017, it was originally called Matic Network, but as the project evolved beyond scaling Ethereum, it rebranded to Polygon in 2021. Polygon focuses on providing a framework for building and connecting Ethereum-compatible blockchain networks, enhancing scalability while maintaining Ethereum's security. At its core, Polygon utilizes a Proof of Stake (PoS) mechanism, where users stake MATIC tokens to validate transactions, ensuring network security. MATIC, the original token, is still used for transaction fees, staking, and governance on the network. One of the standout features of Polygon is its **Polygon SDK**, which allows developers to create custom blockchain networks that are compatible with Ethereum, ensuring interoperability between blockchains. Polygon's primary aim is to address Ethereum's issues with high fees and network congestion by offering a platform where transactions can be processed much faster and at a fraction of the cost. It supports not only Ethereum-based applications but also decentralized finance (DeFi) protocols, decentralized applications (dApps), and non-fungible tokens (NFTs). Major projects like **Aave, Sushiswap**, and **Uniswap** have adopted Polygon to scale their operations while maintaining access to Ethereum's robust security. POL, formerly known as MATIC, represents the upgraded token structure within Polygon's evolving ecosystem. While MATIC was initially the network's main utility token, POL is the rebranded token that extends its use across

Polygon's multi-chain structure. POL aims to reflect the broader capabilities and ambitions of Polygon, focusing on governance and scaling operations across various blockchains, making Polygon a more decentralized, multi-layered platform. The relation between MATIC and POL lies in the transition: **POL** replaces **MATIC** as the core token but still retains all the functionalities of MATIC, including staking, governance, and transaction fees. However, POL introduces enhanced features for governance and multi-chain staking, allowing it to serve the growing needs of the Polygon ecosystem as it expands beyond Ethereum into a multi-chain network. This transformation reflects Polygon's shift from a simple Ethereum scaling solution to a platform enabling interoperability between different blockchains. With this upgrade, POL becomes more central to the governance and security of the platform, as Polygon positions itself as a versatile, multi-chain system while still maintaining its commitment to Ethereum compatibility.

Algorand

Algorand (ALGO) is a blockchain platform designed to enable fast, secure, and decentralized applications. Founded by MIT professor Silvio Micali in 2019, Algorand aims to solve the "blockchain trilemma" by providing a balance between scalability, security, and decentralization. Algorand uses a unique consensus mechanism called **Pure Proof of Stake (PPoS)**, where validators are selected randomly based on the amount of ALGO they hold, ensuring low energy consumption and fast transaction times. The network can process thousands of transactions per second, making it highly scalable for real-world applications like decentralized finance (DeFi), NFTs, and supply chain management. ALGO is the native currency, used for staking, transaction fees, and governance. Algorand emphasizes sustainability, with its blockchain being designed as carbon-negative. It also supports smart contracts and atomic swaps, enabling complex applications and seamless asset exchanges. The Algorand ecosystem is growing rapidly, attracting developers and enterprises looking for efficient, low-cost solutions in blockchain technology. Its focus on innovation, decentralization, and green blockchain technology makes it a promising platform in the crypto space.

Starknet

The Starknet token (**$STRK**) serves as the native cryptocurrency for Starknet. It plays several key roles: it's used for transaction fees on the network, staking to secure the network, and governance, allowing holders to vote on protocol upgrades and changes. Starknet uses **Cairo**, a unique programming language that optimizes for ZK-Rollups, enabling developers to build decentralized applications (dApps) with more flexibility and efficiency. This makes Starknet particularly appealing for applications requiring high scalability, such as decentralized finance (DeFi) and gaming. One of Starknet's core advantages is privacy, as ZK-Rollups inherently offer strong privacy features by validating transactions without revealing all transaction data. Starknet is also Ethereum-compatible, meaning developers can easily build on it using familiar tools and frameworks. The project is developed by **StarkWare Industries**, a team with deep cryptographic expertise, and has already garnered significant attention for its potential to solve Ethereum's scalability challenges. Starknet is positioned to be a major player in the Ethereum ecosystem as Layer 2 solutions grow in importance.

Paypal USD

PayPal USD (**PYUSD**) is a stablecoin launched by PayPal in 2023, fully backed by U.S. dollar reserves. It is designed to maintain a

1:1 peg with the U.S. dollar, ensuring stability in its value. PYUSD is built on the Ethereum blockchain as an ERC-20 token, which allows for broad interoperability with decentralized applications (dApps) and wallets across the Ethereum ecosystem. The primary use of PayPal USD is for facilitating payments, transfers, and transactions within PayPal's network and beyond, including crypto exchanges. Users can easily convert PYUSD to fiat (U.S. dollars) through PayPal's platform or use it for purchases and transfers. It is fully backed by U.S. Treasury bills and other liquid assets, with regular third-party audits ensuring transparency. PayPal USD also targets broader adoption in decentralized finance (DeFi) spaces, offering a secure and regulated stablecoin option. Its issuance marks PayPal's growing involvement in the cryptocurrency sector, aiming to provide users with a seamless blend of traditional and digital finance.

Axie Infinity

Axie Infinity is a blockchain-based game where players collect, breed, and battle digital creatures called Axies. Built on the Ethereum network and using **Ronin**, a sidechain for faster transactions, it introduces play-to-earn mechanics. Players earn **Smooth Love Potion (SLP)** tokens through gameplay, which can be traded or used to breed Axies. The governance token, **Axie Infinity Shards (AXS)**, gives holders a say in the game's future development and can be staked for rewards. Axie's economy centers around its NFT-based Axies, which can be bought, sold, or traded on decentralized marketplaces. Players need at least three Axies to start playing, and each Axie is unique with different traits and battle abilities. Axie Infinity became popular for allowing players, especially in developing countries, to earn real income. However, it faces challenges such as regulatory scrutiny and concerns over sustainability due to fluctuating SLP and AXS prices. Despite these issues, it remains a leading example of blockchain gaming.

Tezos

Tezos is a decentralized, open-source blockchain that enables peer-to-peer transactions and the creation of smart contracts. Launched in 2018, it is designed to be self-amending, allowing upgrades without hard forks through on-chain governance. Tezos uses a Proof-of-Stake (PoS) consensus mechanism, where users can "bake" (stake) **XTZ**, its native token, to validate transactions and earn rewards. Its focus on formal verification ensures smart contracts are mathematically checked for correctness, enhancing security. Tezos emphasizes decentralized governance, allowing XTZ holders to propose and vote on protocol upgrades. This adaptability helps the network evolve without disruptions. Scalability and low fees make it suitable for various decentralized applications (dApps). Tezos has been adopted in areas like DeFi, NFTs, and asset tokenization. Regulatory-friendly, it supports KYC/AML compliance when needed. Its ecosystem continues to grow, driven by an active community and frequent upgrades.

Wormhole

Wormhole Coin (Wormhole) is a cross-chain messaging protocol designed to enable the transfer of tokens, NFTs, and data between multiple blockchains. It acts as a bridge, allowing different blockchain ecosystems like Ethereum, Solana, Binance Smart Chain (BSC), and more to communicate and interact with each other. By wrapping assets on one chain and issuing equivalent tokens on another, Wormhole facilitates seamless interoperability across decentralized applications (dApps). The protocol uses a **Guardian Network of Nodes** to validate and verify transfers, ensuring that assets are securely wrapped and unwrapped. These guardians observe transactions on the source blockchain, sign off on them, and execute the transfer on the target blockchain. This decentralized process minimizes the risk of centralization or failure. Wormhole also supports cross-chain smart contract calls, allowing developers to build dApps that operate across multiple blockchains. This boosts flexibility and scalability for DeFi, NFT platforms, and other projects seeking to leverage multi-chain capabilities. However, users must remain cautious of smart contract risks and liquidity limitations on less popular chains. Wormhole aims to be a key infrastructure for the future of blockchain interoperability.

Ronin

Ronin is a blockchain specifically designed for gaming, created by **Sky Mavis**, the developers of the popular play-to-earn game **Axie Infinity.** Launched in 2021, it operates as an Ethereum sidechain, optimizing for low fees and fast transactions, essential for gaming applications. **RON** is the native cryptocurrency of the Ronin network, used to pay transaction fees and secure the network via staking. Ronin employs a **Proof of Authority (PoA)** consensus mechanism, where trusted validators maintain the network. It focuses on scalability, supporting millions of daily transactions within the Axie Infinity ecosystem. Ronin allows for the seamless transfer of NFTs (like Axie characters and items) and tokens (like SLP and AXS). Sky Mavis controls most validators, raising centralization concerns, but the network aims to decentralize over time. With an emphasis on gaming and NFT applications, Ronin has quickly become a hub for blockchain-based games. The Ronin Bridge enables users to transfer assets between Ethereum and Ronin.

Mina Protocol

The Mina Protocol is a cryptocurrency designed to be light-weight, with a blockchain size that remains fixed at just 22 kilo-bytes, regardless of the number of transactions. This is achieved through its use of **zk-SNARKs** (zero-knowledge succinct non-interactive arguments of knowledge), which allow anyone to verify the blockchain's state without needing to download its entire history. Mina is often called a "succinct blockchain," offering scalability and decentralization. Its native coin, MINA, powers the network, enabling staking and transactions. Mina also features **Snapps** (snark-powered apps), allowing developers to build dApps that preserve user privacy. It aims to make blockchain accessible, decentralized, and scalable, even for devices with limited computational resources.

Decentraland

Decentraland (**MANA**) is a cryptocurrency that powers Decentraland, a decentralized virtual reality platform built on the Ethereum blockchain. Users can buy, sell, and develop virtual land and digital assets within this 3D metaverse. MANA serves as the currency for all transactions, from purchasing land parcels (called **LAND**) to acquiring in-game items and services. LAND parcels are NFTs (non-fungible tokens), giving users true ownership of their virtual properties. Players can create and monetize digital experiences, games, and marketplaces, enhancing the economy within Decentraland. MANA uses ERC-20 tokens, and LAND is an ERC-721 NFT, both supporting Ethereum's blockchain standards. Decentraland also operates as a decentralized autonomous organization (DAO), meaning MANA holders can vote on governance issues and platform changes. The platform combines gaming, social interaction, and crypto economy, making it one of the pioneering virtual worlds in blockchain.

Synthetix

Synthetix (SNX) is a decentralized finance (DeFi) protocol built on Ethereum that allows users to create and trade synthetic assets, known as "**Synths.**" These Synths represent real-world assets like commodities, fiat currencies, stocks, and cryptocurrencies, providing exposure to their value without needing to hold the actual asset. **SNX** tokens are used as collateral to issue these Synths through smart contracts, locking up SNX in return for synthetic versions of assets like sUSD (synthetic USD). The protocol relies on **Decentralized Price Oracles** to track asset prices, ensuring the Synths mirror real-world values. SNX holders are incentivized by earning rewards from staking their tokens and receiving fees generated from trades on the platform. Synthetix enables users to access a wide range of assets from different markets, all while staying within the blockchain ecosystem. However, the system's success depends on maintaining proper collateralization ratios, meaning market volatility can affect the staking and reward process.

Pax Gold

Pax Gold (PAXG) is a tokenized version of physical gold, launched by **Paxos Trust Company**. Each PAXG token represents one troy ounce of a 400-ounce **London Good Delivery Gold Bar**, securely stored in professional vaults. This makes PAXG a digital asset backed by real, physical gold, allowing holders to gain exposure to the value of gold without needing to physically own or store it. PAXG is built on the Ethereum blockchain, adhering to the ERC-20 token standard, which allows for easy transfer and compatibility with various decentralized applications (dApps). Token holders can trade PAXG on exchanges, use it in decentralized finance (DeFi) protocols, or redeem it for physical gold at any time. Each token's corresponding gold bar can even be tracked via a unique serial number. PAXG's primary advantages are its accessibility, lower storage costs compared to physical gold, and the liquidity offered by crypto exchanges. However, the token still relies on Paxos as the central custodian, which means users must trust that the gold backing the tokens is securely held.

PancakeSwap

PancakeSwap is a decentralized exchange (DEX) built on the **Binance Smart Chain (BSC)** that allows users to swap BEP-20 tokens without relying on a central intermediary. It uses an automated market maker (AMM) model, where users trade against liquidity pools funded by other users. These users provide liquidity by depositing tokens into pools and earn liquidity provider (LP) tokens as rewards. In addition to token swapping, PancakeSwap offers various DeFi features, including yield farming and staking. Users can stake LP tokens in farms to earn the platform's native token, **CAKE**, or stake CAKE in **Syrup Pools** to earn more CAKE or other tokens. PancakeSwap also supports lotteries, NFTs, and **Initial Farm Offerings (IFOs)**, where users can participate in new token launches. Its low fees and fast transactions are due to Binance Smart Chain's efficiency, making it popular among DeFi users. However, risks include impermanent loss in liquidity pools, smart contract vulnerabilities, and market volatility.

Zcash

Zcash **(ZEC)** is a privacy-focused cryptocurrency launched in 2016, designed to provide users with the option of fully private transactions. It uses advanced cryptographic techniques, such as **zk-SNARKs (Zero-Knowledge Succinct Non-Interactive Arguments of Knowledge)**, which allow for transactions to be verified without revealing sender, receiver, or transaction amounts. Users can choose between transparent or shielded transactions, giving them control over their privacy. Zcash operates on a Proof-of-Work (PoW) consensus mechanism similar to Bitcoin but with added privacy features. The maximum supply is capped at 21 million coins, like Bitcoin. Zcash has faced regulatory scrutiny due to its privacy capabilities but remains one of the leading privacy coins. It has been listed on major exchanges, though some have delisted it due to privacy concerns. Development is led by the **Electric Coin Company (ECC)** and the **Zcash Foundation**. Zcash also introduced a "Founders' Reward", where a portion of mining rewards goes to the team for development and operations. Despite its privacy focus, it maintains options for transparency, providing flexibility for regulatory and personal use.

Dash

Dash is a cryptocurrency launched in 2014, initially known as **XCoin**, then **Darkcoin**, before adopting the name Dash (short for **"Digital Cash"**). It focuses on fast, low-cost transactions, making it ideal for everyday use. Dash operates on a decentralized blockchain using a Proof of Work (PoW) consensus mechanism, similar to Bitcoin, but with additional enhancements. One key feature is **InstantSend**, allowing near-instant transactions, typically settling in under 1 second. Private Send enables optional transaction privacy by mixing coins to obscure their origins. Dash is governed by a **Decentralized Autonomous Organization (DAO)**, where **Masternodes** (special full nodes) help secure the network and vote on governance decisions, funded through its unique self-funding treasury system. Dash transactions are affordable, with low fees, and the network is designed to be scalable. It has real-world use cases, particularly in regions like Venezuela, where it's widely accepted for payments.

~ 11 ~

TRADING

Cryptocurrency trading involves the buying, selling, or exchanging of digital currencies on a platform. The goal is to profit from the price movements of these digital assets. It has come a long way in just a decade, evolving from simple buy-and-hold strategies into something far more complex and multifaceted. As decentralized finance (DeFi) rises, and digital assets and blockchain technology continue to grow, traders now find themselves with a range of sophisticated financial instruments and methods at their disposal. Among them, spot trading, margin trading, derivatives trading, peer-to-peer (P2P) trading, and over-the-counter (OTC) trading stand as the primary strategies employed by both retail and institutional investors alike.

Spot trading. Spot trading in crypto is where everything happens in real time, right there in the open market. The concept is simple, you buy or sell a cryptocurrency at its current price, the "spot price." There are no future contracts, no obligations tied to time. It's immediate, direct, and driven by the flow of supply and demand. Imagine standing in a marketplace, calling out for Bitcoin or Ethereum, and getting your hands on it the moment you pay. That's spot trading, straightforward and transparent. In the world of crypto, spot trading is often the first experience most traders have. It's simple because the only thing you're focused on is the present price. You're either a buyer, grabbing coins while they're available at a price you find favorable, or a seller, offloading your holdings to someone else on the other end of the trade. Everything happens quickly. The moment the order is matched, the trade is done, and you either own the crypto or the cash equivalent. Exchanges are where the majority of spot trading happens. Platforms like **Binance**, **Coinbase**, **Kraken**, and many others offer a space where buyers and sellers meet. You see it all, the order book displaying prices buyers are willing to pay and what sellers are asking. The system matches orders, and once it does, the assets are exchanged.

If you place a "market order," you agree to buy or sell at whatever the best current price is. If you're more strategic, you might place a "limit order," where you set the price you're willing to accept, and only when someone agrees to it does the trade occur. One of the defining characteristics of spot trading is that it's immediate. Unlike futures or options trading, where contracts may settle at a future date, spot trading is about the present. You want Bitcoin? You pay for it, and it's transferred to your account. You want to sell Ethereum? Someone buys it from you, and you get the agreed-upon amount right away. No waiting, no conditions, just an instant exchange of assets. There's an undeniable appeal to the simplicity of spot trading. You're working with the assets directly, buying and holding the actual cryptocurrency rather than dealing with a derivative or a contract. It's a great entry point for beginners, a way to get acquainted with the volatility and price action of the crypto market without getting tangled in more complex products like futures, options, or margin trades. But spot trading isn't without its nuances. Prices can shift rapidly, sometimes in the blink of an eye, especially in a market as volatile as crypto. One minute Bitcoin might be trading at $30,000, and the next, it could spike or drop significantly. As a spot trader, you're exposed to this volatility. The price you pay is the price you get, and if the market moves against you right after your trade, there's no going back.

You own the asset, and it's up to you to decide whether to hold it or sell it as the market moves. Liquidity is another critical factor. Spot trading depends heavily on liquidity—the availability of assets to buy or sell at any given time. On larger exchanges, like Binance or Coinbase, liquidity tends to be high, meaning it's easy to buy or sell large amounts of cryptocurrency without affecting the market price too much.

On smaller exchanges, liquidity can be thinner, which means your trade could push the price up or down, particularly if you're dealing in larger quantities. The price you see when spot trading reflects what the market believes the cryptocurrency is worth at that exact moment. It's influenced by many factors, news, market sentiment, technological developments, government regulations, and, in the case of Bitcoin or Ethereum, the broader adoption of the technology. When a major event happens, like a regulatory announcement or a big company adopting Bitcoin as a payment method, spot prices can move fast. Traders have to be quick to respond, seizing opportunities as they arise or cutting losses when things go south. Most spot traders tend to take a "buy and hold" approach, especially when they believe in the long-term growth of a cryptocurrency.

They'll buy when prices seem favorable and hold onto the asset, waiting for its value to increase. It's a simple strategy that relies on the belief that over time, the value of cryptocurrencies like Bitcoin or Ethereum will continue to rise. Others take a more active approach, buying and selling frequently to take advantage of short-term price movements. These are the day traders, constantly watching the market, making multiple trades throughout the day in pursuit of quick profits. However, spot trading is not just about Bitcoin and Ethereum. It covers a wide range of cryptocurrencies, from popular altcoins like Ripple (XRP), Litecoin (LTC), and Solana (SOL), to newer, lesser-known projects. The availability of different coins depends on the exchange you're using, and each asset comes with its own level of liquidity, price volatility, and trading volume. Risks are always present in spot trading. The most obvious is price volatility. Cryptocurrency prices can be notoriously unpredictable, and even seasoned traders can find themselves on the wrong side of a price swing. Then there's the risk of hacking or security breaches. While reputable exchanges take significant measures to protect user assets, no system is entirely immune to cyberattacks. It's always wise to move your assets off an exchange and into a secure wallet after trading, especially if you plan to hold for the long term.

Spot trading remains one of the most popular ways to engage with the crypto market because of its simplicity and immediacy. It offers traders the chance to own actual cryptocurrencies, giving them the freedom to decide when to buy, sell, or hold. While it comes with risks—like the volatility that makes crypto so famous—it also presents opportunities for both new and experienced traders to capitalize on the market's movements. It's the most straightforward, intuitive form of crypto trading, and for many, it's where the journey into the world of digital assets begins. The market never sleeps, and in the fast-paced world of crypto, spot traders live and breathe the constant ebb and flow of prices, navigating the peaks and valleys in real-time. Whether you're in it for the long haul or chasing the thrill of quick trades, spot trading gives you the power to own a piece of the future, one transaction at a time.

Margin Trade. Margin trading in crypto is where the stakes get higher. It's not just about buying or selling anymore, it's about amplifying your potential gains, and your potential losses. In the world of crypto, where prices can swing wildly, margin trading can be a powerful tool, but it's also one that requires precision, caution, and a deep understanding of the risks. At its core, margin trading allows you to borrow funds to trade larger amounts of cryptocurrency than you could with your own money alone. Imagine you have $1,000 and want to trade Bitcoin. On a regular exchange, you'd be limited to what that $1,000 could buy. But with margin trading, you can borrow additional funds, sometimes many times your initial investment, giving you the ability to control a much larger position.

The result? Bigger gains if the market moves in your favor. But there's a catch: if the market turns against you, your losses are amplified just as dramatically. The key concept behind margin trading is leverage. Leverage is the ratio of the borrowed funds to your own money. For example, if you're trading with 10x leverage, this means for every dollar of your own money, you control $10 worth of cryptocurrency. If the price of Bitcoin rises 5%, your 10x leverage multiplies that gain to 50%. But if Bitcoin falls by 5%, you don't just lose 5% of your money, you lose 50%. That's the double-edged sword of margin trading. So how does it work? First, you put up collateral, often called the margin, that serves as a security deposit. This margin is a fraction of the total position you want to take. The platform or exchange lends you the rest of the funds to execute the trade. If the market moves in your favor, you can sell the position, repay the borrowed funds, and pocket the profit. But if the market moves against you, things can get tricky. You could face a margin call, where the platform asks you to add more funds to your account to cover the losses. If you can't do that, your position may be liquidated, meaning the platform sells your assets to recover the borrowed funds. Margin trading is available on many crypto exchanges, both centralized and decentralized. Some of the biggest platforms for margin trading include **Binance, BitMEX, Bybit**, and **Kraken**. These platforms allow users to trade popular cryptocurrencies like Bitcoin (BTC), Ethereum (ETH), and many altcoins with leverage, ranging from 2x to over 100x. Let's break it down with an example. Suppose Bitcoin is trading at $30,000, and you believe it's going to rise. You have $1,000 and decide to use

10x leverage, which allows you to control $10,000 worth of Bitcoin. You open a long position, meaning you're betting on the price going up. If Bitcoin rises by 10% to $33,000, your $10,000 position is now worth $11,000. You sell, repay the $9,000 you borrowed, and walk away with a $1,000 profit, doubling your original investment. But here's where it gets risky.

If Bitcoin drops by 10% to $27,000, your $10,000 position is now worth only $9,000. With 10x leverage, you've lost $1,000, wiping out your entire investment. And if the price continues to fall, you could lose even more, potentially facing a margin call or liquidation. There are two main strategies in margin trading: going long and going short. When you go long, you're betting that the price of the cryptocurrency will rise. You borrow funds to buy more than you could with your own money, hoping to sell at a higher price later. When you go short, you're betting the price will fall. In this case, you borrow the cryptocurrency itself, sell it at the current price, and aim to buy it back later at a lower price, profiting from the difference. While the potential for profit is appealing, margin trading comes with significant risks. The volatile nature of the crypto market means prices can swing dramatically in a short period, increasing the chances of losses. Many traders have been liquidated after sudden market movements wiped out their positions before they had a chance to react. Liquidation happens automatically when the value of your collateral falls below a certain threshold, set by the platform, and it can happen faster than expected. To mitigate these risks, platforms offer tools like stop-loss orders, which automatically close a trade if the price reaches a certain level.

This helps limit losses, but in highly volatile markets, prices can sometimes move too quickly for even stop-losses to protect traders. Another key consideration in margin trading is the cost of borrowing. Platforms charge interest or fees on the borrowed funds, which accumulate over time. If you hold a position for an extended period, these fees can eat into your profits or deepen your losses, especially if the market isn't moving in your favor. For those looking to engage in margin trading, understanding how liquidations work is critical. Every platform has a specific liquidation price, the point at which the platform automatically closes your position to protect its loan. This liquidation price is calculated based on your leverage, the amount borrowed, and the cryptocurrency's current market value. The higher the leverage, the closer the liquidation price is to your entry point, making it easier for your position to be liquidated in volatile markets. Despite the risks, margin trading attracts many crypto traders, especially those looking for quick profits in short-term market movements. The allure of turning small capital into large profits is strong, but it requires experience, discipline, and a solid understanding of the market. In conclusion, margin trading in crypto offers both incredible opportunities and significant dangers. It amplifies your position, allowing you to trade with more than you have, but it also amplifies your risk. When used carefully, with a clear strategy and risk management tools, it can be a powerful way to capitalize on market movements. However, without proper caution, it can quickly lead to heavy losses. For those venturing into the world of margin trading, it's essential to understand both sides of the coin—because in crypto, the stakes are always high.

Derivatives Trading. For those looking beyond immediate transactions, derivatives trading offers an advanced approach. Instead of owning the asset itself, you're trading contracts, agreements that lock in a price for a future date. Crypto derivatives are financial instruments whose value is derived from an underlying cryptocurrency. These products allow traders to speculate on future prices, hedge their portfolios, or gain exposure to the market without holding the actual asset.

A derivative is a contract whose value is tied to the performance of an underlying asset, such as Bitcoin (BTC), Ethereum (ETH), or other digital currencies. Common crypto derivatives include **Futures**, **Options**, **Perpetual Swaps**, **Exchange-Traded Funds (ETFs)**, and **Tokenized Derivatives** designed for speculation, risk management, and efficient market participation. Crypto derivatives work similarly to traditional ones. Traders enter contracts to buy or sell an asset at a future date or under specific conditions without owning the cryptocurrency. Leverage plays a significant role here, allowing traders to control large positions with minimal capital. This can amplify both gains and losses, making margin management crucial. Contracts may settle in cryptocurrencies or fiat currencies like USD or stablecoins. Hedging strategies help traders manage volatility by locking in prices, protecting their portfolios from sudden market swings.

Futures Trading. Futures contracts are agreements to buy or sell cryptocurrency at a predetermined price on a set date. Standard futures expire on their due date, while perpetual futures remain open indefinitely, using funding rates to balance buyers and sellers. A futures contract might, for example, allow a trader to buy Bitcoin at $30,000 three months from now, regardless of market fluctuations. Major platforms like **Binance**, **Bybit**, and **CME Group** offer futures trading, catering to both retail and institutional traders.

Options Trading. Options provide more flexibility by offering the choice, not the obligation, to buy (call option) or sell (put option) cryptocurrency at a set price. For example, a trader might purchase a Bitcoin call option with a strike price of $40,000, hoping Bitcoin exceeds that value. If it doesn't, the trader only loses the premium paid for the option. **Deribit**, **Binance**, and **OKEx** are popular platforms for trading options.

Perpetual Swaps. Perpetual swaps resemble futures but without expiration dates. Highly liquid, they allow traders to take long or short positions with substantial leverage. Platforms like Binance, **Bybit**, and **OKEx** dominate this market, with funding rates maintaining the contract's price in line with the actual asset.

Crypto ETFs. For those seeking exposure without holding cryptocurrencies directly, crypto ETFs offer a solution. These funds track the price of various cryptocurrencies or a basket of digital assets. Futures-based ETFs, like the **ProShares Bitcoin Strategy ETF (BITO)** and **VanEck Bitcoin Strategy ETF (XBTF)**, are traded on traditional exchanges such as **NYSE**, while **Canada's Purpose Bitcoin ETF** offers direct exposure to Bitcoin on the **Toronto Stock Exchange**.

Tokenized Derivatives. Innovative platforms like **Synthetix** go further by offering tokenized derivatives, synthetic assets representing real-world instruments but operated on the blockchain. These tools enable traders to explore new opportunities within the market.

The regulation of crypto derivatives varies across jurisdictions. In the **U.S.**, the **Commodity Futures Trading Commission (CFTC)** oversees crypto futures, treating Bitcoin and Ethereum as commodities. The **SEC** focuses on ETFs, allowing futures-based products while being cautious with spot ETFs due to market manipulation concerns. In the **European Union**, **MiFID II** ensures strict regulation of crypto derivatives. **Japan's Financial Services Agency (FSA)** oversees the sector, while **China** has banned crypto derivatives altogether. Offshore jurisdictions, such as the **Cayman Islands**, provide more lenient environments for platforms like **Binance** and **Bybit**, though they face increasing regulatory scrutiny. Stablecoin-based derivatives, settled in USDT or USDC, also attract regulatory attention as oversight grows over these currencies.

Leverage and Risks. Leverage is a double-edged sword in derivatives trading. While it can magnify profits, it also increases the risk of losses. Futures, especially perpetual futures, can settle continuously without an expiration date, requiring traders to stay vigilant. As with all speculative trading, volatility can quickly turn profits into losses, making risk management critical.

P2P Trading. P2P trading in crypto is where the rules of the game shift. There's no need for intermediaries, no need for the towering exchanges that watch over every move. Instead, it's just two people, one with a cryptocurrency to sell and the other with cash in hand, finding common ground. It's personal, direct, and in a world where anonymity is often craved, it's a solution that fits. They meet in virtual spaces, these buyers and sellers, and through whispers of negotiation, they agree on a deal that suits them both. Here, no one is watching. When a seller lists their offer, they throw a line into the sea of traders. They name their price, their conditions, and wait. On the other side, a buyer scours the listings, looking for the right opportunity, the right price, the right method of payment. Some will pay by bank transfer, some by PayPal, others prefer cash. And when the match is made, they connect, silently working out the details. It's all in their hands. The terms, the time, the payment, it all bends to their needs. But it's not without risks. In a world where trust is the most valuable currency, there's always a chance someone won't hold up their end of the deal. That's where escrow comes in. Most platforms act as a silent third party, holding the cryptocurrency safely until the buyer proves they've paid. Only when both sides are satisfied does the trade truly close. It's a safeguard, a layer of trust in an otherwise shadowy exchange. P2P trading offers something traditional exchanges can't, privacy. There's no need to shout from the rooftops, no public order book broadcasting your intentions. Instead, it's a quiet affair, perfect for those who want to stay under the radar. High-profile investors, institutional giants, they've seen the value in this method. Why risk moving markets when you can trade in the dark, without anyone noticing? And then there's the freedom it brings. On the public exchanges, everything is rigid, structured, fixed. But here, in the

P2P world, nothing is set in stone. If you want to pay with cash, you find someone willing to accept it. If you prefer to meet in person, there are platforms that allow it. You negotiate the price, you decide the terms. Flexibility is king, and for those who want to shape the deal their own way, it's the perfect fit. Yet, as with any uncharted territory, there are dangers. Scammers lurk, waiting to pounce on the unsuspecting. They might send fake proof of payment, or worse, initiate a chargeback after the trade is complete. It's a game of trust, and not everyone plays fair. The lack of transparency can be unsettling. Without the clear oversight of a centralized exchange, verifying the deal can feel like navigating through a fog.

Sometimes trades drag out, disputes arise over details, and resolution can be hard to come by. Despite the risks, P2P trading thrives. Platforms like **Binance P2P, LocalBitcoins, Paxful**, they provide the marketplace, but the real action happens between the buyer and seller. There's no rush. Trades might take a little longer than they would on a centralized exchange, but that's the price you pay for control. In these spaces, large trades move without a ripple, without the market ever realizing what happened. And then there are the regions where P2P is more than just an option, it's a lifeline. In countries where centralized exchanges are banned or restricted, P2P offers a way in. It's a global market, open to anyone with the means to access it. Investors who want to move large sums without slipping prices find a haven here. It's a world where deals are struck with precision, and every trade is custom-fit to the needs of its participants. But as much as P2P trading offers freedom, it also walks a tightrope. Regulations are coming, creeping closer. The authorities are watching now, and soon, even these private spaces might find themselves under scrutiny. The landscape is shifting. The need for transparency, for security, is growing, and while P2P trading remains a crucial mechanism for moving large amounts of cryptocurrency quietly and efficiently, its future hangs in the balance. For now, though, the system endures. Buyers and sellers meet, deals are struck, and cryptocurrency changes hands in the shadows. It's a game of trust, a dance between risk and reward, and for those who know the steps, it's where the real action takes place.

Over-the-Counter (OTC) trading. For institutional investors and high-net-worth individuals making large trades, Over-the-Counter (OTC) trading provides an alternative to public exchanges. OTC trading occurs off-exchange, allowing major players to execute large orders without causing significant market disruptions. This is particularly useful when dealing with substantial amounts of cryptocurrency, where executing a trade on a public exchange could dramatically move the market. In OTC trading, deals are negotiated directly between parties, often through specialized OTC desks, bypassing public exchanges. For instance, a whale might purchase 500 Bitcoin in a single deal without impacting the price visible on any exchange. These transactions are highly customized, and both the buyer and seller agree on the terms privately, ensuring that the broader market remains unaffected.

While OTC trading offers the benefit of discretion and reduced market impact, it comes with trade-offs. Lack of transparency is a primary concern, as these trades are not publicly visible, which can create trust issues between parties. Counterparty risk also looms large, without the transparency of an exchange, ensuring the reliability of the trade can be more challenging. Several major OTC desks cater to large-scale investors, offering deep liquidity and personalized services. Among the most prominent players are:

Cumberland: One of the largest OTC desks globally, offering 24/7 crypto trading services.

Genesis Trading: A key player providing access to institutional-grade liquidity across various cryptocurrencies.

Galaxy Digital: A financial services firm specializing in blockchain and cryptocurrency trading, with a focus on large institutional trades.

Kraken OTC: Operated by the popular crypto exchange Kraken, it provides tailored services for high-net-worth clients.

Binance OTC: One of the world's largest exchanges, Binance also offers a dedicated OTC desk for large-volume trades.

OTC trading stands as a pillar of the crypto world. It's the critical mechanism that allows vast sums to move without rippling the waters. But the world is watching, and even the shadows aren't safe forever. As regulators sharpen their gaze, the push for transparency grows stronger. The rules are changing, and the quiet corners of the crypto market may soon find themselves bathed in a light they've long avoided. These different methods of trading, whether immediate and straightforward, or leveraged and speculative, make up the landscape of modern cryptocurrency markets, each offering its own opportunities and dangers. It's a world of risk and reward, where fortunes can be made or lost in the blink of an eye.

~ 12 ~

LEGACY POWER

In the early days of Bitcoin, the relationship between governments and the crypto ecosystem was marked by confusion, skepticism, and outright hostility. Bitcoin, introduced by the mysterious Satoshi Nakamoto in 2009, proposed a radical new financial system that operated outside the control of any government or central bank. For the first time, people could transact value directly, peer-to-peer, without the need for intermediaries such as banks or payment processors. This new technology, blockchain, seemed promising to some but frightening to others. Bitcoin was touted as a currency free from government manipulation, immune to inflation, and private in a way that no fiat currency could be. However, to governments, this very independence was a threat to the established financial order.

In the beginning, most governments dismissed Bitcoin and other cryptocurrencies as fringe innovations, unlikely to gain traction. It was viewed as a technological experiment that would eventually fizzle out. However, as the Bitcoin price soared from fractions of a penny to thousands of dollars in just a few years, governments could no longer ignore it. There were fears that this new, unregulated currency could facilitate illegal activities such as money laundering, drug trafficking, and terrorism financing. Governments, particularly those in the West, began to investigate how to regulate or even ban the use of Bitcoin. At the same time, central banks saw the potential of Bitcoin's underlying technology, blockchain, but remained wary of the currency itself.

On the other side, the traditional banking system, which has operated under government control and regulation for centuries, was immediately at odds with the idea of cryptocurrencies. Banks has served for centuries as intermediaries between individuals, businesses, and the economy, ensuring money flow efficiently and securely, while Bitcoin was promising the complete eradication of the need for these intermediaries. As a consequence, banks resisted cryptocurrencies, fearing they would lose control over financial transactions. Major banks refused to allow customers to use credit or debit cards to buy Bitcoin, and they refused to work with crypto exchanges. These digital currencies were stripping away the need for middlemen, allowing people to exchange value directly, bypassing the traditional gatekeepers.

For banks, it wasn't just a shift in the financial landscape, it was a threat to their existence. On top of that, the shadowy reputation that early cryptocurrencies find themselves tangled in threw fuel on the fire. The dark web, including platforms like **Silk Road**, has sometimes been associated with illegal activities and in its early days, Bitcoin, much like paper dollars, was occasionally used in illicit transactions, such as drug trafficking, weapons deals, and money laundering, often occurring discreetly within the digital realm of the internet. Banks, already skittish about this new technology, now discovered a new potential risk, not only to their reputation but also to their very survival in the regulatory arena. They know that regulators, always watchful, will not turn a blind eye to institutions flirting with such shady activities. The fear of backlash hung heavy in the air. Even beyond the shadowy associations, there was a more profound uncertainty, the regulatory gray zone where cryptocurrencies resided. Banks, burdened by strict regulations, find themselves standing at the edge of this new world, unsure of what awaits. What will the regulators say? How will this new asset class be treated? Banks are accustomed to rules, clear guidelines, and the certainty of compliance. But with crypto, the landscape was blurry.

One wrong step could have plunged them into the murky waters of anti-money laundering laws or other regulations, and they were not willing to take that risk. And then there was the volatility. Bitcoin and its counterparts seem to dance wildly, soaring to incredible highs only to plummet without warning. Compared to the steady, predictable rhythm of traditional fiat currencies, cryptocurrencies were then and are now a chaotic storm. For risk-averse banks, which thrive on stability, the idea of integrating such an unpredictable asset class feels reckless. It's not just an uncharted territory, it's a dangerous one. But the landscape shifts. As cryptocurrencies matured, gaining legitimacy and shedding some of their notorious past, a new kind of financial institution emerged. These are the crypto-friendly banks, the ones who see potential where others see peril. They embrace the digital revolution, offering services tailored to this growing market—crypto custody, fiat-to-crypto exchanges, even lending against crypto collateral. They aren't afraid of the future, they lean into it, ready to guide their clients through the evolving world of blockchain and cryptocurrencies, while the traditional banking world watches from the sidelines, unsure whether to join or resist this digital tide. Here some examples of crypto friendly banks:

Silvergate Bank (USA): A California-based bank that became a leading player in the crypto space by offering banking services to cryptocurrency exchanges and businesses. Silvergate's Silvergate Exchange Network (SEN) allows crypto companies to move U.S. dollars between exchanges in real time, addressing the issue of slow transaction speeds that traditional banks faced.

Signature Bank (USA): Another U.S.-based bank, Signature has actively sought to serve the cryptocurrency industry. The bank's Signet platform allows real-time, blockchain-based payments between customers, making it easier for crypto businesses to access liquidity.

Revolut (UK/EU): A digital bank and financial technology company that offers cryptocurrency trading and storage services alongside traditional banking products. Revolut allows users to buy, hold, and sell cryptocurrencies directly through its app.

Bank Frick (Liechtenstein): Bank Frick is one of Europe's leading banks when it comes to cryptocurrency services. They offer cold storage solutions, direct crypto investments, and work with blockchain companies, providing them access to traditional financial services.

SEBA Bank (Switzerland): SEBA Bank offers both traditional banking services and a wide range of crypto-related services, including digital asset management and custody. It is regulated by Swiss financial authorities and provides services for institutional and professional investors in crypto.

Swissquote (Switzerland): Swissquote offers trading in several cryptocurrencies and is known for its secure crypto trading platform. It supports both individual and institutional investors and provides secure storage solutions for digital assets.

Fidor Bank (Germany): Fidor Bank was one of the earliest adopters of Bitcoin, offering crypto-related services and working closely with crypto exchanges like **Kraken**. It provides seamless integration for those in the crypto space, allowing easy management of both fiat and digital currencies.

Juno Finance (USA): Juno is a modern banking platform that allows users to earn, hold, and manage both cryptocurrencies and fiat. They offer high-interest accounts and easy crypto-fiat conversion, with the ability to make purchases and payments directly from the platform.

Metropolitan Commercial Bank (USA): This bank is known for its partnerships with crypto firms such as **Coinbase** and **Circle**.

They provide services like wire transfers, holding fiat for crypto firms, and issuing debit cards for crypto platforms.

Mercury (USA): Mercury is a digital bank that offers crypto-friendly services, providing tools for startups in the fintech and crypto space. They support integrations with major crypto exchanges and platforms and allow crypto companies to maintain accounts in USD.

Bitbank (Japan): Bitbank is a leading Japanese cryptocurrency exchange that also offers banking services tailored to crypto investors. It provides easy-to-use services for the buying, selling, and storage of digital assets, with a focus on regulatory compliance in Japan.

Solarisbank (Germany): Solarisbank is a fintech company that provides banking as a service and is highly crypto-friendly. They work with crypto companies to provide seamless banking integration and offer a range of services for crypto startups, including fiat accounts and crypto custody.

Xapo Bank (Gibraltar): Xapo is a bank that primarily offers services related to Bitcoin and digital currencies. It provides institutional-grade cold storage for cryptocurrencies and operates as a fully licensed bank, bridging traditional finance with digital assets.

These crypto-friendly banks helped bridge the gap between the traditional financial system and the emerging crypto ecosystem, providing essential services that allowed cryptocurrency businesses to scale and grow. They also demonstrated to the broader banking sector that it was possible to engage with the crypto industry in a compliant and regulated manner. Governments, through regulatory agencies, began working with banks to monitor cryptocurrency activity, flagging suspicious transactions and imposing restrictions on exchanges that dealt with cryptocurrencies. Governments were slow to understand the full implications of cryptocurrencies, but they quickly recognized the potential threat they posed to monetary sovereignty, financial stability, and regulatory control. With the rise of cryptocurrencies, governments feared that people might turn away from national currencies and begin using decentralized alternatives like Bitcoin for daily transactions. If this happened on a large scale, it could undermine the central bank's ability to manage the money supply, control inflation, and respond to economic crises.

In countries experiencing hyperinflation, such as **Venezuela** and **Zimbabwe**, people had already started using Bitcoin as a store of value and means of exchange, bypassing the local currency altogether. This worried governments, especially those that rely on their currency's global position for economic leverage, such as the United States and the European Union. One of the first red flags for governments was the use of cryptocurrencies to evade taxes and launder money. Cryptocurrencies, especially those promising anonymity (like **Monero** and **Zcash**), made it difficult for authorities to track financial flows. The decentralized nature of crypto transactions meant that individuals could hide their wealth from tax authorities or move large sums of money across borders without detection.

Central Bank Digital Currencies

The crypto community feared that governments would try to co-opt blockchain technology for their own purposes, particularly in the form of **Central Bank Digital Currencies (CBDCs)**. While CBDCs represent a recognition of the potential of blockchain technology, they are antithetical to the core principles of decentralized cryptocurrencies like Bitcoin and Ethereum. CBDCs represent a significant shift in how nations are approaching digital currency and blockchain technology. Unlike decentralized cryptocurrencies such as Bitcoin and Ethereum, which operate independently of governments and central authorities, CBDCs are digital forms of a country's fiat currency issued and controlled by central banks. These government-backed currencies aim to offer the efficiency of cryptocurrencies while maintaining the control and regulatory oversight of traditional financial systems. CBDCs are entirely controlled by central banks and governments, and governments would have the ability to track every transaction, control monetary policy directly, and possibly even restrict the use of digital currencies based on certain conditions (for example, prohibiting certain purchases or enforcing negative interest rates). In particular the crypto ecosystem feared that widespread adoption of CBDCs could marginalize decentralized cryptocurrencies and give governments unprecedented control over financial transactions.

China has been one of the most proactive countries in developing a central bank digital currency. The **People's Bank of China (PBoC)** has been working on the **Digital Yuan**, or e-CNY, for several years and is currently running extensive pilot programs across the country. China's motivation for developing the Digital Yuan is twofold. First, the government sees it as a way to modernize the domestic payment system. China is already a largely cashless society, with platforms like **WeChat Pay** and **Alipay** dominating the payments landscape. However, these platforms are controlled by private companies, which the Chinese government views as a potential threat to its control over the financial system. By introducing the Digital Yuan, the government can regain control over the payment infrastructure and ensure that all transactions flow through the central bank. Second, China views the Digital Yuan as a way to challenge the dominance of the U.S. dollar in global trade and finance. By promoting the use of the Digital Yuan in cross-border transactions, particularly in countries that participate in China's Belt and Road Initiative, China hopes to increase the internationalization of its currency and reduce its reliance on the U.S. financial system. The Digital Yuan is designed to be a centralized digital currency, controlled by the PBoC. It operates on a two-tiered system, with the central bank issuing the currency to commercial banks, which then distribute it to consumers. The Chinese government has made it clear that the Digital Yuan is intended to complement, not replace, physical cash. However, over time, it is expected to become the primary means of transaction in the country.

The **European Central Bank (ECB)** has been exploring the development of a **Digital Euro** as part of its broader strategy to modernize the European financial system. The ECB's primary motivation is to ensure that Europe remains competitive in the global digital economy and that European consumers have access to a secure, government-backed digital currency. The ECB has emphasized that the Digital Euro would complement existing forms of payment, such as cash and electronic transfers, rather than replacing them. However, the central bank is concerned that if it does not offer a digital currency, private companies or foreign governments could fill the void, potentially undermining Europe's financial sovereignty. The ECB's vision for the Digital Euro is a currency that is accessible to all European citizens and businesses, regardless of their location or banking status. The central bank is particularly focused on ensuring that the Digital Euro is easy to use, secure, and privacy-preserving. One of the challenges that the ECB faces is finding the right balance between transparency (to prevent illegal activity) and privacy (to protect users' financial data). Unlike decentralized cryptocurrencies, the Digital Euro would be fully controlled by the ECB, with strict regulatory oversight. The central bank is still in the research phase, but it is expected to make a decision on whether to move forward with the project in the coming years.

In contrast to China and the European Union, the **United States** has been relatively slow in developing a **Digital Dollar**. While the Federal Reserve has conducted research into the potential benefits and risks of a CBDC, there has been no formal commitment to issuing a Digital Dollar. One of the reasons for the U.S. government's cautious approach is that the U.S. dollar is already the world's dominant reserve currency. The Federal Reserve is concerned that introducing a Digital Dollar could have unintended consequences for the global financial system, particularly if it destabilizes the banking sector or leads to increased demand for cash withdrawals. The U.S. government is also wary of the impact that a Digital Dollar could have on privacy and civil liberties. There is concern that a government-controlled digital currency could be used to monitor financial transactions, potentially infringing on Americans' right to privacy. Despite these concerns, there is growing pressure on the Federal Reserve to develop a Digital Dollar. The rise of private cryptocurrencies, particularly stablecoins like **Facebook's Diem** (formerly Libra), has raised alarms in Washington. If private companies begin issuing their own digital currencies, they could undermine the government's control over the money supply and financial stability. To address these concerns, the Federal Reserve has been working with other central banks and international organizations, such as the **Bank for International Settlements (BIS),** to explore the development of global standards for CBDCs. While the timeline for a Digital Dollar remains uncertain, it is clear that the U.S. government is paying close attention to developments in the digital currency space.

For many developing countries, CBDCs represent a powerful tool for promoting financial inclusion. In regions where large portions of the population are unbanked, digital currencies offer an opportunity to provide access to financial services without the need for physical bank branches. Countries like **Nigeria**, which launched the **eNaira** in 2021, are using CBDCs to expand financial access to underserved populations. The **Central Bank of the Bahamas** has also taken a similar approach with its **Sand Dollar,** which was the first fully operational CBDC in the world. In these countries, CBDCs are seen as a way to promote economic growth by reducing the costs of financial transactions and increasing access to credit. They also help reduce the reliance on cash, which can be expensive to produce and distribute, especially in remote areas.

Institutional Adoption

While banks and cryptocurrencies were initially seen as adversaries, the reality is that many banks are now collaborating with cryptocurrency companies to offer new products and services. Partnerships become a lifeline, a bridge between the old and the new. Banks, bound by their need for regulatory compliance and risk management, see the advantage in aligning with crypto firms. These collaborations allow them to tap into the expertise of the digital asset world without losing their grip on the careful balance of rules and regulations they are so accustomed to navigating.

The entry of institutional investors into the cryptocurrency market was a key turning point in the relationship between banks and crypto. Once considered a fringe investment, cryptocurrencies became part of the portfolios of hedge funds, pension funds, and family offices. The rise of regulated financial products, such as **Bitcoin Futures** contracts on the **Chicago Mercantile Exchange (CME)**, gave institutional investors a way to gain exposure to digital assets in a familiar regulatory environment. As institutional investors entered the space, banks followed suit. Many banks began offering custody services for cryptocurrencies, allowing clients to store digital assets securely. Banks also developed products such as **crypto-linked exchange-traded funds (ETFs)** and structured notes to cater to the growing demand for digital assets. While banks were initially wary of cryptocurrencies, they quickly recognized the potential of blockchain technology to improve their internal operations. Blockchain's ability to create transparent, immutable records of transactions has applications beyond digital currencies. Several major banks have explored or implemented blockchain technology to enhance their own processes. Examples include:

J.P. Morgan: J.P. Morgan developed its own cryptocurrency, JPM Coin, which is used internally to facilitate instant payments between institutional clients. The bank also launched a blockchain-based platform called Onyx to improve cross-border payments and settlements.

HSBC: HSBC has used blockchain technology to settle billions of dollars' worth of foreign exchange transactions. The bank's FX Everywhere platform uses blockchain to track and reconcile transactions between HSBC's internal balance sheets, reducing costs and improving efficiency.

Santander: Santander was one of the first major banks to issue a bond on the Ethereum blockchain, showcasing blockchain's potential for securitized assets.

Goldman Sachs: Goldman Sachs has been actively engaging in the crypto space by offering clients access to crypto derivatives like Bitcoin futures. The bank does not directly hold cryptocurrency on its balance sheet but has expanded its services to include crypto trading desks and structured crypto-based products. In 2022, Goldman began offering institutional clients exposure to Ethereum (ETH) funds.

Morgan Stanley: Morgan Stanley was among the first major U.S. banks to provide its clients access to Bitcoin funds, and in 2021, the bank started offering institutional clients exposure to cryptocurrency investments. While the bank does not hold crypto on its own balance sheet, it offers investments in Bitcoin-related products, reflecting its cautious but expanding foray into digital asset

DBS Bank: DBS Bank, one of the largest banks in Singapore, launched its own cryptocurrency exchange in 2020, **DBS Digital Exchange**, which allows institutional clients to trade digital assets like Bitcoin and Ethereum. DBS offers cryptocurrency custody services and integrates digital assets into its financial products, making it one of the few traditional banks in Asia with direct crypto involvement.

Standard Chartered: Standard Chartered has made significant moves into the cryptocurrency space, including launching a joint venture called **Zodia Custody**, a cryptocurrency custody service for institutional clients. The bank has explored adding cryptocurrencies to its balance sheet and continues to push for regulatory clarity in the space.

ING Group: ING Group has been involved in cryptocurrency through its blockchain and crypto custody initiatives. ING is developing crypto custody solutions for institutional clients and has been part of multiple pilot projects exploring blockchain technology.

BBVA: BBVA, one of Spain's largest banks, offers its clients Bitcoin trading and custody services through its Swiss subsidiary. BBVA Switzerland allows private banking clients to trade and hold Bitcoin, and the bank is actively exploring broader digital asset services. BBVA is one of the few banks to incorporate cryptocurrency into its operations for high-net-worth clients.

Société Générale: Société Générale has embraced blockchain technology and cryptocurrencies by issuing digital bonds on blockchain platforms like Ethereum. In addition to these experiments with decentralized finance, Société Générale is building infrastructure to support digital assets, though it does not yet hold crypto on its balance sheet.

One of the key challenges that banks face in interacting with the cryptocurrency market is the issue of compliance. Banks are subject to strict regulations regarding anti-money laundering (AML), countering the financing of terrorism (CFT), and know-your-customer (KYC) rules. These regulations are designed to prevent financial institutions from being used to launder illicit funds or finance illegal activities. Cryptocurrencies, particularly in their early days, were viewed as a potential tool for money laundering and tax evasion due to the pseudonymous nature of transactions. This created a significant compliance challenge for banks that wanted to engage with the crypto industry while remaining compliant with existing regulations. Banks that want to offer cryptocurrency-related services must ensure that they comply with AML and KYC regulations. This involves implementing robust processes to verify the identity of customers, monitor transactions for suspicious activity, and report any potential money laundering or illegal activity to regulators. In the U.S., the **Financial Crimes Enforcement Network (FinCEN)** has issued guidance requiring cryptocurrency exchanges and wallet providers to comply with AML/KYC regulations.

Other jurisdictions, such as the **European Union** and the **United Kingdom**, have implemented similar rules, bringing cryptocurrency businesses under the same regulatory framework as traditional financial institutions. In many countries, banks that want to offer cryptocurrency services must obtain the necessary licenses and registrations. For example, in the U.S., banks may need to register with state regulators as money transmitters if they are offering cryptocurrency-related services. They may also need to comply with the rules of the Office of the Comptroller of the Currency (OCC) and other federal agencies. In the European Union, the **Markets in Crypto-Assets (MiCA)** framework, once fully implemented, will create a harmonized set of rules for crypto asset providers, including banks that offer crypto services.

Adoption as Legal Tender

As of now, only a few countries have adopted cryptocurrencies as legal tender. This means they are recognized as official forms of currency that can be used to settle debts and make payments. Here are the most prominent countries that have done so:

El Salvador: Year of Adoption: September 2021, Currency Adopted: Bitcoin (BTC). El Salvador became the first country in the world to adopt Bitcoin as legal tender. The government passed the Bitcoin Law, allowing citizens to use Bitcoin for everyday transactions alongside the U.S. dollar, which was already the official currency. The government launched a digital wallet called "Chivo" to facilitate Bitcoin transactions and set up Bitcoin ATMs across the country. El Salvador has also issued Bitcoin bonds to fund national projects, including "Bitcoin City," a city powered by geothermal energy from a volcano.

Central African Republic (CAR): Year of Adoption: April 2022, Currency Adopted: Bitcoin (BTC). The Central African Republic became the second country to adopt Bitcoin as legal tender. The country introduced a law making Bitcoin an official currency, allowing its use for payments and legal transactions. CAR is also a member of the Central African Economic and Monetary Community (CEMAC), which traditionally uses the Central African CFA franc. The adoption of Bitcoin has been viewed as an attempt to modernize the country's economy and promote financial inclusion. Though not fully adopted as legal tender, some countries are exploring the use of cryptocurrencies or developing frameworks for their potential use:

Panama: Panama has been working on a bill to regulate and potentially use cryptocurrencies, including Bitcoin, for payments in certain sectors.

Ukraine: The government has been working on legislation to create a legal framework for cryptocurrencies, although they are not yet recognized as legal tender.

Paraguay: There have been discussions and legislative initiatives about adopting cryptocurrencies for payments, particularly focused on Bitcoin mining.

~ 13 ~

REGULATORY ECOSYSTEM

The rise of cryptocurrencies has not only transformed financial markets but also triggered significant regulatory challenges. As digital assets like Bitcoin and Ethereum grew in popularity, governments and regulatory bodies across the globe scrambled to understand and manage the risks associated with this emerging technology. The decentralized nature of cryptocurrencies, which promises freedom from traditional financial systems, has proven both revolutionary and disruptive. While enthusiasts champion the ideals of autonomy and innovation, regulators fear the potential for misuse, ranging from tax evasion to money laundering and even threats to the stability of the global financial system. This chapter explores the diverse regulatory responses to cryptocurrencies worldwide, highlighting the efforts of agencies like the U.S. Financial Crimes Enforcement Network (FinCEN), the European Union's Anti-Money Laundering (AML) directives, UAE Regulatory bodies and others that have quickly focused on the risks posed by these new financial instruments.

We will delve, among others, into the fragmented regulatory environment of the United States, where agencies such as the Securities and Exchange Commission (SEC), Commodity Futures Trading Commission (CFTC), and Internal Revenue Service (IRS) interpret cryptocurrencies through different lenses, creating a patchwork of rules and obligations. At the same time, countries like Switzerland, Malta, and Estonia have embraced blockchain technology, positioning themselves as hubs for innovation through crypto-friendly regulations. The chapter will also examine the concerns on both sides: governments, who fear losing control over the financial system, and the crypto community, which views overregulation as a threat to innovation and decentralization. From Initial Coin Offerings (ICOs) to the evolution of stablecoins and non-fungible tokens (NFTs), we will explore the complexities of how these technologies are regulated and the global implications of different regulatory frameworks. Finally, we will consider the future of regulation, particularly in regions like the European Union, where comprehensive frameworks like the Markets in Crypto-Assets Regulation (MiCA) promise to bring clarity and cohesion to this evolving space. As we navigate this complex landscape, it becomes clear that the future of cryptocurrencies will be shaped not only by technological advancements but by the regulatory environments that evolve to govern them. This delicate balance between innovation and control will determine where the next wave of crypto development flourishes, and where it falters.

Regulatory agencies, such as the **Financial Crimes Enforcement Network (FinCEN)** in the **U.S.** and the **European Union's Anti-Money Laundering (AML)** directives, were quick to recognize the potential risks cryptocurrencies posed as vehicles for criminal activity. Governments, apprehensive about the lack of oversight, feared cryptocurrencies could facilitate massive tax evasion and destabilize the broader financial system. A particular concern arose around the volatility of major cryptocurrencies like Bitcoin, whose prices often swung dramatically within hours or even minutes. Such instability, if left unchecked, could not only harm individual investors but also trigger wider economic downturns, especially if significant segments of the population invested heavily in digital assets. Another pressing issue was the potential disruption to the traditional banking system. As decentralized finance (DeFi) platforms and peer-to-peer cryptocurrency exchanges grew, banks, heavily reliant on trust and regulatory safeguards, risked losing customers and deposits. Without a steady inflow of deposits, banks might struggle to issue credit, make investments, or effectively manage financial risk. Recognizing the essential role of banks in maintaining a stable economy, governments and central banks worldwide began to collaborate on mitigating the potential threats posed by this new financial paradigm.

On the other side of the equation, the cryptocurrency community, composed of early adopters like libertarians, technologists, and idealists, was deeply concerned about government overreach. These pioneers envisioned a decentralized financial ecosystem free from centralized control or intervention. However, as regulatory scrutiny increased, particularly from countries like **China** and **India**, the crypto industry feared that excessive regulation could stifle innovation and limit widespread adoption. China's crackdown on Bitcoin mining and India's temporary bans on crypto exchanges caused uncertainty and panic in the market. Meanwhile, in the U.S., the **Securities and Exchange Commission (SEC)** began targeting **Initial Coin Offerings (ICOs),** many of which were unregulated and raised billions without proper oversight. Numerous ICOs were later revealed to be fraudulent, damaging the industry's reputation and prompting fears that excessive regulation would drive innovation away from regions like North America and Asia to more crypto-friendly jurisdictions.

Different governments adopted widely varying approaches. Some, like **China** and **India**, oscillated between severe restrictions and more nuanced regulatory measures. In contrast, countries such as **Japan, Switzerland,** and **Singapore** welcomed cryptocurrencies and blockchain technology, crafting regulatory frameworks that fostered innovation while ensuring adherence to existing financial laws. The **European Union (EU),** adopting a progressive yet cautious stance, introduced the **Fifth Anti-Money**

Laundering Directive (5AMLD) in 2020, which placed crypto exchanges and wallet providers under the scope of AML regulations. Meanwhile, the forthcoming **Markets in Crypto-Assets (MiCA)** framework aims to standardize crypto regulations across the EU, promoting innovation while safeguarding consumers and the financial system.

In the **United States**, the regulatory landscape is particularly fragmented. Different agencies oversee distinct aspects of the crypto industry, leading to a patchwork of rules and classifications. The **SEC** focuses on securities-related matters, particularly token offerings and ICOs, while the **Commodity Futures Trading Commission (CFTC)** regulates cryptocurrency derivatives such as **Bitcoin futures**. The **Internal Revenue Service (IRS)** treats cryptocurrencies as property for tax purposes, meaning capital gains taxes apply to any sales or trades. Simultaneously, **FinCEN** enforces stringent Know Your Customer (KYC) and AML regulations for exchanges, further complicating the compliance landscape for crypto businesses.

As some countries sought to restrict cryptocurrencies, others saw an opportunity to position themselves as havens for the burgeoning industry. **Switzerland**, for instance, became a global hub for blockchain innovation through its "**Crypto Valley**" in Zug. The Swiss government provided clear guidelines on how cryptocurrencies should be classified and taxed, offering a stable environment for blockchain projects. **Malta**, branding itself the "**Blockchain Island**," developed legal frameworks to attract crypto companies, while **Estonia** embraced blockchain on a national level, incorporating it into its e-governance and offering licenses to crypto businesses.

In the **U.S.**, navigating the regulatory environment remains complex. Agencies like the SEC and CFTC interpret cryptocurrencies differently, depending on their function. Bitcoin and Ethereum are generally considered commodities by the CFTC, while the IRS classifies them as property, triggering capital gains taxes when sold or exchanged. The SEC applies its "**Howey Test**" to determine whether a token qualifies as a security, often targeting ICOs and exchanges that list securities without proper registration. The Howey Test, originating from a 1946 Supreme Court case, lays out four key criteria for defining a security: (1) an investment of money, (2) in a common enterprise, (3) with an expectation of profit, (4) derived from the efforts of others. This test has become a pivotal tool in the SEC's efforts to regulate the crypto space. Ripple Labs, for instance, is currently embroiled in a legal battle with the SEC, which argues that Ripple's XRP token constitutes an unregistered security.

Stablecoins, designed to maintain a stable value often pegged to fiat currencies, face additional regulatory scrutiny. Their promise of stability makes them attractive, but governments are wary of their widespread use in payments. Non-fungible tokens (NFTs), representing ownership of unique digital assets, occupy yet another regulatory gray area, with some potentially subject to property taxes.

The **European** regulatory environment for crypto is also evolving. **MiCA** aims to bring order to the diverse regulatory landscape by establishing a unified framework across the EU. It introduces clear classifications for digital assets, cryptocurrencies, stablecoins, and utility tokens, and requires service providers to register with national authorities. MiCA also imposes strict rules on stablecoin issuers, ensuring reserves and redemption rights to maintain public trust. In parallel, anti-money laundering measures like the **EU's 5AMLD** mandate that exchanges and wallet providers comply with rigorous KYC requirements, ensuring that the crypto ecosystem remains transparent and secure.

Despite the variety of regulatory approaches across the world, a few key trends have emerged. Countries like **Japan** and **Singapore** are leading the way with supportive frameworks that encourage innovation while maintaining financial stability. Meanwhile, the U.S. and the EU, though slower to act, are developing more comprehensive regulatory structures that seek to balance innovation with consumer protection and financial integrity. These regulatory developments will shape the future of the cryptocurrency industry, determining where the next wave of innovation will take root and how governments will adapt to this rapidly evolving financial landscape.

United Arab Emirates

With the rapid adoption of virtual assets and the UAE's ambition to become a hub for virtual assets, the government has enacted stringent regulations to oversee virtual asset transactions. This guide aims to help Virtual **Asset Service Providers (VASPs),** a designation used to define entities that handle virtual assets, understand their compliance obligations under UAE law. According to the **Financial Action Task Force (FATF)**, a VASP is any individual or business that engages in activities involving virtual assets. In the UAE, these activities typically include exchanging virtual assets (cryptocurrencies) for fiat currencies or other virtual assets, transferring virtual assets between individuals or entities, safekeeping or providing custodial services for virtual assets, providing financial services related to the issuance or sale of virtual assets (like ICOs), facilitating the trading or investment in virtual assets, often through platforms or exchanges. Virtual Asset Service Providers are subject to specific regulations and compliance standards monitored by dedicated regulatory bodies, to ensure the safety of transactions, prevent money laundering, and support the integrity of the financial system.

There are several key regulatory bodies in the UAE responsible for overseeing VASPs and the virtual asset industry. The **Securities and Commodities Authority (SCA),** a towering presence across six of the Emirates, watches over everything except the DIFC, ADGM, and the emirate of Dubai. Its gaze is unblinking, its mandate clear: protect the markets, shield the investors, and ensure that fairness reigns. Licenses are the SCA's weapon of choice, a key to entry into the world of virtual assets. Without it, no VASP dares to operate. The SCA issues them carefully, watching each move of those it has granted access. It monitors markets, ever-vigilant for fraud, watching for the shadowy hand of manipulation. Investors rest easier under the SCA's protection, knowing that rules are in place to safeguard their interests, transparency brightening every corner of the market. Far from the main hustle, tucked within the sleek confines of the **Dubai International Financial Centre (DIFC)**, the **Dubai Financial Services Authority (DFSA)** operates like a sovereign ruler in its own realm. Here, financial services thrive under the DFSA's watch, with VASPs submitting to its firm but fair control. The DFSA's power lies in its regulatory framework, tight, clear, and built to keep the integrity of the market intact. Audits and inspections are commonplace, a reminder to VASPs that they must toe the line, always. And when the rules are broken, the DFSA is swift to act, its enforcement sharp, cutting down violations with precision. To the south, in Abu Dhabi, the **Financial Services Regulatory Authority (FSRA)** presides over the **Abu Dhabi Global Market (ADGM)**. The FSRA is not just a regulator, it is a gatekeeper to innovation. Within the ADGM's borders, it balances strict oversight with a nurturing hand, allowing the fintech and virtual asset world to blossom while keeping a watchful eye on every new development. Licensing is the first hurdle for any VASP here, followed by rigorous compliance checks, constant reporting, and the weight of risk management. The FSRA knows that with great innovation comes great risk, and it is prepared to manage every potential storm. And then, there is **VARA, Dubai's own Virtual Assets Regulatory Authority**, a newcomer with a singular focus, virtual assets and the vast landscape they inhabit. VARA is the future, Dubai's bold statement to the world that it intends to lead in the crypto space. Here, VASPs must prove themselves worthy, going through a meticulous licensing process. Once inside, there's no room for complacency. VARA's supervision is constant, its expectations high. It enforces rules not just for the sake of order but for the protection of consumers who dare to venture into the world of virtual assets. Safety and transparency are VARA's promises, and it delivers them with a dedication that sets Dubai apart as a beacon in the crypto world. Each authority stands strong, each with its own domain, yet together they form the regulatory web that keeps the UAE's virtual asset ecosystem alive and thriving, balancing risk with opportunity, and ensuring that the future of finance is as secure as its past.

~ 14 ~

METAVERSE

The concept of the Metaverse has evolved from a speculative idea in science fiction to a promising, immersive digital environment with applications across various industries. The term, first coined by Neal Stephenson in his 1992 novel **Snow Crash**, has transformed into a vision of interconnected virtual worlds where individuals can work, play, socialize, and create. Today, the Metaverse represents a combination of technologies—such as augmented reality (AR), virtual reality (VR), blockchain, and AI, that create a persistent, interactive, and immersive digital space. While the term Metaverse originated in Snow Crash, the roots of virtual worlds can be traced back to early text-based environments such as **MUDs (multi-user dungeons)** and **MOOs (MUD, object-oriented)** in the 1970s and 1980s. These were simple, text-based spaces where users could interact and explore virtual worlds. As technology progressed, graphical environments like **Second Life (2003)** became more prominent. Second Life allowed users to create avatars, interact in 3D spaces, build virtual property, and even establish economies, introducing key ideas that would influence future metaverse concepts.

The surge of virtual reality technology in the 2010s, along with advancements in AR, mobile computing, and blockchain, revived the dream of a fully immersive metaverse. Companies like **Meta (formerly Facebook), Microsoft**, and others began investing heavily in developing virtual environments that could cater to entertainment, work, and social interactions. By the early 2020s, the idea of the Metaverse became a dominant tech trend, with platforms and companies competing to define what it would become.

The Metaverse unfolds like a vast, interconnected web, not defined by any single technology but by the convergence of cutting-edge fields that come together to create something entirely new. It draws from the depths of virtual reality (VR), pulling users into immersive, 3D worlds where the sensation of presence is almost palpable. VR headsets, like the **Oculus Rift** and **HTC Vive**, serve as the gateways, transporting users into digital realms that feel as real as the ground beneath their feet. Within these worlds, the boundaries between the physical and digital blur, and the Metaverse begins to take shape. Augmented Reality (AR) adds another layer to this vision. It overlays the digital onto the physical world, not replacing reality but enhancing it. Through the lenses of smart glasses or the screens of smartphones, digital elements merge seamlessly with everyday life. Suddenly, the real world and the Metaverse coexist, each enriching the other in ways never before possible.

At the core of this digital universe is blockchain, the invisible scaffolding that ensures decentralization, ownership, and the flow of economies within the Metaverse. Blockchain platforms deploy non-fungible tokens (NFTs) to anchor ownership, verifying who controls virtual assets, whether it's a parcel of land, an avatar, or a digital artifact. Cryptocurrencies fuel the transactions, weaving an economic web across multiple worlds. Meanwhile, artificial intelligence (AI) breathes life into the Metaverse, crafting responsive environments and dynamic avatars. AI-powered characters and entities move beyond mere scripted behavior, interacting with users in real-time, adapting, and learning. The experience becomes personal, shaped by machine learning algorithms that anticipate desires and refine interactions. But none of this would be possible without the backbone of cloud computing and edge computing. These technologies, working in tandem, power the Metaverse's vast and persistent worlds, rendering complex 3D environments in real time. They provide the computational might necessary to keep these digital worlds alive and interactive. Edge computing ensures that even the most distant user experiences low-latency connections, while 5G networks bring the speed and instant communication required to keep every interaction fluid, every connection seamless. The Metaverse, with all its potential, begins to touch every part of life. Social interaction takes on new forms as platforms like **Meta's Horizon Worlds** open up spaces where people meet, chat, and share moments in immersive environments. Here, avatars become extensions of the self, expressing emotions and gestures, and shared experiences become more vivid, almost tangible. In the world of gaming, the Metaverse finds fertile ground. **Fortnite**, **Minecraft**, and **Roblox** have built sprawling digital landscapes where users not only play but socialize, create, and explore. These games have become more than entertainment, they are full-fledged universes where virtual concerts, movie screenings, and live events thrive, drawing millions into shared experiences that transcend traditional media. The workplace begins to shift too. The Metaverse promises to reshape how we collaborate, with platforms like **Microsoft Mesh** and **Spatial** offering virtual meeting spaces that dissolve the need for physical offices. Teams meet in 3D environments, interacting with holographic models of their work, whether it's architecture, design, or engineering. Education follows close behind, with the Metaverse opening up new possibilities for learning. Virtual classrooms replace traditional settings, immersing students in lessons that go beyond the textbook. Medical students practice surgeries in simulated environments, gaining real-world experience before stepping into the operating room. And in this brave new world, virtual real estate becomes a booming market. Platforms like **Decentraland** and **The Sandbox** offer users the chance to buy, sell, and develop digital land. These plots, much like in the physical world, are valuable, with some selling for millions. The landscape of real estate is redefined, moving from brick and mortar to pixels and code. E-commerce doesn't miss a beat, either. Brands like **Gucci** and **Nike** launch virtual collections, offering fashion for avatars and users alike. Within platforms like **Roblox**, users can purchase clothing, accessories, and even upgrades for their digital selves, paid for in cryptocurrency or platform-specific tokens. The line between physical and digital goods begins to blur, as more and more commerce takes place in the Metaverse. Metaverse-based games like Fortnite lead the charge, evolving from battle royale arenas into expansive digital environments. Concerts, movie screenings, and custom worlds pop up within the game, with events like Travis Scott's 2020 concert drawing over 12 million players, proving that the future of entertainment may well be virtual. Roblox, too, carves out its place, allowing users to create their own experiences, building worlds and games for others to explore. With its user-generated content model, it becomes one of the most vibrant corners of the Metaverse, and its in-game economy allows creators to profit from their innovations. Meanwhile, Decentraland pioneers the concept of virtual real estate on the blockchain, giving users a place to build, explore, and trade. And much like Decentraland, The Sandbox emerges as a space where users buy land and develop it, forming partnerships with celebrities and brands, pulling the real world into their virtual domain. Some platforms aim to become the keystones of this emerging Metaverse. Meta, once Facebook, invests heavily, with its Horizon Worlds at the center of its vision. Meta's goal is a future where users spend their days in this digital universe, working, socializing, and playing entirely within the Metaverse. Microsoft, too, takes a stake with Microsoft Mesh, focusing on business collaboration in virtual spaces, allowing remote workers to come together as if they were standing side by side. And then there's **Somnium Space**, a fully immersive VR metaverse, where users buy land, build environments, and engage in virtual worlds that feel more and more like reality every day. Each platform adds its own piece to the larger puzzle, creating a universe that continues to expand, evolve, and draw users deeper into the Metaverse.

As we stand on the cusp of a new digital frontier, the metaverse promises to reshape how we interact with technology, each other, and the world around us. What began as science fiction is rapidly evolving into a dynamic reality, blurring the lines between the physical and virtual realms. With its vast potential for innovation, commerce, entertainment, and social connection, the metaverse is not just an extension of the internet, it's the next iteration of human experience. As we navigate this uncharted territory, questions of ethics, privacy, regulation, and inclusion will inevitably arise. Yet, just as with the internet before it, the metaverse will ultimately be shaped by how we choose to use it. Whether it becomes a tool for empowerment and creativity or a reflection of our greatest challenges, one thing is certain: the metaverse is no longer a distant dream, but a reality we are building today, step by step, pixel by pixel. The future is virtual, and it is happening now.

~ 15 ~

FURTHER READING

Nakamoto, S. (2008). *Bitcoin: A peer-to-peer electronic cash system.* Reference Website:
Reference Website: https://bitcoin.org/en/

Poon, J., & Dryja, T. (2016). *The Bitcoin Lightning Network: Scalable off-chain instant payments.*
Reference Website: https://lightning.network/

Blockstream. (2015). *The Liquid Network.*
Reference Website: https://blockstream.com/liquid/

Lerner, S., & RSK Team. (2016). *RSK: Bitcoin powered smart contracts.*
Reference Website: https://rootstock.io/

Ali, M., & Nelson, J. (2017). *Stacks: A blockchain for decentralized apps and smart contracts.*
Reference Website: https://www.stacks.co/

Somsen, R. (2018). *Statechains: Sending bitcoin offline.*
Reference Website: https://bitcoinops.org/en/topics/state-chains/

Willett, J. R. (2012). *OmniLayer: Distributed exchange and asset creation.*
Reference Website: https://www.omnilayer.org/

Sztorc, P. (2017). *Drivechain: Enabling multiple blockchains with bitcoin.*
Reference Website: https://www.drivechain.info/

ARK Team. (2017). *ARK: All-in-one blockchain solutions.*
Reference Website: https://ark.io/

Buterin, V. (2013). *Ethereum: A next-generation smart contract and decentralized application platform.*
Reference Website: https://ethereum.org/en/

Poon, J., & Buterin, V. (2017). *Plasma: Scalable autonomous smart contracts.*
Reference Website: https://plasma.io/

Immutable Team. (2020). *Immutable X: Scaling NFTs on Ethereum.*
Reference Website: https://www.immutable.com/

ZK-Rollups.
Reference Websites:
https://matter-labs.io/
https://starkware.co/
https://loopring.org/#/

Optimism Foundation. (2019). *Optimistic Rollups: Scaling Ethereum with optimistic layer 2.*
Reference Website: https://optimism.io/

Coleman, J., Horne, L., et al. (2015). *State Channels: Enabling instant payments on blockchains.*
Reference Website: https://statechannels.org/

Offchain Labs. (2021). *Arbitrum Orbit: A next-gen layer 2 for Ethereum.*
Reference Website: https://arbitrum.io/

Tether Limited. (2016). *Tether: Fiat currencies on the Bitcoin blockchain.*
Reference Website: https://tether.to/en/

Binance. (2019). *Binance Chain: A decentralized exchange blockchain.*
Reference Website: https://www.bnbchain.org/en/bnb-smart-chain

Yakovenko, A. (2017). *Solana: A new architecture for a high-performance blockchain.*
Reference Website: https://solana.com/

Centre Consortium. (2018). *USDC: A stablecoin backed by the U.S. dollar.*
Reference Website: https://www.usdc.com/

Ripple Labs. (2014). *Ripple: A consensus protocol for financial transactions.*
Reference Website: https://ripple.com/

Lido Team. (2020). *Lido: A decentralized staking protocol.*
Reference Website: https://lido.fi/

Markus, B., & Palmer, J. (2013). *Dogecoin: A peer-to-peer electronic currency.*
Reference Website: https://dogecoin.com/

Sun, J., & Tron Foundation. (2017). *TRON: Decentralizing the web.*
Reference Website: https://tron.network/

IOHK. (2017). *Cardano: A blockchain platform for smart contracts.*
Reference Website: https://cardano.org/

Team Rocket & Sirer, E. G. (2020). *Avalanche: Consensus protocol for high scalability.*
Reference Website: https://www.avax.network/

Ryoshi. (2020). *Shiba Inu: A decentralized ecosystem.*
Reference Website: https://shibatoken.com/

Nazarov, S., & Ellis, S. (2017). *Chainlink: Decentralized oracles for smart contracts.*
Reference Website: https://chain.link/

Bitcoin ABC Team. (2017). *Bitcoin Cash: A peer-to-peer electronic cash system.*
Reference Website: https://bitcoincash.org/

Wood, G. (2016). *Polkadot: Vision for a heterogeneous multi-chain framework.*
Reference Website: https://polkadot.com/

Maker Foundation. (2017). *Dai: A decentralized stablecoin system.*
Reference Website: http://makerdao.com/en/

Adams, H. (2018). *Uniswap: A decentralized protocol for automated liquidity provision.*
Reference Website: https://app.uniswap.org/

Lee, C. (2011). *Litecoin: A peer-to-peer electronic currency.*
Reference Website: https://litecoin.com/en/

Monero Core Team. (2014). *Monero: Privacy and decentralization on the blockchain.*
Reference Website: https://www.getmonero.org/

Stellar Foundation. (2014). *Stellar: An open network for storing and moving money.*
Reference Website: https://stellar.org/

Polygon Team. (2019). *Polygon: Layer 2 scaling solution for Ethereum.*
Reference Website: https://polygon.technology/

ETC Team. (2015). *Ethereum Classic: A blockchain for smart contracts.*
Reference Website: https://ethereumclassic.org/

Aave Team. (2020). *Aave: A decentralized lending protocol.*
Reference Website: https://aave.com/

Protocol Labs. (2017). *Filecoin: A decentralized storage network.*
Reference Website: https://filecoin.io/

VeChain Foundation. (2018). *VeChain: Building a blockchain ecosystem for businesses.*
Reference Website: https://vechain.org/

Kwon, J., & Buchman, E. (2016). *Cosmos: A network of distributed ledgers.*
Reference Website: https://cosmos.network/

Micali, S. (2019). *Algorand: A secure and scalable blockchain.*
Reference Website: https://algorandtechnologies.com/

StarkWare Team. (2021). *Starknet: Scaling Ethereum with zero-knowledge proofs.*
Reference Website: https://starkware.co/

PayPal & Paxos. (2023). *PayPal USD (PYUSD): A U.S. dollar-backed stablecoin.*
Reference Website: https://www.paypal.com/us/digital-wallet/manage-money/crypto/pyusd

Sky Mavis. (2018). *Axie Infinity: A decentralized game universe.*
Reference Website: https://whitepaper.axieinfinity.com/

Goodman, L. (2014). *Tezos: A self-amending crypto ledger.* Reference Website: https://tezos.com/

Wormhole Team. (2020). *Wormhole: A cross-chain messaging protocol.*
Reference Website: https://wormhole.com

Sky Mavis. (2021). *Ronin: A sidechain for blockchain gaming.*
Reference Website: https://roninchain.com

Mina Foundation. (2020). *Mina Protocol: A succinct blockchain.*
Reference Website: https://minaprotocol.com/

Decentraland Team. (2017). *Decentraland: A virtual world built on blockchain.*
Reference Website: https://decentraland.org

Synthetix Team. (2018). *Synthetix: Decentralized synthetic assets on Ethereum.*
Reference Website: https://synthetix.io/

Paxos. (2019). *Paxos Gold (PAXG): A regulated digital asset backed by gold.*
Reference Website: https://paxos.com/paxgold/

PancakeSwap Team. (2020). *PancakeSwap: A decentralized exchange for BEP20 tokens.*
Reference Website: https://pancakeswap.finance/

Wilcox-O'Hearn, Z., & Green, M. (2014). *Zcash: Privacy-enhanced cryptocurrencies.*
Reference Website: https://z.cash/

Duffield, E. (2014). *Dash: Digital cash for instant transactions.*
Reference Website: https://www.dash.org/